ELEMENTS OF

QUALITY ONLINE EDUCATION

Edited by John Bourne and Janet C. Moore

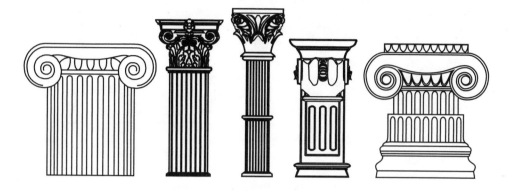

Learning Effectiveness

Cost Effectiveness

Access

Faculty Satisfaction

Student Satisfaction

 THE SLOAN CONSORTIUM
A Consortium of Institutions and Organizations
Committed to Quality Online Education

Volume 3 in the Sloan-C series

Elements of Quality Online Education

Volume 3 in the Sloan-C series

This is the third volume in the annual Sloan-C series of case studies on quality education online. In 1999, 2000, and 2001, the Sloan Foundation selected expert contributors to report on work in progress and to collaborate on research of importance to asynchronous learning networks. Each volume publishes contributions in the form of documented, peer-reviewed scholarly studies of learning and cost effectiveness, access, and faculty and student satisfaction.

Other titles available in this series:

Online Education: Learning Effectiveness, Faculty Satisfaction, and Cost Effectiveness, Volume 2 ISBN 0-9677741-1-X

Online Education: Learning Effectiveness and Faculty Satisfaction, Volume 1 ISBN 0-9677741-0-1

This book was made possible by a grant from the Alfred P. Sloan Foundation.

SCOLE
Sloan Center for OnLine Education
at Olin and Babson Colleges

Sloan-C has its administrative home at the Sloan Center for OnLine Education (SCOLE) at Olin and Babson Colleges. SCOLE has been established as a center that spans the two campus of Olin College and Babson College. SCOLE's purpose is to support the activities of the Sloan Consortium, a consortium of higher-education providers sharing the common bonds of understanding, supporting and delivering education via asynchronous learning networks (ALNs). With the mission of providing learning to anyone anywhere, SCOLE seeks to provide new levels of learning capability to people seeking higher and continuing education. For more information about SCOLE, visit www.scole.olin-babson.org.

For more information about Olin and Babson Colleges, visit www.olin.edu and www.babson.edu.

 Franklin W. **Olin**
College of Engineering

ELEMENTS OF QUALITY ONLINE EDUCATION

Volume 3 in the Sloan-C series

Introduction
   Frank Mayadas, John Bourne, Janet C. Moore 7

Part I. Learning Effectiveness

1. Studies of Effectiveness of Learning Networks
   Star Roxanne Hiltz, Yi Zhang, and Murray Turoff 15

Part II: Cost Effectiveness

1. Linking Quality and Cost
   Tana Bishop and Claudine SchWeber 45

2. Factors in ALN Cost Effectiveness at BYU
   J. Olin Campbell 59

3. Rethinking Cost-Benefit Models of Distance Learning
   Leigh S. Estabrook 71

Part III: Access . . . A Focus on Student Support Services

1. World Campus: Setting Standards in Student Services
   Jean McGrath, Heather Kiris Middleton, and Tamsin Crissman 83

Part IV: Faculty Satisfaction

1. Online Teaching as a Catalyst for Classroom-Based Instructional Transformation
   Peter J. Shea, William Pelz, Eric E. Fredericksen, and Alexandra M. Pickett 103

Part V: Student Satisfaction

1. Pace University's Focus on Student Satisfaction with Student Services in Online Education
   David Sachs and Nancy Hale 127

2. Student Satisfaction and Reported Learning in the SUNY Learning Network
   Peter J. Shea, Karen Swan, Eric E. Fredericksen, and Alexandra M. Pickett 145

3. Immediacy, Social Presence, and Asynchronous Discussion
   Karen Swan 157

4. Student Satisfaction at the University of Phoenix Online Campus
   Anthony P. Trippe 173

Introduction

Frank Mayadas
Program Director
The Alfred P. Sloan Foundation

John Bourne
Director
Sloan Center for OnLine Education
At Olin and Babson Colleges

Janet C. Moore
Managing Editor
SCOLE

In September 2001, the Alfred P. Sloan Foundation invited 40 guests from colleges and universities and from corporate and government organizations to participate in the Sloan Consortium's third annual summer workshop on Asynchronous Learning Networks (ALNs). Participants from throughout the country met to confer on ways to continuously improve online programs that concentrate on the five pillars of quality: learning effectiveness, cost effectiveness, access, student satisfaction and faculty satisfaction.

Hosted by the State University of New York Student Learning Network, participants traveled across the country to meet at Bolton Landing on Lake George in the foothills of the Adirondack Mountains. For centuries the site of successive conflicts among Indians, pioneers, and American revolutionaries, Lake George today is a peaceful place, where the mountain lake atmosphere inspires serious scholarly and creative thinking. In a period closely following the terrorist violence of September 11, scholars set aside other concerns and overcame travel difficulties to meet and study the status of online learning and to share new information from a wide range of perspectives. This introduction serves as an overview of the workshop.

- "Swift trust" is the phrase Starr Roxanne Hiltz of the New Jersey Institute of Technology used to characterize the way successful online teachers quickly establish community and motivation among learners. Hiltz opened the workshop with a survey of empirical research on learning effectiveness. The empirical studies are collected at The WebCenter for Learning Effectiveness Networks Research, which collects, analyzes and synthesizes published studies about online learning. Hiltz synthesizes nineteen studies that favorably compare online learning with face-to-face learning. Of special interest to researchers is breakout information from the studies, tabularized by methods, hypotheses, effectiveness measures and findings. This important work brings together in a cohesive way a first look at findings across the field of asynchronous learning networks. It calls for further research to develop a model for measuring student performance, institutional resources, long-term impacts, and opportunities for learning and teaching in ways not possible before ALN.

- Karen Swan's study of online communication breaks new ground by examining social presence and interaction in ALN. The importance of this work is that it examines a key issue in online learning– the impact of immediacy among communicators. Although people cite lack of immediacy in online learning as a significant drawback, Swan's results show that learners in online courses adapt text-based communications to bond and bridge psychological distance. This paper is a first look at how online learning can be greatly improved by understanding how people communicate with each other. Grounded in the theories of immediacy behaviors in both face-to-face teaching and online teaching, this research offers a significant first step toward greatly improving the way groups learn online.

Studies in the workshop this year reflect the importance of studying cost effectiveness because of its effects on the scalability of courses and programs. Readers will find cost models vary widely according to institutional choices. Some of the implications of the case studies are controversial and provocative, reflecting a continuum of priorities among public, private, and for-profit institutions.

- Tana Bishop and Claudine SchWeber of the University of Maryland University College present a cost effectiveness model developed at the University of Maryland University College (UMUC). With more than 63,000 enrollments, UMUC is one of the largest online systems. The UMUC study presents a framework for maintaining quality that can help institutions decide which methodologies will secure the most significant advances in educational quality. The model is based on the premise that each institution's core mission must be the fundamental guide for costing decisions that effectively link quality choices to the core values unique to each institution.

- Olin Campbell of Brigham Young University reports on cost effectiveness factors related to three delivery modes. At BYU, the development of online learning is motivated by growing demand, coupled with caps on on-campus enrollments and faculty and staff expansion. Hence, accommodating more students through ALN requires finding ways to lower costs and provide greater learning experiences. Of special interest is that BYU has been able to deliver learning in an independent studies program to some 60,000 learners without vastly scaling up the instructor-led component of the program. This finding is at a variance with findings from other researchers who find that numbers of instructors increase as numbers of students increase. For BYU, simulations and other automated activities enable non-linear scaling.

- Tony Trippe of the University of Phoenix reports on a model that uses nearly all adjuncts for teaching almost 30,000 online students. Committed to small learning cohorts of 20 or fewer students, each cohort led by an instructor, the UOP model stands in contrast to the BYU model. UOP employs adjunct instructors as a method for cost reduction while maintaining its distinctive learning model. Planning based on data about student satisfaction is an important component of the UOP model. Examining results from a large UOP study, Trippe reports that students like the modular method of instruction very much. Students enroll in courses sequenced according to the curricula and take one course at a time; courses are condensed into short, 5-6 week semesters; and courses require intense interaction—a model quite different from traditional university learning models. Training for faculty is mandatory, both before teaching the first course with the assistance of a mentor, and throughout the time faculty are affiliated with UOP.

- Leigh Estabrook of the University of Illinois Library and Information Science School demonstrates how a relatively small school (currently enrolling 165 students) can move to an online learning environment and make the activity financially viable while integrating it with the traditional culture of the program. Her paper is notable because it outlines the program's expenses and income over time with an economic model that does not operate as a separate cost center—faculty, students, and tuition rates are the same whether online or on campus. Readers will find analyses of the program's income and expense table useful. Of special note also are Estabrook's comments about how income must be carefully analyzed to balance in-state and out-of-state tuition rates for cost effectiveness.

- David Sachs and Nancy Hale of Pace University provide a look at progress on a three-year grant from the Fund for the Improvement of Postsecondary Education (FIPSE) Learning Anytime Anywhere Program (LAAP). This study examines how student services are provided in the National Coalition for Telecommunications Education and Learning (NACTEL) program, an online Associate of Science program for telecommunications workers. The Pace model shares costs with telecommunications companies who sponsor their employees' enrollments in the program.

- Jean McGrath, Heather Kiris Middleton, and Tamsin Crissman of the Pennsylvania State University World Campus emphasize that Penn State has developed student services for more than 20,000 enrollments based on feedback from students themselves. World Campus finds that services online and by telephone greatly improve the learning experience. The call center handles a high volume of requests, and has become quite popular. A significant contribution of this study is its description of the ways Penn State has changed its orientation to view students as customers; support services are a priority, critically important to learners' decisions to matriculate and to continue learning online. Policies to facilitate support for adult learners online are integrated as closely as possible with traditional student services, so that the World Campus mission is part of the fabric of Penn State University.

- Peter Shea, Karen Swan, Eric Fredericksen and Alexandra Pickett of SUNY provide a tour-de-force in a detailed paper showing results from its ongoing study of student satisfaction. SUNY has experienced substantial growth in courses, from 8 in 1995-96 to over 1500 in 2000-01, and in enrollments from 119 in 1995-96 to more than 20,000 in 2000-01. Data from surveys of more than 8,000 faculty and student respondents confirm that:

  - Good practice encourages contact between student and faculty;
  - Good practice encourages active learning methods;
  - Prompt feedback is important;
  - Measuring time on task enhances outcomes.

- Peter Shea, William Pelz, Eric Fredericksen and Alexandra Pickett of SUNY show that instructors teaching online become better teachers face to face because of the specific discipline and practices that online teaching requires. Typically online instructors spend significant time rethinking their face-to-face courses for online delivery. Instructors need to create highly structured course materials with explicit instructions in advance; they need reflect on ways to create community-building activities; and they often collaborate with others in planning and revising based on learning outcomes and student feedback. Surveys of faculty in the SUNY system reveal that their classroom teaching is greatly enhanced through their experiences with online teaching. Most instructors enthusiastically confirm that student performance and interaction with teachers and peers is greatly enhanced online.

- At Herkimer County Community College, one of SUNY's 53 colleges, where there is an institutional cap of 15% limiting online enrollments, the online program has grown during the past four years from a program in which 3 faculty taught 36 students, to a program in which 48 faculty teach more than 1800 enrollments. HCCC reports 100% faculty willingness to teach online again, and William Pelz reports that: "The courses are the same; the books are the same; the teachers are the same; and the quality and quantity of interaction and learning are better."

For schools considering developing an online environment, SUNY notes that while success requires time, money and effort, certain benchmarks suggest the effort is worthwhile:

- 71% of students report they spend more time studying for online courses
- 85% of faculty report online teaching improves face-to-face teaching
- 86% of students report putting more thought into discussions online
- 87% of students report their satisfaction with timely, constructive feedback
- 91% of 255 faculty in different subjects at different degree levels report online learning is equivalent to or better than learning online
- 97% of faculty report online teaching improves understanding of teaching with technology

Faculty and learners are enthusiastic about the revolutionary possibilities online learning offers, and providers are demonstrating considerable ingenuity in meeting unprecedented demand for increased access to higher education. Nevertheless, critics may complain that online learning cannot match the classroom for academic excellence. They fear that online learning may obstruct relationships with professors and peers and foster isolation and alienation. Online education, critics claim, costs too much, undermines academic freedom, lures students away from classrooms, and burdens faculty with yet more work for which they are not recognized or rewarded.

In response to criticism, and more importantly, to help realize the enormous potential of online learning, leaders in American higher education have provided guidelines for ensuring quality in developing online programs. Among the most well known guidelines and recommendations are those developed by the American Council of Education, by the

American Federation of Teachers, by the American Distance Education Consortium, by the Congressional Commission on Web-Based Education, by the Institute for Higher Education Policy, by the Southern Regional Electronic Board, and by the Western Cooperative for Educational Telecommunications for the interregional accrediting commission. These guidelines share the common goal of using technology to make the best in educational opportunities available online so that all American citizens can access lifelong learning. As Ralph Gomory, president of the Alfred P. Sloan Foundation, envisions it, higher learning should become "an ordinary part of everyday life."

For nearly a decade, the Sloan program for learning outside the classroom has encouraged academic leaders to open new doors for learning and continually improve quality. The Sloan Consortium has grown as a voluntary organization of colleges and universities that includes hundreds of programs for online learners. Membership in the Sloan Consortium is free for institutions that demonstrate commitment to quality as defined by the five pillars and the quality framework that is based on them.

Readers may find useful this brief version of the Sloan-C™ pillars of quality framework, which illustrates some ways to put the pillars into practice, measuring progress towards the goal of educating all who value learning as a lifelong endeavor:

GOAL	PROCESS/PRACTICE	METRIC	PROGRESS INDICES
LEARNING EFFECTIVENESS			
Quality of learning online is demonstrated as at least as good as the quality the institution provides in traditional programs	Academic integrity and control reside with faculty in the same way as for traditional programs at that institution.	Faculty perception surveys or sampled interviews compare learning effectiveness in delivery modes

Learner/graduate/employer focus groups or interviews measure learning gains | Faculty report online learning is equivalent or better

Direct assessment of student learning is equivalent or better |
| **COST EFFECTIVENESS** | | | |
| Institutional business practices generate and support stable, high-quality educational programs and expansion to meet needs | The institution demonstrates financial and technical commitment to its online programs

Tuition rates provide a fair return to the institution and best value to learners at the same time

Tuition rates are equivalent or less than on-campus tuition | Institutional stakeholders show support for participation in online education

Effective practices identified | The institution sustains the program, expands and scales upward as desired, strengthens and disseminates its mission and core values through online education |
| **ACCESS** | | | |
| All learners who are qualified and motivated are enabled to succeed and complete a course/degree/ program through online access to learning in any discipline (continually enlarging the pool of learners) | Program entry processes inform learners of opportunities, and ensure that qualified, motivated learners have reliable access

Integrated support services are available online to learners | Administrative and technical infrastructure provides access to all prospective and enrolled learners

Quality metrics measure Information dissemination; learning resources delivery; and tutoring services | Qualitative indicators show continuous improvement in growth and effectiveness rates |

FACULTY SATISFACTION			
Sustain and increase faculty participation in online teaching Expand and deepen faculty awareness of and satisfaction with online teaching Integrate faculty online and face-to-face with online purposes and practices	Process to ensure faculty participation in matters particular to online education (e.g. governance, intellectual property, royalty sharing, etc.) Process to ensure adequate support for faculty in course preparation and course delivery	Repeat teaching of online courses by individual faculty indicates approval Addition of new faculty shows growing endorsement	Data from post-course surveys show continuous improvement: At least 90% of faculty believe the overall online teaching/learning experience is positive Willingness/desire to teach additional courses in the program: 80% positive
STUDENT SATISFACTION			
Every learner who completes a course is satisfied with the: Level of interaction with faculty and other students Learning outcomes matching the course description Adequacy and appropriateness of technology and support	Faculty/learner interaction is provided timely and substantive Adequate and fair systems assess course learning objectives; results are used for improving learning	Metrics show growing satisfaction: Surveys (see above) and/or interviews Alumni surveys, referrals, testimonials Outcomes measures Focus groups Faculty/Mentor/Advisor perceptions	Satisfaction measures show continuously increasing improvement Institutional surveys, interviews, or other metrics show satisfaction levels are equivalent to or better than those of other delivery modes for the institution

The framework is a work in progress, designed to be adaptable for a wide array of educational organizations. A more complete version of the quality framework is available online at http://www.sloan-c.org/effectivepractices, and readers are welcome to contribute to its development by sharing and discussing effective practices there. Drawn from the research and experience of Sloan-C schools such as this volume represents, the framework-in-progress signifies the visionary spirit Alfred P. Sloan claimed for his legacy:

> The greatest real thrill that life offers is to create, to construct, to develop something useful. Too often we fail to recognize and pay tribute to the creative spirit. It is that spirit that creates our jobs. There has to be this pioneer, the individual who has the courage, the ambition to overcome the obstacles that always develop when one tries to do something worthwhile, especially when it is new and different.

May the studies in this volume be useful to you as you work to make quality education accessible to all.

The Sloan Consortium Mission Statement

"A consortium of institutions and organizations committed to quality online education."

The purpose of the Sloan Consortium (Sloan-C) is to make education a part of everyday life, accessible and affordable for anyone, anywhere, at any time, in a wide variety of disciplines. Sponsored by the Alfred P. Sloan Foundation, Sloan-C™ is primarily a consortium of accredited higher education providers and organizations that provide equipment, tools and infrastructure support for these providers. Sloan-C™ encourages collaboration, sharing of knowledge and effective practice to improve online education in the areas of learning effectiveness, access, affordability for learners and providers, and student and faculty satisfaction.

Sloan-C™ maintains a catalog of degree and certificate programs offered by a wide range of regionally accredited member institutions, consortia, and industry partners; provides speakers and consultants to help institutions learn about online methodologies; hosts conferences and workshops to help implement and improve online programs; publishes a newsletter, the Journal of Asynchronous Learning Networks (JALN), and annual volumes of applied research studies; and conducts research, surveys and forums to inform academic, government and private sector audiences. Sloan-C™ also offers services such as awards, conferences and workshops, an effective practices database, and a listing in the Sloan-C™ catalog for members with complete online degree and certificate programs.

Sloan-C™ generates ideas to improve products, services and standards for the online learning industry, and assists members in collaborative initiatives. Members include (1) private and public universities and colleges, community colleges and other accredited course and degree providers and (2) organizations and suppliers of services, equipment, and tools that support quality online learning. Membership in Sloan-C™ is open to nonprofit and for-profit organizations that practice the Sloan-C™ quality principles. Associate membership is available to institutions that share an interest in online education and Sloan-C™ goals, but currently offer no online courses. Membership is free at this time.

LEARNING EFFECTIVENESS

Studies of Effectiveness of Learning Networks

Starr Roxanne Hiltz
Yi Zhang
Murray Turoff
New Jersey Institute of Technology

- The evidence is overwhelming that ALN tends to be as effective or more effective than traditional modes of course delivery at the university level. What we need is more research that will enable us to make online learning even more effective, especially as new technologies proliferate.

- The WebCenter for Learning Networks Effectiveness Research (www.ALNResearch.org) increases the quality, quantity, and dissemination of results of research on the effectiveness of Asynchronous Learning Networks (ALN).

- Many studies do not distinguish Asynchronous Learning Networks, which emphasize extensive student-student and teacher-student interaction, from distance modes that simply post materials on the web and use individual email assignments, without any collaborative learning activities or formation of a "class" of interacting students. An empirical research study must include research questions or hypotheses, describe data collection methods, include a reasonable number of subjects, and report empirical results.

- In colleges and universities and corporations all over the US and the world, new online courses and programs are being designed and introduced. Faculty need to be able to learn what pedagogical techniques work best in this environment.

- It is time to start looking at the evaluation of ALN beyond the single course and consider the full range of evaluation variables. A top down model structures evaluation variables: student performance measures; resource measures; opportunity measures (including organizational impacts of doing things not possible before, and doing things differently than before); long term impacts; and significant intervening variables.

I. THE LEARNING NETWORKS EFFECTIVENESS RESEARCH PROGRAM

This paper describes the goals of the program and the contents of a "WebCenter for Learning Networks Effectiveness Research." One of its main components is a knowledge base of empirical studies. Studies currently in this collection that compare measures of student outcomes for ALN and traditional modes of delivery are analyzed in order to describe the methods that are being used, and the findings of such studies to date.

A. Need for the Program

Almost daily, there are articles in the press about online courses that approach the subject from either a negative or positive angle. Most of these articles cite a few faculty members or students who have been interviewed, or cite a single study of a single course, with unknown quality of research methods. Many of them do not distinguish Asynchronous Learning Networks, which emphasize extensive student-student and teacher-student interaction, from distance modes that simply post materials on the web and use individual email assignments, without any collaborative learning activities or formation of a "class" of interacting students.

Claims and counter-claims are likely to persist unless a comprehensive and authoritative knowledge base of information about evaluation research studies of ALN is created and made available to the public, on the Web as well as in published journals.

Meanwhile, in colleges and universities and corporations all over the US and the world, new online courses and programs are being designed and introduced. Faculty need to be able to learn what pedagogical techniques work best in this environment. Those assuming the role of researchers—either because it is necessary to evaluate the online programs in connection with accreditation activities, or because they are interested in pursuing research on this relatively new phenomenon—need to know what theories, methods, and previous findings are available to help them in designing their research.

There is currently no place where faculty, researchers, potential students, or the press can go to find out what information exists about the following:

- What empirical studies have been conducted about ALN? What were the methods, variables, and findings?
- What is the current overall picture of these research findings, in terms of comparing the effectiveness of ALN with other modes of delivery of college-level courses? What do we know about relatively effective and ineffective ways of doing ALN?
- Who are the leading researchers in ALN, are they willing to be contacted by the press, and if so, how can they be contacted?
- What methods and research instruments (questionnaires, interview guides, etc.) are available for use by ALN researchers?
- What are the strengths and weaknesses of various research methods for studying ALN, and what methods are recommended by experts in the field as especially appropriate for understanding this form of educational medium?
- What theoretical foundations are there for the field of ALN? What theories are most appropriate for framing research studies in this area? And which methods best match different theoretical frameworks?

The Learning Networks Effectiveness Research Project aims to make the above information available, with a primary mission of serving researchers on ALN effectiveness, and also to provide a place where the answers to the above questions are available to all who are interested. The objective is to create an online research community, to which users will contribute materials on an ongoing basis. Community members should be able to contribute to, discuss, and learn from the community's knowledge, and from each other.

B. Project Objectives

The goal of this research program, which began in January of 2001, is to increase the quality, quantity, and dissemination of results of research on the effectiveness of Asynchronous Learning Networks (ALN). It will synthesize existing knowledge and create new knowledge about the methods and findings of research on the determinants of effectiveness of ALN, and make the results available worldwide via a project web site. The major activities will be to:

- Create a "Web Center for Learning Networks Research." It will include a series of online knowledge bases that are regularly updated and will be available through the project web site to researchers, faculty, the press, and the public. Users are invited to contribute to these knowledge bases, as well as to use the information already there.

- Build/strengthen an ALN evaluation research community that will create and share improved research methods, theoretical frameworks, and instrumentation for assessing the outcomes of online learning. Face to face workshops and asynchronous communication will be used to achieve this. The results of these activities will be used to enhance the materials on the web site.

C. Creating a knowledge base of ALN research results

The "alpha" version of the WebCenter appeared at the end of January 2001. By August, we had completed coding of studies and creation of a database for approximately 50 empirical research articles related to the effectiveness of learning networks. In this paper, we will summarize the subset of these studies that explicitly compare ALN effectiveness to that of traditional courses.

Learning networks are defined as groups of people who use computer networks (the Internet and World Wide Web) to communicate and collaborate in order to build and share knowledge. The emphasis for studies in the database of empirical research is on asynchronous (anytime, anyplace) use of networks, but the project includes studies of courses that emphasize use of synchronous (same time) technology or which compare face-to-face, synchronous and asynchronous learning processes. Secondly, the emphasis will be on post-secondary, for-credit courses, but information will also be collected about studies of the use of ALN in pre-college courses and in continuing professional education (not for academic credit) courses or learning communities. Effectiveness is defined in this project as focusing on learning outcomes for students, and on positive or negative impacts on faculty. To the extent that other measures of effectiveness are reported in empirical studies (e.g., fiscal impacts on educational institutions, cost-benefit analysis, or societal impacts in terms of educational access and equity), they will be included in a separate database of other papers to be created in the future.

D. Criteria for Inclusion in the Published Research List of Papers

1. Papers included in the ALNResearch database must be empirical studies of the effectiveness of learning networks and have been published in a refereed journal or conference proceedings, in the English language. They must be full papers, not just extended abstracts. A full paper is operationally defined as at least five pages in length.

2. "Learning networks" technology and pedagogy refer to the use of computer-mediated communication among students as well as between instructors and students, for a substantial part of the course work. Learning networks may be used asynchronously and/or synchronously, though we are mainly concerned with courses that include substantial use of asynchronous (anytime) media. They may be used alone or in combination with other media, such as face-to-face lectures, videotapes, Web postings of lecture or reading or tutorial material, etc. Not all web based courses use learning networks; some just post lecture type materials or exams for downloading, do not involve extensive interaction among students in a class, and therefore do not qualify as "learning networks" courses. One synonym for learning networks is "computer-supported cooperative learning" (CSCL).

3. "Effectiveness" is defined as primarily concerned with learning outcomes for students, but also includes effectiveness from the instructor's point of view. It thus includes studies that look at student perceptions, student performance, or faculty perceptions, satisfaction, or performance in this mode of course delivery.

4. To be considered as an empirical research study, the paper must include research questions or hypotheses (at least implicitly), describe some data collection methods, and report some empirical results. In order to be considered an adequate empirical study, it must have a reasonable number of subjects on which conclusions are based. We have operationally defined a reasonable number for the time being as a minimum of at least 20 subjects included in the study.

E. Coding of the studies for the Database

Appendix 1 shows a partial list of papers in the database. Users can view the abstract, the coded database entry, and if the publisher gave permission, the full text of the article. Most of the coding of studies is done by Ph.D. students working under the direction of the project director, who checks them over and ascertains that the study "qualifies" according to our criteria. One complete database entry is included as Appendix 2, showing all of the information that is recorded for each study. One objective is to make this WebCenter the first stop for the literature review of ALN researchers who are planning a new study or article. This should save researchers time and assure them a more complete overview of related prior research than they are likely to obtain on their own.

For this paper, we decided to focus on analysis of a key subset of the papers: those that compare the effectiveness of ALN courses in terms of student outcomes, to that of traditional face to face (FTF) courses (Appendix 3). We identified 19 of the studies that clearly meet this criterion. We have included only the most important study characteristics in the charts and in the analysis presented here: the research methods, the way effectiveness was measured, and the results. As for the remaining studies in the database, they tend to be case studies of ALN rather than comparative studies measuring comparative effectiveness, or to be concerned primarily with variables that are correlated with good outcomes in ALN, or to be focused on different outcomes, such as faculty satisfaction. In the future, we will probably add more studies to the 19 included here.

F. Procedure: Coding of the Studies for this Paper

Two of the authors categorized the types of individual measures used, and whether each individual finding reported showed ALN to be better than traditional courses, no different, or worse. The second step was that all of the results for each study were categorized in terms of whether they showed ALN to better, worse, or no different on the whole.

II. RESEARCH MODELS, METHODS, AND MEASURES FOR ASSESSING THE EFFECTIVENESS OF ALNS

Asynchronous Learning Networks may be considered to be one type of information system: a computer-based system designed to support the work of teachers and learners. There are two dominant research models in Information Systems and in other fields using social science methodologies to study human subjects: the "positivists" and the "interpretivists." Positivists strive to follow the model of scientific inquiry developed in the natural sciences, with the objective being to specify quantitative measures of all variables, state hypotheses, collect data using random sampling and other proce-dures that will enable the testing of hypotheses with inferential and descriptive statistics, and then analyze the data, and report the results and their limitations. Interpretivists strive for an in depth understanding of the processes in human social systems; they generally start with research questions, and use qualitative methods such as participant observation, unstructured or semi-structured interviews, and content analysis to obtain a rich description of the phenomenon and arrive at an interpretation of why and how things work— or do not work [1]. The most sophisticated research projects combine both quantitative measures (describing quantitatively "what" is happening) and qualitative measures (describ-ing "why" the results are occurring, in terms of the details of behavior and interaction that transfer an input of course materials provided in various modes to an output of what the student does or does not learn.)

To qualify as an empirical study using generally accepted methods, a research project should start with specific hypoth-eses and/or research questions, which guide the selection of methods and measures. Unfortunately, the majority of publications related to ALNs do not have any explicit research questions, let alone specific hypotheses. They tend to be accounts by instructors of courses they designed and of their experiences and impressions; the value of such studies in building a scientific body of knowledge is questionable.

The paradigm of positivist research has enshrined experimental design as the most valid method for determining "cause and effect," specifically, the "pre-test, post-test, control group design" using random assignment of individual subjects to conditions. It is basically impossible to randomly assign students to take a traditional section or an ALN section of a course; they may be unable to travel to campus if they live 2000 miles away, or unable to take an ALN section if they have no PC and Internet provider. One is therefore left with quasi-experimental designs at best, in which students self-select the mode of course delivery, but the study designer and instructors try to hold constant everything else, such as the syllabus, assignments and exams. The pre-test, post-test design means that ideally one measures the dependent variable (such as knowledge about accounting or data bases or English Literature) before the course, then measures again after the course, to determine amount learned as the difference between scores. Most ALN studies do not do this either, since it is not usual to give students the equivalent of a final exam on the first day of the course, and in many project-based courses, it is not appropriate, since there will be no final exam either. (One exception is the Worrell et al. study of a graduate accounting course [2], for which standardized professional exams are readily available to test knowledge of accounting). Thus, we often do not know whether differences in grades at the end of the course are caused by differences in mode of course delivery, or differences among the students who self-selected the different modes. Positivists would thus tend to say that most ALN research to date is not very rigorous.

Several different types of measures of effectiveness of ALNs for students are commonly used. Objective measures of performance and subjective assessments by students have been used about equally (see Table 1). The number of studies shown in Appendix 3 using each of the following objective measures is noted in parentheses:

- Grades, for specific projects or exams or for the entire course, compared to sections or students using other delivery modes (16).
- Measures of the quality of work (e.g., group projects may be judged on creativity, completeness, length, etc.) (9). Such judgments may be biased if they are made by the instructor who designed the online course, and who knows who did a particular piece of work and the mode that student was in. Thus, procedures need to be designed to make the quality of work measure as reliable as possible by using multiple judges, who are blind to the identity and course delivery condition of the student (e.g., see Fall, 2000).
- Course completion rates (3 studies).
- Counts or measures of activity levels or patterns (5).

"Subjective" measures are frequently used in the current body of ALN research on effectiveness, though they are not usually considered as valid as objective measures. These include student self-assessments (through questionnaires or interviews) of course learning outcomes (absolute or compared to traditional courses; 8 of the studies included in this paper use such a measure); the effectiveness of the mode or system used for delivery (including convenience, motivation, usability, time required, access to professor; 18 studies); or of the quality of the instruction or materials (3 studies). Note that the total number of studies using each type of measure adds up to more than 100% of the studies, since many used more than one measure of effectiveness. Generally, multiple measures enhance the reliability of the conclusions about effectiveness.

Table 1: Summary of Measures and Results for All Nineteen Studies

Measures	Positive for ALN	No Difference	Negative for ALN
Objective Measures			
Course grade	2	6	
Final exam grade	2	1	
Midterm/quiz grades	2	3	
Quality of work rated by instructor	3	2	
Assignment Measures Length of Report	1		
Rated by Judges Forgetting		1	
Content Quality	1		
Completeness	1		
Amount of Collaboration		1	1
Amount of Activity / Participation	2		
Female participation	1		
Course completion	1		2
Use of instructor who does not prepare materials	1		1
Subjective measures via students Learning more		5	
Skill development			
Quality of work		2	1
Quality of course materials		1	
Quality of discussion			2
Motivation/Interest	3	1	1
Progress to degree	2		
Access to degree	2		
Access to instructor	1		
Access to educational resources	1		
Usability of technology	2	1	2
Participation			1
Social Presence			1
Totals	28	24	12

III. RESULTS: ALN VS. TRADITIONAL FACE-TO-FACE COURSE DELIVERY

A. Summary Tables of Results

Most of the studies measure effectiveness in more than one way (e.g., grade distributions plus subjective student assessments) and/or study different courses, resulting in many "mixed results." We have classified results as falling into one of two categories, those generally show ALN to have better outcomes than traditional courses (Table 2), and those that tend to show no difference, overall (Table 3).

Table 2: Summary for eight studies with largely positive ALN findings

Measures	Positive for ALN	No Difference	Negative for ALN
Objective Measures			
Course grade	2	2	
Final exam grade	2		
Midterm/quiz grades	2		
Quality of work rated by instructor	3		
Assignment Measures Length of Report	1		
Rated by Judges Forgetting		1	
Content Quality	1		
Completeness	1		
Amount of Collaboration			
Amount of Activity / Participation	1		
Female participation			
Course completion	1		
Use of instructor who does not prepare materials			
Subjective measures via students			
Learning more	6		
Skill development	1		
Quality of work			1
Quality of course materials			
Quality of Discussion			
Motivation/Interest	3		
Progress to degree	2		
Access to degree	2		
Access to instructor	1		
Access to educational resources			
Usability of technology			
Participation			
Social Presence			

For these eight studies in Table 2, the preponderance of the evidence is that ALN is more effective than traditional courses. All of the results indicate ALN is better, or else some results show ALN as better and others show "no difference." The studies that are judged to be in this category include those by Alavi [3]; Andriole [4]; Benbunan-Fich et.al. [5], Hiltz [6]; Hiltz & Wellman [7]; Hsu et.al. [8]; Thoennessen et. al [9]; and Turoff and Hiltz [10].

For the remaining 12 studies, the preponderance of the evidence shows "no significant difference" between ALN and the traditional courses or sections or experiences that are compared. Either all the results show "no significant difference," or there are mixed results with results better for ALN for some courses or measures, and worse on others (e.g., in the SCALE projects at Illinois [11], there are some conflicting results related to the course and/or experience of the instructor.).

There are no qualifying empirical studies for which ALN is clearly shown to be less effective than traditional modes of course delivery, on the whole.

The first important point to note is that the "no significant difference" cases really indicate that ALN is just as effective as face to face and when this is added to the positive results for ALN there is a four to one ratio of positive results to negative results in these 19 studies. Furthermore, if we realize there are only four instances of objective measures that are negative and none of them includes direct measures of learning, we find that the results rather overwhelmingly support the hypothesis that ALN is a meaningful alternative to the classical face to face class; ALN tends to be as effective or more effective, depending on the circumstances of the particular implementation and the measure used.

In terms of some of the negative results, the course completion or drop out rate is probably higher than it should be because of mistaken expectations by students, either because they are new to the use of ALN or because they do not have the student network to warn them away from particular offerings where the course might not live up to the description. In fact, many studies of ALN show that the role of the instructor and his or her ability to deal with this new mode of learning is a principal factor in ALN success. Teaching ability is important, as well as experience in the mode of delivery. A lot of face to face courses may be taught by less than perfect instructors, but the face to face environment can tolerate a wider range of instructor abilities. We must evolve a mechanism to specify in evaluation work the competence of instructors, or results can easily be confounded.

Most universities have a standardized survey for measuring student reactions to an instructor at the end of the course. It is only this year that the union at NJIT agreed to a slightly modified version of a teaching evaluation course to be put online for all ALN courses, so all online courses will receive the same survey and those teaching online sections can be directly compared with respect to their face to face sections and with others teaching the given course. It is this sort of data that should be assessed longitudinally to determine how the performance of the instructor evolves over time, and which instructors are the important ones to carefully debrief to determine relative success factors in the teaching of a given course.

Table 3: Summary for eleven studies with largely mixed or No Difference" ALN findings

Measures	Positive for ALN	No Difference	Negative for ALN
Objective Measures			
Course grade		4	
Final exam grade		1	
Midterm/quiz grades		3	
Quality of work rated by Instructor		2	
Assignment Measures Length of Report			
Rated by Judges Forgetting			
Content quality			
Completeness			
Amount of collaboration		1	1
Amount of activity / participation	1		
Female participation	1		
Course completion			2
Use of instructor who does not prepare materials	1		1
Subjective measures via students			
Learning more		5	
Skill development			
Quality of work		2	
Quality of course materials		1	
Quality of discussion			2
Motivation/interest		1	1
Progress to degree			
Access to degree			
Access to instructor			
Access to educational resources	1		
Usability of technology	2	1	2
Participation			1
Social presence			1

Some of the variables that are related to the degree of effectiveness of a particular course implementation are suggested by the various correlations with learning effectiveness reported in the studies included in this analysis. These are shown in Table 4. There are not enough replications that test specific relationships to reach any firm conclusions on these relationships at this point, but the studies do suggest hypotheses to be tested in future studies.

Table 4: Correlations or Interactions Reported for the Positive Studies

- Perceived collaboration correlates with perceived learning
- Activity by individuals correlates with perceived learning
- Perceived collaboration correlates with motivation
- Higher objective grades in Computer Science correlate with the use of ALN
- SAT Scores and/or GPA are the dominant correlation with course grades (independent of ALN or face-to-face)
- Initial subjective expectations correlate with later actual participation
- Course type and mode of delivery interact
- Degree of collaboration correlates with satisfaction with course

Correlations or Interactions Reports (unique to one study) for the Mixed or No Difference Studies

- Use of quizzes (for feedback only) improves learning perceptions by instructors and students
- Collaboration falters when there is not sufficient critical mass
- Laboratory use and collaboration are correlated in a Chemistry course
- Collaborative groups online have higher satisfaction than individuals online
- Group Communications with Learning Game led to higher learning levels than with either alone
- No benefit found for use of telephone communications
- Dense hyperlinks interfere with ease of learning
- More efficient management of distance students possible
- Larger courses in distance possible.
- Technology problems correlate with student dissatisfaction

With respect to student feedback, it is not surprising to find from a number of studies that face to face students often think that the quality of their work or the quality of discussion is better face to face, when in fact the opposite may be true when expert judges are used. This perception is similar to that of someone who changes from using a manual technique to using a computer to handle tasks. The way one is used to doing work is usually felt to be a better way than having to learn a new way. It often takes a long time for people to get used to a new way of solving problems or learning and to begin to actually realize improvement.

It is also time to capitalize on student records to begin to conduct some longitudinal analyses. We need to relate students' subjective opinions about an ALN course to how many such courses they have taken. We must view their grades and overall grade averages in relation to how they have performed in prerequisite courses, to help to control for possible effects of self-selection of mode of delivery. In this manner we can begin to get a handle on the true long-term impacts of ALN. One would suspect that longitudinal analyses will begin to show that those who actually desire to use the ALN alternative (as compared to those who are basically "forced" to take an ALN section because there are no available alternatives) do better than those in comparable face to face classes.

IV. CONCLUSIONS AND DISCUSSION

The evidence is overwhelming that ALN tends to be as effective or more effective than traditional modes of course delivery, at the university level. There really is no need for more studies to explore this question. What we need is more research that will enable us to make ALN even more effective, especially as new technologies proliferate. For example, most early ALN's were "text-only" discussion; many now include multi-media web based tutorials instead of or in addition to a textbook, and possibly audio and/or video interaction with the instructor. How important is multi-media in student teacher and student-student interaction, and how may it best be used? With very small and pervasive devices coming into use (e.g., wireless and pocket PCs), how can these devices best be used to further improve convenience of access to ALNs? What forms of collaborative learning vs. individual assignments are most appropriate for different kinds of courses or class sizes? As Alavi and Leidner [12] point out in their call for "greater depth and breadth of research" on technology-mediated learning, research in this area must look at *how* technology influences learning, which involves an "explicit consideration of relationships among technology capabilities, instructional strategy, psychological processes, and contextual factors involved in learning). We need to develop more sophisticated and more comprehensive theoretical frameworks, and also more valid methods and instruments than those that have characterized a majority of studies to date.

In conclusion, it is time to start looking at the evaluation of ALN beyond the single course and consider the full range of evaluation variables. Consider the following top down structure of evaluation variables that might form an overall model for the study of ALN effectiveness and impacts:

Evaluation Measures

Student Performance Measures
- Amount of learning
- Time to Degree
- Satisfaction
- Motivation
- Enjoyment
- Participation

Resource Measures
- Effort to Learn
- Time to learn
- Time to educate
- Cost of resources
- Effort to access learning
- Cost of learning resources
- Availability of course as needed
- Convenience of courses

Opportunity Measures

Do new things not possible before
- Accessibility for new populations
- Reduce or eliminate distinction between distance and regular students
- Make direct use of human resources not normally available in a course
- Introduce new programs

25

Do things differently than before (organizational impacts)

- Change the nature of courses
- Change the nature of degree programs
- Change the nature of educational institutions
- Change the nature of departments
- Change the nature of teaching
- Change the evaluation criteria of faculty

Long Term Impacts

- Impact on individual (job, earnings, advanced study. etc.)
- Reputation of Program
- Reputation of Institution
- Accreditation of Program

Significant Intervening Variables

- Type of Students (objectives, part time, learning abilities, gender, age, experience, and other demographics)
- Type of Course (laboratories, skill, subject area, etc.)
- Teaching Methodologies employed (e.g., is discussion graded, are individual or group assignments and activities used)
- Size of course
- Information on courses available to potential students
- Technology employed (media mix, usability, functionality)

From the above and the preliminary correlations based upon courses as well as our understanding of higher education, it is time to begin formulating testable models that involve many of the key variables, and to begin to use meaningful historical data to verify or improve our models.

For all the talk of university research, as with most commercial organizations, universities are reluctant to expose the critical historical data that they have, for fear of negative publicity. Historically, in industry, the few times that this has succeeded, it has tended to be the work of an independent and non-competitive organization that guaranteed the anonymity of detailed data when it came to the publication of the resulting analysis reports. The incentive for the participating organizations was to be able to compare their performance with others, and in so doing, have a better idea of how to make decisions to improve their situation.

It might be that the formulation of such an independent depository of historical information is one of the next important steps in furthering the evaluation of ALN. While we have done a reasonable job, as an academic community, in proving the viability of ALN, our form of distance learning is probably still a minority in terms of the methods whereby distance learning is being offered. ALN researchers tend to believe that approaches that do not include extensive communication and interaction among students and faculty are inferior to ALN approaches as well as face to face education, but this message has not "gotten through" to a lot of distance course designers. We need to increase our evaluation and research dissemination efforts and use the opportunity presented to provide a deeper understanding of higher education effectiveness than exists to date.

V. ACKNOWLEDGEMENTS

This work is partially supported by a grant from the Alfred P. Sloan Foundation, by NJIT, the New Jersey Center for Multimedia Research, and the New Jersey Center for Pervasive Information Systems. David Spencer and Jayalamathy Sadagopan contributed many of the article reviews for the database. Razvan Bot has primary responsibility for the database of papers and other aspects of the web site construction and maintenance.

VI. REFERENCES

1. **O. Ngwenyama and Lee, A.** Communication Richness in Electronic Mail: Critical Social Theory and the Contextuality of Meaning. MISQ June 1997. Available at http://saturn.vcu.edu/~aslee/ngwlee97.htm

2. **Worrell, M., Hiltz, S.R., Turoff, M. and Fjermestad, J.** An Experiment in Collaborative Learning using a Game and a Computer Mediated Conference in Accounting Courses, Proceedings, Hawaii Int'l Conference on System Sciences, 28th Annual, pp.63-71, 1995.

3. **Alavi, M.** Computer-Mediated Collaborative Learning: An Empirical Evaluation, MIS Quarterly, June, pp.159-174, 1994.

4. **Andriole, S. J.** Requirement-Driven ALN Course Design, Development, Delivery & Evaluation, JALN, Vol 1, No 2 - August, 10p., 1997. http://www.aln.org/alnweb/journal/issue2/andriole.htm

5. **Benbunan-Fich, R., Hiltz, S.R., and Turoff, M.** A comparative content analysis of face-to-face vs. ALN mediated teamwork. Proceedings of the 34th Hawaii International Conference on System Science, IEEE Computer Society, 2001.

6. **Hiltz, S. R.** Correlates of learning in a virtual classroom, Int'l Journal Man-Machine Studies, Vol.39, pp.71-98, 1993.

7. **Hiltz, S.R. and Wellman, B.** Asynchronous Learning Networks as Virtual Communities. Communications of the ACM, Sept. 1997, 44-49.

8. **Hsu, E. Y. P, Hiltz, S.R. and Turoff, M.** Computer-Mediated Conferencing System as Applied to a Business Curriculum: A Research Update, Int'l Business School Computer Users Group, 20th Annual North American Conference, pp.214-227, 1992.

9. **Thoennessen, M., Kashy, E., Tsai, Y. and Davis, N.E.** Impact of Asynchronous Learning Networks in Large Lecture Classes, Group Decision and Negotiation, Vol.8, pp.371-384, 1999.

10. **Turoff, M and Hiltz, S.R.** Effectively Managing Large Enrollment Courses: A Case Study. In Bourne, J. and Moore, J.C., eds, Online Education: Volume 2. Learning Effectiveness, Faculty Satisfaction, and Cost Effectiveness, pp. 55-80. Needham, MA, Sloan Center for Online Education, 2000.

11. **Arvan, L., Ory, J., Bullock, C.D., Burnaska, K.K., and Hanson, M.** The SCALE Efficiency Projects, JALN, Vol 2, No 2 - September, 27p., 1998. http://www.aln.org/alnweb/journal/vol2_issue2/arvan2.htm

12. **Alavi, M. and Leidner, D.E.** Research commentary: Technology-mediated learning— A call for grater depth and breadth of research. Information Systems Research, 12, 1 (March), 1-10, 1991.

13. **Alavi, M., Yoo, Y., and Vogel, D.R.** Using Information Technology to Add Value to Management Education, Academy of Management Journal, Vol 40, No 6, pp.1310-1333, 1997.

14. **Arbaugh, J.B.** Virtual classroom versus physical classroom: An exploratory study of class discussion patterns and student learning in an asynchronous internet-based MBA course, Journal of Management Education, Vol.24 Issue 2 Apr., pp.213-233, 2000.

15. **Benbunan-Fich, R. and Hiltz, S.R.** Impacts of Asynchronous Learning Networks on Individual and Group Problem Solving: A Field Experiment, Group Decision and Negotiation, Vol.8, pp.409-426, 1999.

16. **Fallah, M.H., How, W. J. and Ubell, R.** Blind Scores in a Graduate Test: Conventional Compared with Web-based Outcomes. ALN Magazine, Vol. 4, Issue2, December 2000.

17. **Hadidi, R and Sung, C.** Pedagogy of Online Instruction – Can it be as Good as Face-to-face? Proceedings of the American Conference on Information Systems, Long Beach, California, Aug 2000, pp. 2061-2065, 2000.

18. **Hiltz, S.R.** The Virtual Classroom: Learning Without Limits Via Computer Networks. Norwood, NJ, Ablex Publishing (Human-Computer Interaction Series), 1994. (Currently available from Intellect at www.intellect-net.com)

19. **Hiltz, S.R., Benbunan-Fich, R., Coppola, N., Rotter, N., and Turoff, M.** Measuring the Importance of Collaborative Learning for the Effectiveness of ALN: A Multi-Measure, Multi-Method Approach. JALN 4, 2 , 2000. http://www.aln.org/alnweb/journal/jaln-vol4issue2-3.htm

20. **Ocker, R.J. and Yaverbaum, G.J.** Asynchronous Computer-Mediated Communication versus Face-to Face Collaboration: Results on Student Learning, Quality and Satisfaction, Group Decision and Negotiation, Vol.8, pp.427-440, 1999.

21. **Sandercock, G.R.H. and Shaw, G.** Learners' Performance and Evaluation of Attitudes Towards Web Course Tools in the Delivery of an Applied Sports Science Module, ALN Magazine Vol.3 Issue 2 Dec., 9p., 1999. http://www.aln.org/alnweb/magazine/Vol3_issue2/sandercock.htm

22. **Sener, J. and Stover, M.L.** Integrating ALN into an Independent Study Distance Education Program: NVCC Case Studies, JALN, Vol. 4 Issue2, 2000.

23. **Wade, V. P. and Power, C.** Evaluating the Design and Delivery of WWW Based Educational Environments and Courseware, ACM, ITICSE Proceedings, July, pp.243-248, 1998.

APPENDIX 1: LIST OF PAPERS IN THE KNOWLEDGE BASE: PARTIAL DISPLAY

Users can choose to view an abstract of the articles included, the full text (when permission is granted to post, by the copyright holder), and most importantly, the database entry with coding and analysis of the important aspects of the methods and findings of the study.

APPENDIX 2: DATABASE ENTRY FOR ONE STUDY

Database Entry

[1] Author, Date, Paper Title and Reviewers

Author(s): Alavi, Maryam
Year: 1994
Full Title: Computer-Mediated Collaborative Learning: An Empirical Evaluation
Reviewer(s): not available

[2] Theories/Concepts

Collaborative Learning: active learning, knowledge construction, group-oriented learning, transforming mental models-problem solving; emergent knowledge.

[3] Study Design

- Field Experiment
- Comparative Analysis of treatment groups (treatment: teaching theater with GDSS-2 groups, non-GDSS-traditional classroom-1 group)
- Level of Analysis: Individual

[4] Class Size	[5] Grade Level	[6] Institution(s)	[7] M/F Ratio
40-50	MBA	Univ. of Maryland	Not Available

[8] Subjects

127 MBA students, with 79 in GDSS condition and 48 in non-GDSS condition

[9] Study Methods	[10] Media
Experimental	SynchronousSameRoom
Comparative	AsynchronousEmail
Survey	

---

[11] Hypothesis

(Implicit)
Individuals in GDSS groups have higher collaborative learning effectiveness than individuals in non-GDSS groups.

[12] Measures of Dependent Variables

Dependent Variable: Collaborative learning effectiveness

Measures of the dependent variable: Perceived skill development, self-reported learning, learning interest, class evaluation, group case evaluation, expected grade, exam scores.
Note: The first five measures emanate as factors from the principal component analysis of 28 self-reported learning and class evaluation variables. The last measure is an objective measure of effectiveness.

[13] Results

- Higher perceived skill by participants in GDSS groups was extremely significant ($p < 0.001$)
- Higher collaborative learning effectiveness for participants in GDSS groups, in terms of self-reported learning, learning interest, class evaluation, and group case evaluation, was supported at the 5% significance level ($p < 0.05$)
- There was no significant difference in mean expected grades between the treatment groups
- Mid-term exam scores were not significantly different between the treatment groups, but participants in the GDSS groups achieved significantly higher final exam scores ($p < 0.01$)

[14] Comments/Conclusions

Author

- Students' affective reactions to computer-mediated collaborative learning process were more positive than reactions to manual collaborative learning process
- Implication of finding significantly higher final exam scores (but not mid-term scores) for GDSS participants, is that the impact of computer-supported group learning processes on student achievement may be cumulative
- GDSS contributes to collaborative learning effectiveness by enhancing cooperation and teamwork
- Limitations include uncontrolled inter-group interactions, experimenter bias (instructor was the experimenter as well), novelty effect (of GDSS technology) as a potentially vitiating factor, and comparison of unequal groups.

APPENDIX 3: 19 STUDIES COMPARING ALN AND TRADITIONAL COURSES

1. Alavi, M. Computer-Mediated Collaborative Learning: An Empirical Evaluation, MIS Quarterly, June, pp.159–174, 1994. [3]

Method

- Field Experiment
- Comparative Analysis of treatment groups (treatment: teaching theater with Group Decision Support Systems (GDSS)-2 groups, non-GDSS-traditional classroom-1 group)
- 127 MBA students, with 79 in GDSS condition and 48 in non-GDSS condition

Hypothesis

(Implicit) Individuals in GDSS groups have higher collaborative learning effectiveness than individuals in non-GDSS groups.

Measures of Effectiveness

Dependent Variable: collaborative learning effectiveness.
Measures of the dependent variable: Perceived skill development; self-reported learning; learning interest; class evaluation; group case evaluation; expected grade; exam scores.
Note: The first six measures emanate as factors from the principal component analysis of 28 self-reported learning and class evaluation variables. The last measure is an objective measure of effectiveness.

Findings

- Higher perceived skill by participants in GDSS groups was extremely significant ($p<0.001$).
- Higher collaborative learning effectiveness for participants in GDSS groups, in terms of self-reported learning, learning interest, class evaluation, and group case evaluation, was supported at the 5% significance level ($p<0.05$).
- There was no significant difference in mean expected grades between the treatment groups.
- Mid-term exam scores were not significantly different between the treatment groups, but participants in the GDSS groups achieved significantly higher final exam scores ($p<0.01$).

2. Alavi, M., Yoo, Y., and Vogel, D.R. Using Information Technology to Add Value to Management Education, Academy of Management Journal, Vol 40, No 6, pp.1310–1333, 1997. [13]

Method

46 MBA students, with 21 students at Univ. of Maryland and 25 at the Univ. of Arizona.

- Case Study
- Comparative analysis of groups (in-class learning experience-local/distance students)
- Implicit longitudinal analysis (in-class learning experience: time of measurement is a main effect)
- Cross-sectional analysis (out-of-class learning experience)

Hypothesis

(Implicit)
H1: Information-technology-enabled partnership in management education is less effective than the traditional classroom pedagogy.
H1a: In-class experiences of students in remote locations are different from the experiences of local students, when classes are linked in virtual space.
H1b: In-class experiences of students vary with the time of sampling/measurement. (Times of measurement: Weeks 4, 9,13 of the semester)

Measures of Effectiveness

Dependent Variable: pedagogical effectiveness
Measures of the dependent variable

- In-class learning experience- Perceived learning, participation in learning, social presence, classroom evaluation. All four measures are factors emanating from the principal component analysis with varimax rotation; the first two factors emanated from the learning variables, the last two from the classroom assessment variables.
- Exam Scores

Findings

In-class learning experience

No significant main or interaction effects of time or location were found on students' perceived learning or participation in the learning process.

- Distant students rated both social presence and classroom dynamics significantly lower than the local students.

Out-of-class learning experience

- Student scores for satisfaction with learning experience and with participation, were significantly higher than the respective mid-points, interpreted by the authors as a positive response to the information-technology-enabled partnership.
- Individual students' self-reported learning scores were not significantly different from the mid-point for the questionnaire.

3. Andriole, S. J. Requirement-Driven ALN Course Design, Development, Delivery & Evaluation, JALN, Vol 1, No 2–August, 10p., 1997. http://www.aln.org/alnweb/journal/issue2/andriole.htm [4]

Method

- Students from 3 FTF and 3 ALN courses taught by the same instructor (number not available), for comparative evaluation of student performance
- 207 students from 17 courses, for student survey (course evaluation)
- Case study
- Concurrent design and evaluation of an ALN course
- Comparative evaluation of Face-to-Face (FTF) and ALN courses

Hypothesis

(Unstated, but tested, albeit informally)

- Student performance (in "Systems Analysis & Design" Courses) is consistently superior in the ALN mode relative to the FTF mode.
- Student evaluations of ALN courses are more positive relative to their evaluation of FTF courses.

Measures of Effectiveness

Dependent Variable #1: student performance

Measures: Quality of (a) requirements models, (b) prototypes, (c) prototype evaluation, (d) software specifications, (e) documentation, (f) teamwork; overall creativity, ability to use design tools, timeliness.

Dependent Variable #2: student evaluation

Measures: Perceived learning, extent of communication, access to instructor, and overall attitude.

Findings

Student Performance

ALN students always performed at least as well and often better than their conventional counterparts on all measures. Prototype quality was consistently higher in the ALN courses than for the conventional courses.

Student Evaluation

- Only 28% of students preferred interaction times during the daytime.
- 97% of students felt they had more access to the instructor in ALN courses.
- 80% of the students felt that conventional courses were more boring than ALN courses.
- 67% of the students felt they had more communication with fellow students in ALN courses.
- 66% of students felt they had learned more in the ALN course.
- 99% of the students felt that seeing the ideas and assignments of others was useful.

4. Arbaugh, J.B. Virtual classroom versus physical classroom: An exploratory study of class discussion patterns and student learning in an asynchronous internet-based MBA course, Journal of Management Education, Vol. 24 Issue 2 Apr., pp.213–233, 2000. [14]

Method

60 MBA students, with 33 in traditional classroom and 27 in the Internet-based section

- Field Experiment
- Comparative Analysis of treatment groups (traditional/Internet-based classes)
- Inclusion of control variables in the study? Age, gender, GPA

Hypothesis

(Implicit)

H1: Student participation and interaction are different between traditional classroom sections and internet-based course sections.

H1a: Student participation and interaction are different across groups classified by class section jointly with gender.

H2: Student learning varies between traditional classroom and internet-based course sections.

Measures of Effectiveness

Dependent variable #1: Student participation and interaction

Measures:Participation in class/group discussions - # of comments

Interaction difficulty, interaction quality, interaction dynamics (factors generated by principal component analysis on a 10-item instrument with variables on student attitudes about class interaction)

Dependent variable #2: student learning

Measures: Pre-test, post-test scores (50-question multiple choice exam)

Findings

- Participation patterns were significantly different between the two class sections ($p < 0.002$), with more than 70% of the participation coming from the internet course.
- Participation patterns were also significantly different between groups classified according to class section by gender ($p < 0.005$). Further, in the classroom section, men contributed 55% of the comments, in the internet section, women contributed about 65%.
- Class interaction difficulty was found significantly higher for the internet section than for the traditional classroom section ($p < 0.001$).
- There were no significant differences between the sections, on class interaction quality and interaction dynamics.
- As for student learning, the classroom pre-test group significantly outperformed the Internet pre-test group, but there were no significant differences between the groups in the post-test scores.

5. Arvan, L., Ory, J., Bullock, C.D., Burnaska, K.K., and Hanson, M. The SCALE Efficiency Projects, JALN, Vol 2, No 2–September, 27p., 1998. http://www.aln.org/alnweb/journal/vol2_issue2/arvan2.htm [11]

Method

8000 undergraduate students, with subjects in individual case studies ranging form 110-200

- Case Study
- Comparative Analysis of groups (ALN/non-ALN, ALN/ALN)
- Implicit Longitudinal Analysis (Performance through the term)
- Cost-benefit analysis

Hypothesis

(Implicit)

H1 (not formally tested): ALN achieves lower operational cost per student relative to traditional classroom.

H2 (formally tested in some cases): ALN results in lower instructional quality relative to traditional classrooms.

Measures of Effectiveness

Dependent Variable #1: Operational cost per student

Measures: Class size, student-faculty ratio, total instructional hours, and distribution of instructional hours over full-time faculty, graduate and undergraduate TAs

Dependent Variable #2: Instructional Quality

Measures: Exam Scores, Student assessment (difficulty of the material, perceived learning, overall experience, recommendation to self/peers, ease of use of the Web, overall Web experience

Findings

Overall, mixed results on differences between ALN and traditional, which can be summed up as "no significant differences." This depends on the specific measure, course, experience of the instructor and more.

6. Benbunan-Fich, R. and Hiltz, S.R. Impacts of Asynchronous Learning Networks on Individual and Group Problem Solving: A Field Experiment, Group Decision and Negotiation, Vol. 8, pp.409–426, 1999. [15]

Method

140 undergraduate students distributed across conditions as: 42-Individual/Manual, 42-Individual/Online, 28-Groups/Manual, and 28-Groups/Online

- Field Experiment
- Two-by-two factorial design, crossing two modes of communication (manual-offline vs. asynchronous computer conference) and two types of teamwork (individuals working alone vs. individuals working in groups)

Hypothesis

H1a: Groups will produce higher quality solutions to ethical dilemmas.
H1b: Participants working through an ALN will produce higher quality solutions.
H2a: Groups will submit longer reports.
H2b: Participants working through an ALN will submit longer reports.
H2c: Interaction: ALN-supported groups will produce the longest reports.
H3a: Group participants will perceive higher levels of self-reported learning.
H3b: ALN-supported participants will perceive higher levels of learning.
H4a: Solution satisfaction will be greater for those participants working in groups.
H4b: Solution satisfaction will be lower for ALN-supported participants.
H4c: (Interaction) Individuals working through an ALN will be the least satisfied.
H5a: ALN-supported groups will report lower levels of discussion quality.

Measures of Effectiveness

Dependent Variable #1: Task performance
Measures: Solution quality (Expert panel evaluation of reports based on clarity, organization of ideas, concept application, correctness and effectiveness of recommendations); Length of reports
Dependent Variable #2: Learning
Measures: Perceived (self-reported) learning, perceived collaborative learning, final exam grades
Dependent Variable #3: Satisfaction
Measures: Solution satisfaction (self-reported), perception of discussion quality

Findings

- ALN-supported participants had significantly better solution quality than their manual counterparts ($p=0.05$) [H1b supported].
- Group reports were significantly longer than individual reports ($p<0.0001$); online conditions submitted longer reports ($p<0.0001$); average length of reports produced by computer-supported groups was significantly higher than the average length of individual manual reports ($p<0.01$) [H2 fully supported].
- As for perceived learning, no significant main effects were found; no significant differences among conditions were found for perceptions of collaborative learning [H3d] and final exam scores; but there was a significant interaction effect between teamwork and technology [H3c supported]. Groups /online reported better perceived learning than all the other conditions.
- Groups reported significantly higher levels ($p<0.03$) of solution satisfaction than individual participants [H4a supported]; individuals online reported the lowest levels of solution satisfaction [H4c], but this interaction effect was not statistically significant.
- Manual groups reported significantly better perceptions of discussion quality than ALN-supported groups [H5a supported].

7. Benbunan-Fich, R., Hiltz, S.R., and Turoff, M. A comparative content analysis of face-to-face vs. ALN mediated teamwork. Proceedings of the 34th Hawaii International Conference on System Science, IEEE Computer Society, 2001. [5]

Method

50 students, with 28 in the FTF (control) condition, and 22 in the ALN (experimental) condition. The 28 subjects in the FTF condition were (randomly) grouped into 5 teams, and the 22 subjects in the ALN condition were also organized into 5 teams.

- Field Experiment
- Comparative analysis of groups (experimental (ALN)/control (FTF))
- Level of analysis: group
- Pilot tests to determine the appropriate allocation of time for task completion, for each condition.

Hypothesis

H1: ALN supported groups will have broader discussions than will their manual counterparts.

H2: When transferring the contents of their discussion to the final report, face-to-face groups will incur a greater loss of information than ALN-supported groups.

H3: ALN-supported groups will submit more complete reports than their manual counterparts.

H4: ALN-supported groups will produce longer solutions to the case than will their manual counterparts.

H5: ALN-supported groups will report lower levels of discussion quality than will face-to-face groups.

H6: ALN-supported groups will tend to follow parallel or pooled coordination approaches, while face-to-face groups will adopt a more tightly coupled mode.

Measures of Effectiveness

Dependent Variables:

- Discussion Breadth
- Efficiency in Information Transfer
- Completeness of reports
- Report Length
- Discussion Quality
- Coordination Approach

Measures:

- % Of issues discussed, with reference to a master list created prior to the experiment.
- % Of the issues discussed that were represented in the final report.
- % Of the issues in the master list, represented in the final report
- Word count
- Perceived Discussion Quality- overall quality, process effectiveness, outcome satisfaction, quality of execution of discussion, adequacy of exploration of issues, development of content
- Research Assistant's assessment of coordination approach in-group task completion, based on discussion transcripts. (5 mutually exclusive and exhaustive approaches for the purposes of this study: parallel, pooled, concurrent, sequential, reactive/ reciprocal)

Findings

- Asynchronous groups had broader discussions than their manual counterparts. On average ALN groups mentioned about 72% percent of the issues while face-to face covered about 52% of them.
- H2 was not supported by data. Under both conditions the experiment revealed a similar amount of lost items (about 15%) in the process of transferring the contents of the discussion to the final report.
- The hypothesis of more complete reports generated by ALN groups, predicted by H3, holds. Data supports H3 at p=. 02.
- H4 was also supported (p=. 0002) The ALN-supported groups were able to produce longer reports (682 words on average) than their manual counterparts (average of 405 words).
- Manual groups reported significantly better perceptions of discussion quality than ALN groups. The data supports H5 at a significance level (p=. 0001).
- ALN groups adopted coordination approaches with the lowest degree of interdependence (parallel/pooled), while FTF groups adopted approaches with medium degree of interdependence (concurrent/sequential). H6 was supported (p<0.01).

8. Fallah, M.H., How, W. J. and Ubell, R. Blind Scores in a Graduate Test: Conventional Compared with Web-based Outcomes. ALN Magazine, Vol. 4, Issue 2, December 2000. [16]

Method

19 graduate students, with 7 in the experimental (Web-campus) condition and 12 in the control (on-campus) condition

- Field Experiment
- Comparative analysis of experiment (Virtual Classroom) and control (Conventional Classroom) groups
- Blind study procedure: Grading of (identical) mid-term exams of students in both conditions by the instructor ignorant of the identities of individual students (and hence the conditions associated)

Hypothesis

(Implicit) Student performance in the Web-campus condition is different from student performance in the on-campus condition.

Measures of Effectiveness

Dependent Variable: Student Performance
Measure: Mid-term exam scores

Findings

The average score for the online class was slightly higher than that of the conventional class; the dispersion was much lower for the online class than for the conventional class; however, a comparison of means (standard t-test) could not reject the null hypothesis of equal means.

9. Hadidi, R and Sung, C. Pedagogy of Online Instruction—Can it be as Good as Face-to-face? Proceedings of the American Conference on Information Systems, Long Beach, California, Aug 2000, pp. 2061–2065, 2000. [17]

Method

MIS students
- Comparative
- Survey

Hypothesis

(Implicit) There will be no difference in quality of education between the online and face-to-face sections.

Measures of Effectiveness

Grades and 6 questions on evaluation of the course and instructor

Findings

No significant differences between the FTF and online classes in any of the subjective satisfaction measures, self-reported motivation, or in grades.

10. Hiltz, S. R. Correlates of learning in a virtual classroom, Int'l Journal Man-Machine Studies, Vol. 39, pp.71–98, 1993. [6]

Method

Longitudinal, comparative and quasi-experimental study of 315 undergraduates in ALN and traditional courses in a variety of disciplines on three campuses, mid- 1980s

Hypothesis

H1: There will be no significant differences in scores measuring mastery of material taught in the virtual and traditional classrooms.
H2: Students will report that the virtual classroom, as compared to the traditional classroom, improves the overall quality of the learning experience.
H3: Those students who experience "group" or "collaborative" learning in the virtual classroom are most likely to judge the outcomes of online courses to be superior to the outcomes of traditional courses.
H4: Differences among students in academic ability (e.g. as measured by SAT scores of Grade Point Average) will be strongly associated with outcomes in the virtual classroom. High ability students will experience more positive outcomes than low ability students.
H5: Students with more positive pre-course attitudes towards computers in general and towards the specific system to be used will be more likely to participate actively online and to perceive greater benefits from the VC mode.
H6: Students with a greater "sphere of control" on both the personal and the interpersonal levels will be more likely to regularly and actively participate online and to perceive greater benefits from the VC mode.
H7: There will be significant differences in process and outcome among courses, when mode of delivery is controlled (an interaction effect between mode and course).

Measures of Effectiveness

Pre-post questionnaires, grade distributions in matched sections of courses

Findings

H1: Supported. In one of five courses [Computer Science), VC final grades were significantly better.
H2: Supported.
H3: Supported.
H4: Supported. Though students with the highest SAT scores (500 and above) received the higher grades and gave the highest subjective ratings to the VC, even students at the lowest levels, were, on the average, able to perform at a satisfactory level in the VC.
H5: Supported.

H6: Not supported.

H7: There are significant differences among courses in grade distributions; no consistent differences between modes of course delivery, and some interaction between course and mode.

11. Hiltz, S.R., Benbunan-Fich, R., Coppola, N., Rotter, N., and Turoff, M. Measuring the Importance of Collaborative Learning for the Effectiveness of ALN: A Multi-Measure, Multi-Method Approach. JALN 4:2, 2000. http://www.aln.org/alnweb/journal/jaln-vol4issue2-3.htm [19]

Method

A three-year longitudinal field study of 26 courses that are part of an undergraduate degree in Information Systems compared the process and outcomes of learning using an online anytime/anywhere environment to those for comparison sections taught in the traditional classroom .

An embedded field experiment looked at the separate and joint effects of working online versus in the classroom and of working individually versus in groups.

Hypothesis

P1: ALNs can improve ACCESS to education, as compared to traditional face-to-face classrooms.

P2: ALNs can improve the rate of progress towards the degree.

P3: ALNs can improve the quality of learning as self-reported by students.

H1: ALNs can improve quality of learning as measured by grades or similar assessments of quality of student mastery of course material.

Such improvement will be contingent upon a favorable set of circumstances characterizing the use of the ALN; in particular, they will be more likely if:

H2: The student actively participates in online learning.

H3: The instructor utilizes collaborative pedagogical strategies.

H4: Participating in a collaborative (group vs. individual) assignment will increase an online student's motivation, and thus both the amount of active participation and the quality of learning.

Measures of Effectiveness

- Access to education was measured by student self-reports in the field study of 26 courses.
- The rate of progress towards the degree was measured by student self-reports in the field study.
- Quality of learning as student self-reporting was measured by questionnaire results from the field study of 26 courses and from the quasi-experimental study of one course.
- Quality of learning as measured by grades or similar assessments of quality of student mastery of course material.
- Student participates in online learning measured by correlation in the field study.

Findings

P1: ALNs can improve ACCESS to education.

P2: ALNs can improve the rate of progress towards the degree.

P3: ALNs can improve the quality of learning as self-reported by students.

H1: ALNs can improve quality of learning as measured by grades or similar assessments of quality of student mastery of course material.

H2: The student actively participates in online learning and improves learning.

H3: The instructor utilizes collaborative pedagogical strategies improves learning.

H4: Participating in a collaborative (group vs. individual) assignment will increase an online student's motivation, and thus both the amount of active participation and the quality of learning.

12. Hsu, E. Y. P, Hiltz, S.R. and Turoff, M. Computer-Mediated Conferencing System as Applied to a Business Curriculum: A Research Update, Int'l Business School Computer Users Group, 20th Annual North American Conference, pp.214–227, 1992. [8]

Method

Third and fourth year engineering students taking an introduction to management course who were full time day students who could also be expected to be able to meet outside of class hours.

Over a two-year period, five introductory management courses were divided into competitive teams and participated in their virtual companies over a semester long period.

Hypothesis

(Implicit) The current limitation on the effectiveness of learning through gaming was imposed by a lack of communication facilities among the players.

Measures of Effectiveness

Dependent Variable #1: Effectiveness of learning management

Dependent Variable #2: Quality of business decision

Measures:

(a) a group summary report

(b) a composite index derived from the final performance scoreboard built into the game model

Findings

The use of "Virtual Management Lab" had the effect of facilitating group efforts in arriving at sound business decisions and in composing a meaningful group report reflecting their learning of management concepts and skills.

The power of 'Virtual Management Lab" has its origin in two basic philosophic concepts: asynchronous connectivity and structurization of communication.

Asynchronous connectivity greatly expands the probability of making contacts with members of the organization by removing the spatial and temporal barriers.

Structurization of communication is, of course, a solution to the general problem of information overload, which is the result of the information explosion and the advancing technology of connectivity, both synchronous and asynchronous.

The incorporation of CMC technology into the gaming environment provides the possibility for the use of games as a management support tools.

13. Ocker, R.J. and Yaverbaum, G.J. Asynchronous Computer-Mediated Communication versus Face-to-Face Collaboration: Results on Student Learning, Quality and Satisfaction, Group Decision and Negotiation, Vol. 8, pp.427–440, 1999. [20]

Method

43 graduate students participated in the experiment. 40 were part-time students with 38 of full-time employment.

The experiment uses a single factor, counter-balanced, repeated measures design.

Factor: communication mode

Experimental groups completed two back-to-back collaborative assignments. For the other assignments, groups met face-to-face for the initial meeting.

Hypothesis

H1: There will be no difference, in terms of learning, between asynchronous and FTF groups.

H2: There will be no difference, in terms of the quality of written case analyses, between asynchronous and FTF groups.

H3: There will be no difference, in terms of content of the written case analyses, between asynchronous and FTF groups.

H4. FTF groups will be more satisfied with the group interaction process the synchronous groups.

H5. FTF groups will be more satisfied with the discussion quality than asynchronous groups.

H6. There will be no difference, in terms of solution satisfaction, between asynchronous and FTF groups.

Measures of Effectiveness

Dependent variable: learning performance

Measures:

- Post-experiment questionnaire for satisfaction with the case study solution and satisfaction with the process
- Quality of the written case analysis was rated by two judges
- A multiple choice quiz was administrated to subjects at the end of each two-week experimental period

Findings

All hypotheses were supported by the collected data.

Learning measure: The difference was not significant. (p=0.846)

Quality Measure: The difference was not significant. (p=0.235)

Content Measure: The difference was not significant. (p=0.868)

Process satisfaction measure: The difference was not significant. (p=0.023)

Discussion quality measure: Subjects collaborating FTF were more satisfied. (p=0.004)

Solution satisfaction measure: No significant difference between the ranking of subjects in the FTF and asynchronous treatment. (p=0.656)

14. Sandercock, G.R.H. and Shaw, G. Learners' Performance and Evaluation of Attitudes Towards Web Course Tools in the Delivery of an Applied Sports Science Module, ALN Magazine Vol. 3 Issue 2 Dec., 9p, 1999. http://www.aln.org/alnweb/magazine/Vol3_issue2/sandercock.htm [21]

Method

80 first-year Sports Science/Sports Therapy students (median age 19.5, I.Q. Range 19–23) took part in the study.

- A control group took the module in semester A while the experimental group took the module in Semester B supplemented with WebCT.
- Attitudes towards the module were assessed in both using a standard end of module questionnaire.
- Attitudes of the control group compared to the WebCT experimental group were assessed using an online questionnaire constructed by the author.

Hypothesis

The aim of the present study was firstly to determine the effects of providing learning material and support of learners through the use of the WebCT environment on their performance in a preliminary level sports science module. Secondly the experiences of those learners using the package were also evaluated

Measures of Effectiveness

- Gender and age distributions within the groups were tested using chi squared and Mann Whitney U-test analyses respectively.
- Independent t-test comparing A-Level points were carried out to determine if any differences in previous academic achievement existed between the groups.
- Differences between the two groups in attitude towards the module in either semester were analyzed using an independent t-test.
- Correlations between the frequency of use of the WebCT site and performance in both course work and examinations were carried out in the test group.
- Descriptive statistical analysis was performed on the results of the questionnaire to assess the attitudes of the test group to the use of WebCT.

Findings

- No statistically significant (p >0.05) differences between the 2 groups in either age or gender mix respectively.
- No significant (p >0.05) difference in A-Level points between the two groups.
- No significant difference between the course work and examination marks for each group. A similar relationship existed with examination results.

15. Sener, J. and Stover, M.L. Integrating ALN into an Independent Study Distance Education Program: NVCC Case Studies, JALN, Vol. 4 Issue 2, 2000. [22]

Method

Sample: 8 ALN undergrad and grad course courses at NVCC in different majors: Chemistry, Engineering, Mathematics and Information Systems Technology. Courses varied from 4 to 88 students and were offered from 1995–1999.

Hypothesis

Research questions: What factors explain ALN success?

Measures of Effectiveness

Focus groups, faculty and student questionnaires, grade distributions

Findings

A. Faculty Perceptions of Learning Effectiveness

- Chemistry: Having several on-campus lab sessions resulted in a more productive learning environment, produced more collaboration, resulted in more productive online interactions. Computer conferencing, interactive CD-ROM, electronic homework software and video tapes works well for students. Telephone communication was not particularly effective.
- Engineering: The success of this online collaboration was largely dependent on the number of enrolled students and their particular characteristics. The online collaborative assignments did not work well when roughly fewer than about a dozen students participated in it.
- Mathematics: The use of quizzes to enable students to practice performance without punishment has proved to be an effective means for the instructors to provide feedback and monitor progress more frequently.
- Introduction to Internet Service: Too much writing text on the screen, course materials too densely hyperlinked to be printed out, slow access to online software impeded learning effectiveness. Allowing students to resubmit substandard assignments

is a more mastery learning-oriented approach. ELI students often seemed to learn more in-depth than students in on-campus courses.

B. Students Perception of Learning Effectiveness: A large majority (84%) of students overall felt that they had equal (74%) or greater (10%) access to learning resources in ELI. Two-thirds (over 70% in the case study courses) felt that ELI ALN courses were an equal or more effective than on-campus experience in Engineering courses.

C. Course Grades ELI courses have a higher student withdrawal rate than on-campus courses.

- Students who started case-study courses have success rates comparable to their on-campus counterparts. ELI courses grade are following a pattern of polar success/failure. With same instructor, same semester, the students overall grade are the same with ELI ALN and on-campus courses.

16. Thoennessen, M., Kashy, E., Tsai, Y. and Davis, N.E. Impact of Asynchronous Learning Networks in Large Lecture Classes, Group Decision and Negotiation, Vol. 8, pp.371–384, 1999. [9]

Method

1997, at MSU, the ALN was added to CAPA in an introductory physics class for engineers with over 500 students.
A longitudinal study was carried during year 96 and 97.
A comparison of learning performance between using ALN and not using ALN has been conducted.

Hypothesis

Personal attention increases student comprehension.
ALN used in large lecture classes will be seen as personal attention.
Interactive computer-assisted personalized approach (CAPA) increases student comprehension.
Students who use ALN and CAPA are more motivated to learn.
Students contacted using computer-generated email will improve their grades.

Measures of Effectiveness

Dependent variable: learning performance
Measures: grade, drop-rate

Findings

- Students taking the ALN/CAPA available class received 20% higher mid exam grades than students in previous traditional classes.
- In classes with ALN/CAPA, students using the ALN received approximately 10% higher grades and missed 12% fewer classes.
- Students receiving computer-generated email exhorting better performance were able to raise their final grade by nearly one point.

17. Turoff, M and Hiltz, S.R. Effectively Managing Large Enrollment Courses: A Case Study. In Bourne, J. and Moore, J.C., eds, Online Education: Volume 2, Learning Effectiveness, Faculty Satisfaction, and Cost Effectiveness, pp. 55–80. Needham, MA, Sloan Center for Online Education, 2000. [10]

Method

Student post-questionnaires were used to measure effectiveness.
Student questionnaires (N= 2069), conference transcript analysis for one CIS course, faculty perceptions
Case study

Hypothesis

- Results of earlier project on CIS undergraduates only will be replicated for wider variety of subject matter and student levels.
- Careful structuring and management of large online courses requiring extensive student-student interaction can make them as successful as smaller online courses.

Measures of Effectiveness

Effectiveness: "Virtual Classroom Overall" index scale (More efficient, better quality, learned more, etc. than traditional course) and Instructor Overall index scale

Findings

- Overall student ratings of their experiences are generally positive.
- Principles for successfully conducting large-enrollment sections based on required student-student interaction include:
Provide the students with a guide to the structure you are going to use, and make clear the need to follow content guidelines on the placement of material.
Utilize a large number of separate discussion spaces either as separate conferences or discernible topics within a single

conference structure.

Utilize software that allows an instructor to edit and/or delete any contributions by a student so the correct placement of contributions can be enforced by the instructor.

Use software that allows the instructor to determine the status of each student with respect to their activity and when they were last on the system.

Use software where the students doing collaborative projects can have their own private conferences to be able to work on their projects as a group.

Keep the class in synchronization so that everyone focuses on the same set of activities at the same time.

Encourage the "Montessori" technique, where students help others to minimize the overload on the instructor.

Use collaborative approaches for the class as a whole so that an atmosphere for sharing knowledge is encouraged.

18. Wade, V. P. and Power, C. Evaluating the Design and Delivery of WWW Based Educational Environments and Courseware, ACM, ITICSE Proceedings, July, pp.243–248, 1998. [23]

Method

300 students over 3 years in a course on relational databases
- Field study of two groups of learners, full time university seniors in computer science
- "Corporate" students from 4 European nations who could access materials from work
- Using a "Virtual Learning Environment" incorporating messages and multimedia materials

Hypothesis

Premise: WWW courses that follow good design guidelines can be successful.

Measures of Effectiveness

Dependent Variable: Effectiveness
Measures: informal interviews, oral exam, feedback form

Findings

Successful.
Quality of instruction "at least as effective as traditional lecture."
More in-depth exposure to subject matter.
Less contention for time and resources from the lecturer and library staff.
More efficient administration and management of students and curriculum.
Students dislike reading from screens.
Access from noisy labs detracted from learning.
Students requested more tutorial questions, after every unit.

19. Worrell, M., Hiltz, S.R., Turoff, M. and Fjermestad, J. An Experiment in Collaborative Learning using a Game and a Computer Mediated Conference in Accounting Courses, Proceedings, Hawaii Int'l Conference on System Sciences, 28th Annual, pp.63–71, 1995. [2]

Method

191 graduate students attend the study.
- Introduce a game and CMC to improve accounting information systems and auditing education.
- The game and CMC environments were tested under fewer than four conditions.

Hypothesis

Given the combination of a game and a CMC (ALN):
- Students would learn more about design, fraud, and auditing. Course experience would be improved.
- Group decision-making would improve. Students would have more favorable attitudes about computers.

Measures of Effectiveness

- Learning effect measured by test
- Perception of learning measured by end-of-course questionnaire
- Attitudes toward computers measured by 10 questions in the end of course tests

Findings

- Overall learning was supported by CMC but not in all sub areas.
- Neither the game nor the availability of a CMC individually had a group impact on learning, but the combination of the two was significant.
- The game produced significant results in awareness of business problems, which is consistent with its nature.
- Students felt they contributed to group decisions with the game, but having a CMC available made no difference.
- Both the game and the availability of a CMC improved group behavioral problems individually and in total.
- Only the availability of a CMC produced significant results in improved attitudes toward computers.

VII. ABOUT THE AUTHORS

Murray Turoff is Chairperson and Distinguished Professor in the Department of Information Systems, New Jersey Institute of Technology.
Contact: Murray Turoff, New Jersey Institute of Technology, Newark NJ 07102;
Phone: 973-596-3399; Email: Turoff@NJIT.edu; URL: http://eies.njit.edu/~turoff.

Starr Roxanne Hiltz is Distinguished Professor and Director of the Ph.D. in Information Systems.
Contact: Starr Roxanne Hiltz, New Jersey Institute of Technology, Newark, NJ 07102;
Phone: 973-596-3388; Email: Hiltz@NJIT.edu; URL: http://eies.njit.edu/~hiltz.

Yi Zhang is majoring in Information Systems at the New Jersey Institute of Technology, Newark, NJ 07102.
Contact: Yi Zhang, Department of Information Systems, College of Computing Sciences, New Jersey Institute of Technology, Newark NJ 07102; email: yxz1847@njit.edu; URL: http://web.njit.edu/~yxz1847.

COST EFFECTIVENESS

Linking Quality and Cost

Tana Bishop
Claudine SchWeber
University of Maryland University College

- Online learning is restructuring higher education.
- It is time to restructure distance learning discussions by examining the dynamic, positive, mutually desirable goals of and cost-effectiveness, and by consciously seeking strategies that accomplish both aims within the framework of unique institutional cultures and commitment.
- Respect institutional uniqueness; beware evaluation templates. Models need frequent reevaluation and consideration of new indicators.
- Quality occurs at the intersection of excellence and funding. Linking cost measures and cost strategies with quality indicators can help institutions make decisions about quality in student support, faculty support, curriculum development and delivery, and evaluation and assessment.
- UMUC's model asks:
    1) Which quality alternatives will produce a specified level of effectiveness for least cost, or
    2) Which quality alternatives will produce the highest level of effectiveness for fixed $$ amount?

I. INTRODUCTION

A. Distance Learning at UMUC

University of Maryland University College (UMUC) has a 54-year history of serving adult, part-time students. As one of 11 degree-granting institutions in the University System of Maryland, UMUC is recognized as the System's leading provider of educational programs to adults. This non-traditional student population has provided the university with the unique opportunity to explore a variety of course delivery methods. As a result, UMUC offered undergraduate courses for many years through a distributed learning model by employing a variety of delivery modes, such as voice mail, interactive television, and interactive video networks. In 1996, UMUC began offering both graduate and undergraduate online courses. Since that time, UMUC's online offerings have grown exponentially at both the graduate and undergraduate levels.

Today, UMUC offers 24 bachelors and master's degrees completely online. In addition to its virtual offerings, the university has retained a significant presence in on-site facilities. Currently, there are more than 60,000 enrollments[1] in virtual classes worldwide (See www.umuc.edu).

Most UMUC courses and programs were developed first for the traditional classroom and then adapted to the online environment. The standards and curriculum for the online courses and programs mirror those required of the traditional face-to-face offerings. In recent years, certain curricula have been designed primarily for the online learning environment. In the Graduate School, for example, the Master of Distance Education was designed exclusively for online delivery and the Master of Business Administration was developed initially for online learners.

B. Reshaping the Distance Learning Discussion

The focus on institutional accountability and the distance learning movement of the late 1990s refueled debates and discussion regarding educational productivity and quality. Between 1995 and 1998, distance programs grew 72 percent (National Center for Education Statistics, 1999). Those concerned with the restructuring of the higher education model challenge both the quality and cost-effectiveness of this new delivery model. As a result, many institutions that offer online courses focus their efforts on responding to concerns regarding quality and justifying the new modality as an effective teaching and learning platform.

In addition to addressing quality issues, institutions face questions about the costs of distance delivery from legislators, stakeholders, and critics. The discussion focuses on two key concerns: 1) whether or not technology-driven education can provide a quality learning environment, and 2) if the benefits of the distance education modality outweigh the costs of its delivery. Consequently, much of the discussion has reflected a reactive posture and focused on quality assurance as a problem that needs solving (Twigg, 2001).

Providers of online education have a unique opportunity to lead the discussion of quality in a more meaningful direction. Few would disagree about the need for institutions to provide assurance that quality concerns are considered. Rather than viewing quality and cost-effectiveness as mutually exclusive aims, we posit that the two can be considered simultaneously as desirable goals. Toward that end, we examine both quality and cost issues of online learning courses and programs at a leading provider of online education today, UMUC.

II. RATIONALE

A. Institutional Context and Commitment

UMUC is a learner-centered institution that emphasizes teaching, faculty development, student learning outcomes, lifelong learning partnerships with students worldwide, and innovative delivery of high-quality educational programs and services. UMUC's principal constituency worldwide consists of citizens in the workforce and members of the

---

[1] Enrollment data reflect individual course enrollment, not headcount.

armed services who wish to begin, continue, or complete college degrees and to do so by continuing their studies along with work and family commitments.

UMUC's programs, instructional formats, and infrastructure for academic support services are designed expressly to serve this unique student population, with an emphasis on relevance, rigor, and accessibility. The growth of the university's online programming is a direct result of the institutional commitment to providing educational opportunities to the adult student population. As the demand for online courses has grown, so has the university's commitment to delivering quality programming in this new learning model. This institutional context and commitment provides the core from which quality is measured.

III. SELECTION OF QUALITY INDICATORS

The concern regarding quality in online education prompted the eight regional accrediting commissions to determine the "best practices for electronically offered degree and certificate programs" and other policy bodies to identify specific quality assurance areas. The indicator areas selected as components of best practices include: institutional context and commitment, curriculum and instruction, faculty support, student support, and evaluation and assessment (Middle States/Regional Accrediting Guidelines, 2000). Other policy bodies agree, in general, with the Middle States guidelines, but also stress the importance of technology (Benke, et al., 2000) as well as "time-on-task measures" and "goals and outcomes" (Phipps, Wellman & Merisotis, 1998).

In practice, UMUC similarly seeks to ensure the quality of its online education offerings in specific activity areas. With institutional context and commitment at the core, the university examines quality using seven broad areas: faculty knowledge/skills; student knowledge/skills; faculty-student interaction; student engagement in learning; curriculum, technology and information resources; and assessment and feedback (Allen, 2001). For purposes of this paper and in keeping with the current literature, we organize the discussion around four major indicators: student support, faculty support, curriculum development and delivery, and evaluation and assessment. Technology underpins each of the four UMUC quality indicators discussed below. It is an explicitly stated measure in the student support and faculty support indicators, and technology is imbedded in online curriculum development and delivery and evaluation and assessment.

The four indicators and their measurements include the following:

- **Student support**— as measured by student advisement, worldwide information resources/library services, and 24/7 support services (including online application and registration, course status and textbook information, and technology help).

- **Faculty support**— as measured by recruitment, selection, class size, training, and 24/7 information technology support.

- **Curriculum development and delivery**— curriculum development as measured by content experts, instructional designers, editors, file management support, peer review/curriculum committee review; curriculum delivery as measured by facilitating interaction (in teams and among and between students and faculty), developing critical thinking, and fostering the application of appropriate web resources in problem-solving.

- **Evaluation and assessment**— as measured by student course evaluations, periodic program reviews, special longitudinal assessments of new programs, individual course assessments conducted by faculty, and alumni surveys.

While UMUC has used these indicators for many years, the digital environment has resulted in the adaptation or addition of new measures in the indicator categories. For example, "faculty support" now includes "training about teaching," an integral component that is critical for success in the online environment, but is absent from the traditional classroom model. The desirable class size has been reduced from an average of 35 in the face-to-face setting to an average of 25 in the online classroom.

The type of support provided students and faculty also has changed dramatically as a result of the online environment. For example, the library services area has been transformed from a primarily print and residential service to a 24/7 full-service digital and global environment. In addition, information technology has shifted from being primarily an auxiliary service to a dominant and high-priority service. In fact, we now measure one aspect of student and faculty support in terms of 24-hour access.

The "curriculum development and delivery" quality indicator also has been adapted to include measures not required in face-to-face classes. The technological nature of the design and delivery has created a pedagogical shift from the standard classroom approaches. In addition, curriculum development at UMUC now requires a greater collaborative process than in the past. For example, faculty work closely with instructional designers to develop courses that are pedagogically sound. In the evaluation area, the need to identify and measure student learning outcomes systematically is another addition to the quality process. This latter requirement— of measurable outcomes— is a direct result of the concerns about the overall transformation of higher education to a digital learning environment.

As noted in the literature, it is critical that each indicator "work[s] in concert with the others to ensure…[a] quality learning experience" (Benke, et al., p 34). At UMUC, these components are closely connected and form part of the cost analysis when developing a new program and when conducting annual budget reviews. This paper will examine the link between quality and cost by examining the interplay of these dimensions at UMUC.

IV. THE EXAMINATION OF COST

Finite resources and the demand for accountability and efficiency in organizations are the basis for the examination of costs. It is little wonder so much attention is focused on the costs of online education. More than ever before, higher education institutions are expected to reflect more productivity with fewer, or minimal, resources. This prevailing condition suggests the need to identify institutional priorities and determine how to produce the desirable results most economically. As a result, cost analysis has become an integral component of strategic planning.

How we measure cost reflects the evaluative approach selected. Levin and McEwan (2001) apply an economic framework in their discussion of cost analysis and divide the analysis into four distinct categories: *cost-effectiveness, cost-benefit, cost-utility*, and *cost-feasibility*. The selection of a particular approach reflects the analytical line of questioning. For example*, cost-effectiveness* analysis is an appropriate model in the determination of which alternative produces X level of effectiveness for the least cost. The *cost-effectiveness* approach also works well in determining which alternative produces the highest level of effectiveness for a set amount.

Cost-benefit analysis differs from cost-effectiveness because it focuses on benefits. The question posed in this analysis is which of the alternatives produces X benefits at the lowest cost. *Cost-utility* measures which of the alternatives produces X utility level most economically (or highest level of utility at X cost). *Cost-feasibility* is the simplest of the four cost analysis approaches since its driving question is simply whether a certain alternative can be produced within the confines of a specified budget.

This array of cost analysis models is a convenient but simplistic overview of cost approaches widely utilized. [For a thorough treatment of each of these cost models, see Levin and McEwan (2001).] The cost analyses conducted at UMUC most often apply a cost-effectiveness analytical model. That is, we typically want to determine:

- Which alternative, or combination of alternatives, will produce a specified level of effectiveness for the least cost, or
- Which alternative, or combination of alternatives, will produce the highest level of effectiveness for a fixed dollar amount.

V. COST-EFFECTIVENESS AS AN INSTITUTIONAL PRIORITY

Cost is an important consideration at UMUC. The application of a cost-effective model is not only a good management strategy but also a practical necessity for the university. UMUC currently receives only 10% of its stateside budget from state funds, and this level of support is not guaranteed for the future. Although the state funding formula is improving, for most of the 1980s and 1990s the state contribution was negligible. The modest level of state support the university receives has helped foster an entrepreneurial culture focused on a business "return on investment" financial model. As such, the cost-effectiveness of programs is one factor in the determination of strategic direction. The university insists on programmatic excellence and, with that as the desired result, we examine various alternatives to determine how to achieve this quality goal with minimal cost.

Those who are skeptical about the restructuring taking place in asynchronous learning environments often view quality and cost-effectiveness as competing goals in higher education. Our view is that these are not opposing aims since cost-effectiveness compares alternative means for achieving a desirable goal— quality— and examines the costs associated with those alternatives, and maximizes effectiveness by selecting the option that will achieve the goal at minimal cost. The cost-effective analytical framework applied in this paper reflects the intersection of quality educational programming and affordability.

VI. BACKGROUND: INSTITUTIONAL IDENTITY

UMUC's mission is to extend access to post-secondary educational opportunities for individuals who combine work with study, with a special emphasis on Maryland's professional workforce education needs. UMUC meets those needs through innovative online and classroom-based credit and noncredit programs, using a variety of delivery formats and scheduling options.

UMUC's global mission is to sustain international eminence by extending access to American post-secondary degrees and noncredit programs worldwide. UMUC's international mission is twofold: to serve U.S. citizens and their families overseas and to expand into international markets that, in turn, will enhance Maryland's economic development as a center for global commerce.

VII. METHODOLOGY

Quality is imperative to the development of *all* of UMUC's academic programs. As noted earlier, UMUC's primary quality indicators align with those identified in the best practices literature and include the areas of student support, faculty support, curriculum development and delivery, and evaluation and assessment. The model we propose for the examination of cost and quality contains four steps: 1) the identification of the institution's quality indicators; 2) the identification of the measures for each indicator; 3) the determination of the desired impact or goal for each measure; and 4) the application of a cost model. [We apply a cost-effectiveness model in this study.]

The examples below show how UMUC applies these steps for *one* measure in each of the quality indicators. Each example reflects how we examine cost-effectiveness and quality. The cost-effectiveness analytical model utilized is an adaptation of the approach employed by Levin and McEwan (2001). In the examples that follow, we use the following scale:

    1 = low cost or low effect
    2 = low-moderate cost or low-moderate effect
    3 = moderate cost or moderate effect
    4 = moderate-high cost or moderate-high effect
    5 = high cost or high effect

Since dollars are relative to an institution's budget and desired goals/impact, they have less meaning than relational data. Therefore, the data presented in our examples reflect ratios rather than absolute dollar figures. Ideally, institutions would want to achieve a 1:5 cost-effectiveness ratio— that is, low cost and high effect— but this is difficult to achieve in environments with so many competing resource demands and finite revenue streams.

A. Quality Indicator: Student Support
Indicator Measure: Library Services
The student support quality indicator includes measures such as student advisement, worldwide information resources/ library services, and an array of 24/7 services, including online application and registration, course status and textbook information, and technology help.

Table 2: Linking Quality and Cost II: Faculty Support (Recruitment)
Desired Impact/Goal: Recruit 200 part-time faculty in 2001-02

Alternatives	Projected Cost	Measure Effect (Impact)	Cost/Effectiveness Ratio
Option #1 • Increase current faculty load (full-time and part-time) • Apply word-of-mouth strategy to recruit part-time, qualified colleagues of faculty members	1 (Low cost)	2 (Low-moderate effect) Increasing load is a short-term approach, and word-of-mouth has unpredictable results	1:2 (L cost: L-M effect)
Option #2 • Apply word-of-mouth strategy to recruit part-time, qualified colleagues of faculty members • Advertise in 1 or 2 general publications that direct candidates to UMUC recruitment website	3 (Moderate cost)	3 (Moderate effect) Unpredictable results based on word-of-mouth strategy are offset by the typical strong response rate to print advertising	3:3 (M cost: M effect)
Option #3 • Apply word-of-mouth strategy to recruit part-time, qualified colleagues of faculty members • Advertise in 1 or 2 general publications that direct candidates to UMUC recruitment website • Advertise in online environments (list-servs, banner ads) • Target recruitment advertising in specialized papers and journals • Contact specialized organizations, such as professional associations	5 (High cost)	5 (High effect) The strategy includes both general and targeted advertising	5:5 (H cost: H effect)

UMUC likely will need to utilize a combination of these options to meet the goal of recruiting 200 new part-time faculty in 2001-2002. For example, to recruit faculty in highly specialized areas such as software engineering or e-commerce, the strategies delineated under Option #3 may be necessary. When searching for faculty in more traditional fields, such as history and English, either Option #1 or #2 may be sufficient, depending upon faculty availability and the number of faculty needed.

C. Quality Indicator: Curriculum Development and Delivery
Indicator Measure: Curriculum Development

The development of online curriculum and the ability to effectively deliver and update the course(s) involves the following measures: the use of content experts, instructional designers, file managers, editors, and peer review/curriculum committee approval. In 2001-02, the Undergraduate School anticipates developing 70 online courses, and the Graduate

School plans to develop over 30 new online courses. The example below reflects the combination of various alternatives considered to achieve a cost-effective approach to developing the 70 undergraduate level courses. Varying costs are associated with each of these strategies, and we classified the costs from low (1) to high (5) based on cost data gathered. In addition, we analyzed the likely effect, or impact, of each of these strategies, drawing on information provided by undergraduate course development staff. As with cost data, we classified the measured effect from low (1) to high (5). After we identified the projected cost and impact (or effect) of each of the alternative strategies, we presented the cost-effectiveness ratio. The ratio represents how many units of cost are required to produce X level of effect.

Table 3: Linking Quality and Cost III: Curriculum Development
Desired Impact/Goal: Develop 70 online undergraduate courses per year

Alternatives	Projected Costs	Measure Effect (Impact)	Cost/Effectiveness Ratio
Option #1 • Individual author/content expert • Curriculum specialist • Editor • Primarily text-based • Generally fully developed at one time	1 (Low cost)	3 (Moderate effect) Appropriate for quick turnaround and for revisions. Uses some technology.	1:3 (L cost: M effect)
Option #2 • Team authorship • External peer reviewer • Text-based plus graphics and programming • Editor • Developed in stages	3 (Moderate cost)	3 (Moderate effect) Developmental time is longer than Option #1. Model uses an external reviewer and more technology than Option #1 to support the learning.	3:3 (M cost: M effect)
Option #3 • Team authorship • External peer reviewer • Text-based plus graphics and programming • Editor • Developed in stages • Additional experts in sub-topical areas • Multimedia (video, animation) • Specialized software (e.g., mathematical analyses)	5 (High cost)	2 (Moderate-high effect) Utilized for a selected number of "super" courses that have high enrollments or academic content that lends itself to a multimedia rich environment.	5:2 (H cost: M-H effect)

The selection of a single option will not achieve the desired result since the 70 courses targeted for development represent an array of disciplines with varying requirements. For example, certain courses are more adaptive to a highly specialized multi-media environment. Selective courses with large enrollments also have been designated as appropriate for sophisticated multi-media development. These courses fall into the Option #3 classification. Many of the 70 courses that need to be developed this year do not require that level of customization to be highly effective. Typically the largest percentage of online course development requires the selection of Option #2.

D. Quality indicator: Evaluation and Assessment
Indicator Measure: Course Evaluations

At UMUC, various measures of evaluation and assessment are in use, including: student course evaluations, periodic program reviews required by the university or the state, special longitudinal studies of new programs, individual course assessments by faculty and alumni surveys (UMUC Middle States, 2001). Course evaluations are processed by one office for all stateside classes. In spring 2001, approximately 17,000 online evaluations were processed, analyzed, and disseminated to administrators plus 700 individual faculty. Annually, this involves about 50,000 evaluations and dissemination to administrators and over 1,500 individual faculty. As you will note in Table 4, the costs for processing and distributing course evaluations increase as one moves from Option #1 to Option #2. The illustration presented below reflects a hierarchical model similar to that described in Table 2 (Library). However, with respect to course evaluations, Option #3 will provide the greatest impact (effect) but not necessarily at a greater cost over time. Varying costs are associated with each of these strategies, and we classified the costs from low (1) to high (5) based on cost data gathered. In addition, we analyzed the likely effect, or impact, of each of these strategies, drawing on information provided by the course evaluation staff. As with cost data, we classified the measured effect from low (1) to high (5). After we identified the projected cost and impact (or effect) of each of the alternative strategies, we presented the cost-effectiveness ratio. The ratio represents how many units of cost are required to produce X level of effect.

Table 4: Linking Quality and Cost IV: Course Evaluations
Desired Impact/Goal: Collect, process, analyze, and disseminate approximately 17,000 online course evaluations per semester (Adelphi campus)

Alternatives	Projected Costs	Measure Effect (Impact)	Cost/Effectiveness Ratio
Option #1 • Automate data collection, processing, and analysis • Use current staff of 1.5 FTE (plus student workers) for dissemination of results to Deans, Provost, faculty • Provide supervision for quality control of evaluation data and IT processes • Provide supervision of student workers and interface with IT staff	2 (Low-mod cost)	3 (Moderate effect) Data processing and analysis completed quickly after data collection. Dissemination process slow. Periodic problems because all databases not fully integrated. Online response rates irregular or low unless mandatory.	2:3 (L-M cost: M effect)
Option #2 • Automate data collection, processing, and analysis • Hire additional staff for specialized analyses and report production • Automate dissemination to Deans and Provost; faculty dissemination remains offline • Provide supervision for quality control of evaluation data and IT processes, and liaison with IT staff • Provide supervision for dissemination	3 (Moderate cost)	3 (Moderate effect) Data processing and analysis completed quickly after data collection. Dissemination process faster than Option #1. Online response rates irregular unless mandatory. Ability to do specialized reports at request of deans, provost; can enhance frequency of feedback.	3:3 (M cost: M effect)
Option #3 • Automate data collection, processing, analysis, and dissemination to deans, provosts, individual faculty • Provide supervision for quality control of evaluation data and IT processes • Provide specialized reports on regular basis	5* (*Initially high cost, eventually moderate -- amortized)	5 (High effect) Data processing, analysis, and dissemination completed quickly after data collection. Automated quality control feedback mechanisms. Online response rates irregular unless mandatory.	5*:5 (Initially H cost, then →M cost: H effect)

At present, UMUC is using Option #1 as the best application of its resources and technical limitations, while administrative support systems are in process to move us shortly to Option #2. Ideally, course evaluation processing would have sufficient funding, technological infrastructure, and administrative support to be able to apply Option #3. While the initial costs of Option #3 are expected to be high, these costs will decrease amortized over time. This would require the ability to conduct evaluations and to disseminate analyses and data electronically for all online and face-to-face classes worldwide. In 2000-01, enrollments worldwide rose above 225,000. Such a volume presents significant challenges to an effective and efficient evaluative process.

VIII. CONCLUSIONS

In the digital educational environment, it is critical that we view quality and cost-effectiveness as mutually desirable goals and that we consciously look for strategies that enable us to accomplish both aims within the framework of our institutional cultures and commitment. We have suggested several categories of cost analyses (cost-effectiveness, cost-benefit, cost-utility, and cost feasibility) and focused specifically on the cost-effectiveness approach utilized at UMUC. Typically, our cost-effectiveness analysis begins with establishing the desired goal or impact of a particular quality measure. After goal identification, we array various alternatives, or combination of alternatives, to determine which will produce either: a) a specified level of effectiveness for the least cost, or b) the highest level of effectiveness for a fixed dollar amount.

In this case study, we identified the four primary quality indicators that guide our institution—student support, faculty support, curriculum development and delivery, and evaluation and assessment—and several of their associated measures. As noted earlier, technology is an integral component of each of the quality indicators, because technology underpins the ability to provide a quality digital learning environment. The model we proposed for the examination of cost and quality contains four steps: 1) the identification of the institution's quality indicators; 2) the identification of the measures for each indicator; 3) the determination of the desired impact or goal for each measure; and 4) the application of a cost model. By linking quality measures and cost strategies, we offered examples of how UMUC focuses on the achievement of both goals simultaneously.

Our institutions and our stakeholders will benefit from such an effort to link quality with cost. Without such clear linking, online education is prey to the critics who argue that profitability, rather than pedagogy, dominates the agenda of higher education institutions. To date, the response from providers of online education tends to follow a defensive posture. We suggest that it is time to reshape the distance learning conversation. Institutions of higher education that provide online education have the opportunity to lead the discussion and analysis of teaching and learning in an increasingly dynamic technological world.

In the process of linking quality and cost, the first step is to identify the desired goal. Identification of the goal must be done within an institutional context. That is, the impact must reflect the desired outcome of a specific quality measure of a particular program or institution. The recent interest in cost analysis has led to the suggestion that cost templates can easily be adapted to identifying costs and decision-making (Jones, 2001; Morgan, 2000). However well intentioned the suggestion is, we have concerns about the promotion of templates as a key solution to complex cost issues. Each institution must develop models that fit the organizational culture, commitment, and resources. In addition, models need to be reevaluated periodically to assess their compatibility with the desired goals.

Finally, the identification of quality indicators and measures also needs to be evaluated periodically. The dynamic digital learning environment requires that we remain vigilant regarding newly emerging indicators of quality and the ways they are measured. For example, student learning outcomes has become a critical measure of an institution's quality and a primary focus of attention. Similarly, student persistence in the online environment is another measure that has garnered recent interest. At UMUC, we are beginning to evaluate measures of learning outcomes and persistence systematically. New quality indicators and measures need to be linked with appropriate cost analyses. By reshaping the discussion to focus on the co-existing relationship between cost and quality, we all have the opportunity to direct the agenda to where we believe it should be— the positive relationship between funding and excellence.

IX. REFERENCES

1. **Allen, N.** (2001). Lessons learned on the road to the virtual university. *Continuing Higher Education Review,* Vol. 65, pp. 60-73.
2. **Benke, M., Brigham, D., Jarmon, C.G. and Paist, E.** (2000). Quality indicators for distance education programs. In *Rethinking quality assurance: Examining established practices exploring new strategies.* Paper presented at Annual Accreditation and Quality Assurance Conference of the Middle States Commission on Higher Education, Philadelphia, PA.
3. **Commission on Higher Education, Middle States Association of Colleges and Schools.** (2001). Statement of commitment by the regional accrediting commissions for the evaluation of electronically offered degree and certificate programs.
4. **Jones, D.** (2001). Technology costing methodology casebook 2001. Boulder, CO: Western Cooperative for Educational Telecommunications.
5. **Levin, H. and P. McEwan.** (2001). *Cost-effectiveness analysis, 2nd ed.* Thousand Oaks, CA: Sage Publications, Inc.
6. **Morgan, B.** (2001). Is distance learning worth it? Helping to determine the costs of online courses, http://www.marshall.edu/it/onlinecosts/distancelearning.pdf.
7. **Phipps, R. and J. Merisotis.** (2000). Quality on the line: Benchmarks for success in internet-based education. Washington, D.C.: Institute for Higher Education Policy.
8. **Phipps, R., Wellman, and J. Merisotis.** (1998). Assuring quality in distance learning: A preliminary review. Washington, D.C.: Institute for Higher Education Policy.
9. **Twigg, C.** (2001). Quality assurance for whom? Providers and consumers in today's distributed learning environment. Troy, NY: Center for Academic Transformation, Rensselaer Polytechnic Institute.
10. **U.S. Department of Education, National Center for Education Statistics.** (1999). Distance education at postsecondary education institutions: 1997-98. Statistical Analysis Report No. 2000-013, by L. Lewis, K. Snow, E. Farris, D. Levin, and B. Greene. Washington, DC: National Center for Education Statistics.

X. ABOUT THE AUTHORS

Tana Bishop is the Associate Dean for Administration in the Graduate School at University of Maryland University College. Prior to that, she was Assistant Director for the United Kingdom and Iceland with UMUC's European Division. She also worked in Japan as the Executive Director of the Navy Relief Society, a non-profit financial institution. Other professional experience included many years as an educator. She spent more than a decade living and working outside the United States. That international experience has influenced her interest in offering asynchronous courses and degree programs to diverse student populations. She holds a master's degree in Japanese Studies. Tana recently successfully defended her dissertation in the College of Education at the University of Maryland College Park and anticipates receiving her Ph.D. in December 2001. Her areas of specialization include the economics of education, educational leadership, and international teaching and learning. She currently serves as President of the Maryland Association of Higher Education.

Contact: Tana Bishop, Graduate School, University of Maryland University College, 3501 University Blvd. East, Adelphi, MD 20783; Phone: 301-985-7200; Fax: 301-985-4611; E-mail: tbishop@umuc.edu.

Claudine SchWeber is Associate Provost, Office of Distance Education and Lifelong Learning at the University of Maryland University College. She is also a Graduate professor in the Executive Master's Degree Program at UMUC. Her work in distance education is the result of earlier activities as a mediator (especially for ADA cases) and her interest in using technology to bring services to the client. She has written about distance education, and given innumerable presentations and workshops. Recently the State Department sent her to Australia to discuss Distance Education and the issues faced in the U.S. In addition to her administrative work, Dr. SchWeber is an online faculty member, and she formerly trained Graduate School faculty in the pedagogy and practicality of online teaching. Prior to coming to UMUC, Dr. SchWeber was the training director for the Council of Better Business Bureaus Mediation-Arbitration Division, and before that an Associate Professor of Criminal Justice with specialties in labor relations, conflict management, and ethics. Claudine SchWeber is the author of dozens of articles, a book on the aftermath of court-mandated change, and hundreds of presentations. She currently serves as a Commissioner in the University Continuing Education Association (UCEA) Commission on Learning and Instructional Technologies and is a member of the Appeals Board for the Better Business Bureau Privacy Project.

Contact: Claudine SchWeber, Office of Distance Education and Lifelong Learning (ODELL), University of Maryland University College, 3501 University Blvd. East, Adelphi, MD 20783; Phone: 301-985-7777; Fax: 301-985-7845; E-mail: cschweber@umuc.edu; URL: http://www.umuc.edu/distance/odell/; Personal URL: http://polaris.umuc.edu/~cschwebe/claudine/csmain.html.

Factors In ALN Cost Effectiveness at BYU

J. Olin Campbell
Brigham Young University

- The first factor in cost effectiveness is to increase effectiveness by improving learner knowledge, skills and attitudes (e.g., by providing simulations and tutorials on demand for difficult concepts, or by formative interactions with mentors). This can improve cost effectiveness for learners.
- The second factor is to decrease fixed costs per learner (e.g., by decreasing development costs and increasing the number of learners).
- The third factor is to decrease variable costs per learner (e.g., by substituting capital for labor through automated grading and record keeping, or by developing online learning programs or videos to replace faculty lectures, so the same number of faculty can support more learners or provide more mentoring).
- To meet rapidly increasing demand for a BYU college education while meeting its institutional mandates for fixed on-campus student enrollment, fixed square foot space limits, and fixed FTE faculty and staff, BYU has three online programs:

  The Bachelor of General Studies (BGS) uses cost effective courses to enable learners to earn a degree from an accredited university.

  Independent Study (IS) is evolving from a paper format to include web-based courses that use a discussion board and email for students and faculty, with immediate grading and feedback on quizzes.

  Semester Online (SO) provides online versions of high enrollment courses across the curriculum, decreasing time to earn a degree by making courses available when they are needed, avoiding construction of new buildings as enrollment increases by moving courses or parts of courses online, and supporting faculty in creating online modules for high enrollment courses.
- The Center for Instructional Design (CID) substitutes capital (development of online modules) for labor (faculty time in lectures). It is designed to decrease labor costs per learner by 40 percent while enabling faculty members to work individually or in small groups with students.

59

I. INTRODUCTION

Brigham Young University in Provo, Utah, is part of the education system of the Church of Jesus Christ of Latter Day Saints (LDS). It is one of several higher education LDS Church schools, and is the largest, with an enrollment of 29,000 students. All of the LDS Church schools are heavily supported by tithing and donations from members. As the Church grows rapidly worldwide, it becomes increasingly difficult to provide quality higher educational opportunities to widely dispersed members, and admission has become more selective— decreasing access to a highly valued resource. Church leaders have considered divesting the Church schools, as they have divested other institutions such as department stores and banks that were set up in the mid 1800's because there were no such institutions in the Utah desert. However the decision has been made— repeatedly— to maintain the Church schools as a vehicle to develop men and women from many nations who will be leaders in their own communities.

BYU has high incentives to control or reduce costs and increase academic productivity. The following describes the reasons:

The Growth of BYU's Clientele: While some universities are facing a slowdown in growth, BYU is experiencing the opposite problem— an increasing population of eligible individuals who would like to attend BYU. The LDS Church heavily underwrites tuition (currently $1530 per semester for full time students). The membership of the LDS Church is now over 11 million and growing, with over 100,000 of its youth turning college-age each year. Presently, Brigham Young University is only able to admit about 6,000 of the applicants each year.

Philosophy: The University's sponsor is very interested in providing a BYU education to as many eligible individuals as possible. The philosophy is one of access and inclusion. However, the costs of operating a university campus constrain access. In order to contain costs BYU's Board of Directors has implemented several cost limiting efforts, such as a cap on on-campus enrollment, a moratorium on new positions, and a moratorium on building space (detailed below), all of which may be affected by using technology to increase productivity.

Enrollment Cap: The Board of Trustees has capped BYU's on-campus enrollment at 30,000 students to help control costs. Maintaining this cap has caused entrance requirements to rise. Scores for a typical entering freshman have risen from an unadjusted high school GPA of 3.3 up to 3.7 (on a four-point scale) and an average ACT score of 22 up to 27. BYU must find a way to extend its reach to more than just this narrow range of outstanding high school students eligible for admission to the university. However, no limits have been placed on online enrollments— the enrollment cap only affects on-campus students. Both the Board of Trustees and the administration are looking to online courses as a way to alleviate the pressure to admit more students while maintaining or increasing quality and honoring the enrollment cap.

Moratorium on FTEs: Closely related to the enrollment cap is a long-standing moratorium on full-time equivalencies (FTEs) in paid positions. Online courses may also allow existing staff to serve a growing student body.

Moratorium on Square Footage: In another move to control costs, BYU's Board of Trustees has also placed a moratorium on building space on campus. Several buildings on campus have recently been rebuilt, on the condition that equal square footage was torn down to make room for the new square footage. It is hoped that better use of technology will create a "bricks to clicks" situation, allowing many more students to be served in the same physical space.

Changes in the LDS Church Education System: In addition to BYU in Provo, Utah, the LDS church owns and operates three other degree-granting post-secondary institutions:

- BYU-Idaho in Rexburg, Idaho, with an enrollment over 8900
- BYU-Hawaii in Laie, Hawaii, with an enrollment nearly 2300
- LDS Business College in Salt Lake City, with an enrollment of approximately 900

The LDS Church's Commissioner of Education has said that all the church-owned post-secondary institutions in the USA will be required to rely on BYU to build their online offerings.

In this context, the access to and cost effectiveness of educational opportunity have become vital issues to the Church and the University. The focus in this paper is on factors in the cost effectiveness of ALN. To bring forward the issues and alternatives, three related BYU learning programs are considered: Semester Online (SO, created in 1999); Independent Study (IS, created in 1921); and Bachelor of General Studies (BGS, created in 1999). Semester Online materials may be a complete course, a simulation, or parts of a full course, depending on the need. IS and BGS typically provide complete courses.

The programs vary in purpose, history, and methods for achieving cost effective learning, but all are part of or contribute to an established curriculum. In addition, IS supports family history (e.g., genealogical research) and other non-curricular learning programs. Many of the Semester Online and Independent Study courses are also available in face-to-face classes. IS has a complete high school curriculum, with transcripts provided. It has also had a very small high school diploma program, with the diploma being awarded from two local school districts. IS does not grant degrees, but the courses that it develops may be used toward a degree— either a traditional BYU degree or the Bachelor of General Studies (BGS).

To support these initiatives, the University Administration created a new Center for Instructional Design (CID) in 1999. This center provides the design and development expertise for high quality college-level courses and for special projects. This centralized development is similar to that used by the British Open University. As part of the centralized development operation that uses substantial university resources, the University holds copyright and distributes proceeds. In the case of traditional faculty's creative works where only nominal use of university resources is involved, the faculty member maintains copyright, subject to the provision that the author grants to the University and the Church a license to use the intellectual property for internal, noncommercial purposes.

II. RATIONALE

A. Related Work on Cost Effectiveness

1. Describing Cost Effectiveness

The description of cost effectiveness presented here draws from prior work on use of computer-aided and distributed learning as a means to increase access and decrease costs while providing learning equivalent to or better than methods used in the typical classroom. Hiltz, Derry, Goldman-Segall, and Turoff [1] analyzed empirical studies of ALN that asked research questions, collected data (qualitative or quantitative), reported results, and were published in refereed conference proceedings or journals, in the English language. From the 15 papers in which the effectiveness of ALN was compared to that for face-to-face classes, 2/3 reported it was more effective, and the remainder reported "no significant difference."

This result is congruent with broader but less rigorous compilations of studies on distributed learning by Russell, termed The Significant Difference Phenomenon [2] and The No Significant Difference Phenomenon [3]. They are also congruent with earlier work by Kulik and Kulik [4] on computer-based instruction, and by Fletcher [5] on interactive videodisc instruction.

2. Cost Effective Learning Methods

The investigation of cost effective learning methods includes interpersonal skills and laboratory courses. For example, Campbell, Lison, Borsook, Hoover, and Arnold [6] investigated use of computer and video technologies to develop interpersonal skills. They found that by using interactive video modeling and peer coaching they could save two-thirds of the instructor's time and produce significantly better results than classroom methods to help students develop and use interpersonal skills. The learners' performance was judged by detailed ratings of specific statements in role-playing and also by qualified independent raters who were blind to the treatments used.

3. Electronic Laboratories

With regard to electronic laboratories for learning, Campbell, Bourne, Mosterman, and Brodersen [7] found that students who used seven simulated labs and two practice sessions in physical labs performed as well on a criterion physical lab as those who learned using all physical labs. Moreover the students tended to prefer simulated labs because of the flexibility to complete labs when and where they are most convenient. Oakley [8] discusses similar work at the University of Illinois on electronic labs.

4. Intelligent Agents

Work in a lab at Vanderbilt University by Thaiupathump, Bourne, and Campbell [9] investigated use of intelligent agents (software) to facilitate faculty's and other instructors' learning to create online courses using HTML and Microsoft FrontPage. These intelligent agents (or knowledge robots— knowbots) remind students of assignments and invoke themselves to check student work when the assignment is due (e.g., by verifying that the correct HTML tags are used). Students can also invoke knowbots as tutors to check partially completed assignments. The latter function was acutely important to some learners who became frustrated when they could not understand how to use a particular function late at night when the assigned human tutor was not available. The use of knowbots was positively correlated with workshop completion rates. This work lends credence to the notion that such intelligent agents may help improve completion rates, learner satisfaction, motivation, or cost effectiveness of distributed learning.

Taken together, these studies provide initial evidence that the scope of distributed learning need not be limited to basic topics, but that some aspects of complex human interactions and laboratory work may be amenable to cost effective methods that leverage faculty and teaching assistant time.

5. Automated Lesson Generation

The work noted above relates primarily to cost effectiveness of learning methods. The results can be highly leveraged because they represent the variable costs required to support each learner. These variable costs increase as the number of learners increases. However there may also be large fixed costs for course development that need to be addressed. The fixed costs can be spread over large numbers of learners. Thus the fixed cost per learner typically decreases as more students use the course. Nevertheless, large teams of developers working on instructional design projects that change rapidly can be both a scheduling and a financial nightmare.

A very large instructional design program in the aerospace industry used automated lesson generation to speed development and cut fixed costs [10]. The automated lesson generation methods produced a savings of 17 person years of labor in the first project. These design and development systems use templates for instructional strategies, screen layout, and user navigation, and provide a configuration control board that responds to and manages requests for changes to the design system. Because some of our work at BYU in the Center for Instructional Design and in Independent Study requires centralized development and teams of developers, related forms of template and automated lesson generation methods are being considered and used.

6. Evaluating Learning Outcomes

Kirkpatrick [11] provides a method to evaluate learning outcomes at several levels, beginning with learner reaction (e.g., ratings) and progressing to performance in the learning environment, performance on the job, and impact on the organization that uses the learners. Phillips [11] discusses means to estimate return on investment (ROI) in training. Both of these are primarily oriented to businesses, but they can provide instructive ideas for faculty and administrators in higher education, especially as the notion of accountability grows among accreditation boards.

B. Semester Online

Semester Online was introduced at BYU to improve cost effectiveness, given the same total number of students on campus and square feet of buildings. The intended audience is primarily traditional on-campus college students. Semester Online is currently a hybrid online (including ALN) and face-to-face classroom program that was initiated by senior administration. There are several goals:

1. Facilitate higher throughput by more flexible scheduling, so fewer students need to wait a semester to take a course they need, and may thereby graduate more rapidly.

2. Reduce the number of class sessions students are required to attend in physical classrooms. Doing so can free up classrooms for additional courses.

3. Provide centralized high quality course design and development for online courses and modules in high-volume courses.

Semester Online courses range widely in their methods, but all provide online learning in place of some classroom lectures, and meet less often than regular courses. This added flexibility allows students to schedule classes, and allows faculty in class meetings to focus on discussing content and answering questions. SO courses are offered over the Internet at no additional cost to tuition-paying students. These courses allow students to progress at their own pace within the semester, and may also provide immediate feedback, chat rooms, and links to other resources. Students in many Semester Online courses can purchase from the bookstore a CD-ROM containing course-related multimedia resources, allowing use of large media files even if students have slow Internet connections.

Semester Online courses typically include discussion of content with other students in the course, as well as with the instructor, both online (ALN) and in person. Students can do many of their assignments completely online from home, the library, or a campus computer lab. Assignments with objective questions (multiple choice, matching, and true/false) are graded and returned to the student within seconds. For each missed item the learner receives a specific feedback statement from the instructor. Examinations for Semester Online courses are proctored by the BYU Testing Center. (This discussion is adapted from the University's Semester Online web site at http://ar.byu.edu/so/.)

Two examples of the cost effectiveness effort are CID's development of video and online courses such as Accounting 200 and English 115. Accounting 200 registers 1200 students each semester and is taught almost entirely using video and distributed learning components.

English 115 is one of the most recent CID projects. It is a redesign of the traditional classroom course, which enrolls 3280 students each academic year in 87 sections per semester, with 20 students per section. It is taught primarily by graduate instructors in the English Department's MA program. The project is expected to reduce the cost of teaching each section by 33 percent, for an annual savings in excess of $200,000. This project is funded by a large Pew grant, and substitutes capital (development of online modules) for labor (faculty time in lectures). It is designed to allow faculty members to work individually or in small groups using face-to-face or ALN discussions with students. When complete, it will reduce the need for classroom space from approximately 80 classrooms per semester to 30 classrooms. The English Department also plans to double the availability of sections at popular times and increase student mentoring.

C. Independent Study

BYU's Independent Study (IS) program is one of the largest in the country, with approximately 66,000 enrollments in the 2001 calendar year (where each course is counted as an enrollment, but testing out of a course is not counted). The predicted enrollment for the following year is well in excess of that. The program's intended audience is learners who need college, high school, and personal enrichment courses. Independent Study began offering traditional correspondence courses in 1921. It is expected to more than recover its costs.

All IS courses support emailed student questions to faculty, though such email may first be reviewed by staff members, who answer logistical questions, and then forward content issues onward. A growing number of IS courses also support ALN faculty and student interaction via a discussion board. Tests are proctored at approved centers.

The table below presents the number and type of IS courses as of December 2001:

Table 1: Number & Type of IS Courses

Current Courses	Web	Paper
University	146	320
High School	78	211
Personal Enrichment	49	96
Total	273	627

Some courses for Family History/Genealogy are free and are very heavily used. For example the cumulative enrollments from two of these free courses grew from 415 at the end of January 2001 to 19,584 at the end of July. The University can provide these free courses because the incremental cost of adding one new user is practically nothing. These free courses are not included in counts of Personal Enrichment courses or in enrollment numbers.

In 1996 BYU Independent Study began offering courses over the Internet. Web courses now account for 25% of IS enrollments. The introduction of Internet courses resulted from the twin goals of improving the quality of educational offerings and reducing operational and management costs— in other words improving both cost and effectiveness. Scability, the ability to support large numbers of learners at a low cost per learner, was one of the key principles. Some outreach models in education increase faculty burden so much that faculty are not motivated to continue. This approach is designed instead to leverage faculty time and talent.

Because of its low costs and high revenues, Independent Study funds other programs on campus. In 1993 IS developed Speedback, which uses a computer to grade assignments. Instructors write the questions, and then write feedback for every allowable response. This information is stored in a computer database, so when a paper assignment is submitted it is immediately graded, and feedback provided for the student. This essentially reduces turnaround time to that of mail transit for those who use paper versions of the course.

For Web Speedback, the response is immediate— and the time and personnel cost to process and mail student materials is eliminated. Creating Speedback responses can be challenging, since the instructor must anticipate the reasons for errors and provide a response for each error. In Speedback, the instructor is setting the standards and providing individualized feedback, then coaching and grading via software. In this environment the faculty provide learning guidance via the course materials, and respond to questions as needed.

Web-based Speedback can decrease variable costs that go up for each learner, by substituting *capital* (the hardware and software to support the system) for instructor *labor* to grade each person's assignments. Because the instructor must anticipate common errors, Speedback offers another teaching opportunity. For large numbers of learners, Speedback may provide more rapid and individual feedback than a classroom teacher can give.

Although BYU Independent Study offers paper versions of its courses, the Web versions provide much more rapid response to learners. This is a qualitative improvement as well as quantitative improvement for learners, because immediate response changes the learning experience from "do and wait" to "do and revise."

There are three main categories of courses at Independent Study: college, high school, and personal enrichment. Each category has different types of students.

- College courses
  Students take IS college courses for many reasons. Some cannot fit a required class into their schedule because the course is offered only one semester each year. Instead of waiting for that semester, Independent Study

students can start a course any time, and finish any time within a year. In addition, some high school students take college courses to get a jump-start on college, or to fill concurrent enrollment requirements. Others need to make up a class.

- High school courses
  Several types of students take Independent Study high school courses: those who are required to take courses because they are failing, those who want to take a course to graduate early or for convenience, and home-schooled students who need curriculum. The latter are part of a growing population that takes courses from Independent Study. These students are typically good at working on their own.

- Personal enrichment courses
  These courses often attract motivated learners who want to learn for the sake of learning. They are not concerned about a grade—they just want knowledge, and to be able to do something with what they learn. Often these are older students who already have a degree, or just want to brush up on a subject.

The table below presents projected IS enrollments for 2001.

Table 2: Projected IS enrollments for 2001

University	High School	Personal Enrichment	Total
22,000	47,000	1000	70,000

Of these projected enrollments approximately 19,000 are expected to be web-based.

Some people are concerned that Independent Study attracts large numbers of students because the courses are easier, or because of the LDS "brand." With regard to this, Independent Study courses at the college level have long been developed and controlled by BYU faculty departments. They are now also being merged into the on-campus curriculum. Thus students attracted to the BYU brand who are taking college courses online are the beneficiaries of the same review and accreditation procedures as other University courses.

D. Bachelor of General Studies

This degree completion program was initiated by senior administration in 1999. Many students at BYU marry and move away from the University before completing their formal education, then return online to complete their degree. The Bachelor of General Studies (BGS) serves these students. The typical learners in BGS courses are those who have started college but not completed a Bachelors degree. The BGS requires a 30-credit hour BYU campus residency out of the 120 total credits required. The BGS program is continuously accepting enrollments, and does not use the cohort model where students are admitted in groups. Its learners are typically adults. These and other IS courses are readily available and are migrating to an online format.

BGS courses are offered in an ALN format because the learners are widely dispersed. The courses are part of the University's established curriculum, provided through Independent Study. They are in many cases similar to those used on campus. The program requires at least 30 hours on campus of the total 120 hours of courses. This is an always-open program (i.e., not a cohort).

BGS students can study at their own pace and often do not need to return to campus to complete their degrees. Economically, this means that they can remain at home, can retain their jobs, and can progress toward the degree.

The Center for Instructional Design (CID) at BYU creates most of the college level courses for IS, which are then used by the BGS program. As of July 2001 the average age for BGS students was 39 years, with 88 percent female and 12 percent male. Seventy eight percent were from the Western States, Alaska, and Hawaii. Other countries of BGS students included Canada, China, Germany, Guam, Japan, Kuwait, Mexico, and Thailand.

BGS is cost effective for students because tuition is reasonable; they can remain employed or work at home; and they may not need to return to campus. Initial financial expectations for BGS to increase revenues and at least break even are reasonable. Fixed costs for development are important, but the largest factor in cost effectiveness for the University is the variable cost per learner, and this is typically low for courses from Independent Study.

As of July 2001, the new BGS had formally admitted 920 students, with 337 provisionally accepted based on completion of a one-hour prerequisite course. The program has 8 areas of emphasis. The following present specific data on BGS learners:

Table 3: Percentage of Bachelor of General Studies Students in Each Area of Emphasis

Area of Study	Percentage
American Studies	4
English and American Literature	8
Family History	8
Family Life	32
History	7
Management	20
Psychology	12
Writing	8

Note: numbers do not sum to 100% because of rounding.

As of July 2001 there were 20 graduates of the program, with another 8 expected to graduate in August 2001.

The demographics of formally admitted students are as follows:

Gender: Female 88%, Male 12%

Age: Average for females is 40, average for males is 36, and average for the total is 39, with an overall range of 22 to 71.

Table 4: Geographic Distribution

Area	Percentage
Utah County	13.6
Salt Lake/Davis Counties	14.0
Other Counties in Utah	4.3
Western States, Alaska, Hawaii	45.7
Central States	9.2
Eastern States	10.7
Other Countries and APO (Canada, China, Germany, Guam, Japan, Kuwait, Mexico, Thailand)	2.5

Table 5: Prior College Work

Description	Percentage
Former BYU students	82
Transfer Students	16
No Previous College	2

III. BACKGROUND INFORMATION FOR THE PROGRAMS

ALN in the sense of a discussion board and direct email access to the instructor has become more common in college level Independent Study courses. Unless the instructor incorporates discussion into the course and actively uses it, or discussion is required, few students typically become involved. On the other hand, it is not uncommon for ALN faculty who encourage online discussions to comment that they enjoyed the interactions but would be wary of doing an ALN course again because they had not learned how to manage the volume of discussion. Because faculty are often more directly involved in Semester Online courses, this may be the target of opportunity to encourage further use of ALN.

To be successful, we will need to provide ALN discussion training and peer mentoring for both faculty and students. The central issue is to train students and faculty to use ALN tasks and discussion while maintaining the cost effectiveness of the ALN program.

One possibility that we are investigating to keep costs down while increasing the use of ALN is to focus on peer mentoring. In this scenario, students who have completed an assignment receive credit for mentoring a fellow student who has not yet completed that assignment. This approach requires monitoring by the faculty, but it is potentially a considerably lower time commitment than committing full time faculty to actively contributing to multiple threads in a discussion. Another possibility is to charge an additional fee for online tutoring via ALN. University leaders are in discussion about how to mentor ALN discussions as we scale up.

We are currently implementing a decision support system (DSS) that can give us information such as the cost per credit hour for a student. This DSS is central to continuous quality improvement because it makes visible some of the effect of our interventions. Such data can be very helpful as we discuss how to most productively implement ALN and facilitate mentoring.

Where our planned enrollment is 100,000 (as it is will be with Independent Study), planning and monitoring indicators of vital signs is critical. Changing incremental costs only slightly can make or break a program. Even at our current enrollment of 60,000 in Independent Study and 29,000 on-campus students, it is to our advantage to hone the system that generates and supports courses, rather than leaving each course a unique creation. We see few limits to growth using this approach, and the distinct possibility to deal with a fundamental issue we face— how to extend the educational opportunities to those who cannot come to BYU. Our goal is to bring BYU to them.

The level of growth planned for the future has not been set. First we must satisfy ourselves that the system we are using will scale up to the next level, that remote ALN learners compare favorably to the learners on campus, and that we can support the learning with appropriate access at a cost that learners can afford.

IV. METHOD

Our goal is to use technology to offload some of the teaching responsibilities of faculty and increase the number of students per instructor. It is also to encourage the "mentored student" who works closely with a faculty member on a project of worth. The goals of decreasing cost per student credit hour and increasing individual mentoring may not be mutually exclusive. By using ALN methods to replace some classroom lecture time for faculty, we open the door to more students per faculty member (because much of the faculty member's instruction is available online) and also provide more faculty time for individual mentoring. In sum, we are attempting to decrease variable costs per learner and increase quality by redeploying faculty resources.

We are using multiple methods to compute costs and benefits. Complex formulas and manual data collection will not work in the long run. One computational method is the student/faculty ratio for a course, program, or individual instructors. Another method is to compute the cost per student credit hour for programs and courses. The decision support system (DSS) will support these computations.

In the Bachelor of General Studies and Independent Study programs we have already gained experience increasing service responsiveness for students and driving out variable costs by using online courses. We are in the process of gaining additional experience in Semester Online.

The following briefly describes a new Semester Online project that is an experimental investigation of redesigning a high volume beginning English course. The goal of this redesign is to decrease faculty time required for classroom interactions by 40%, which will allow us to offer more sections of an advanced class.

BYU recently won a large grant from the Pew Foundation for "Redesign of a First Year Writing Course." This project represents many of the innovations in which we are currently engaged. The focus of this Semester Online course is as follows:

- Ensure more consistent teaching among graduate instructors by standardizing learning objectives and curriculum across sections of first-year writing.
- Improve student learning overall and specifically by reducing lecture time and increasing individual or small group faculty-to-student interaction.
- Reduce preparation time by capturing the best practices of many teachers, instantiating these practices in the multimedia course materials, and sharing them with present and future teachers.
- Prepare students for lifelong learning by shifting more of the learning responsibility to students, encouraging them to become more independent learners.
- Provide more flexibility to students and faculty to determine where and when they will interact.
- Free up classroom space to allow more students the flexibility of taking first-year writing at their preferred times.
- Maintain the important "home room" function of first-year writing, but at a significantly lower cost.
- Create capital-for-labor cost savings that will allow the English department to offer more sections of our advanced writing course, where there is more demand than we can currently meet.

V. RESULTS

Semester Online courses increasingly provide distributed learning and incorporate capital for labor substitution. Similarly, some IS courses are becoming ALN by incorporating online discussions and collaboration. Independent Study courses tend to be moneymakers. For paper and pencil IS courses, the break-even point is reached after approximately 20 students enroll. This takes into account all aspects of producing the course: designing, writing, editing, proofreading, formatting, printing, and mailing. Most Independent Study courses enroll more than 20 students. The highest enrolling courses have over 1000 students per year.

Web IS courses are typically less costly than paper IS courses because they do not incur the printing and mailing costs of paper courses. Web courses may recover their costs and break even after 5 to 10 enrollments. One reason is that the course is already written in the paper and pencil format, and conversion costs to put the course on the Web are usually minimal. Since most Independent Study Web courses come with a CD-ROM containing videos of the instructor, there is still a small mailing cost. Even this may disappear as high-speed Internet connections become more common. Once those fixed expenses are recovered, a high proportion of the tuition dollars for IS Web courses drop to the bottom line.

As we move more courses to an ALN format, online help and discussion may be provided by other students who mentor and collaborate as part of their course work. Some may come from teaching assistants. Some may come from automated software tutors, and some from staff. But some of the learning will require faculty participation, handling unanswered questions, and acting as role models and mentors.

Classroom and Semester Online courses are typically more expensive to produce than Independent Study courses (fixed costs) and require more continuing faculty involvement (variable costs) than IS courses. Our study of the new Semester Online version of English 115 can help us learn how to reallocate and leverage faculty time. Our learning from these initiatives will help us blend the cost effectiveness of Independent Study courses with the collaboration, mentoring, and simulations of Semester Online and classroom courses. In doing so, we may be able to open doors of opportunity for many more potential students, including those in developing countries.

VI. REFERENCES

1. **Hiltz, S. R., Derry, S. J., Goldman-Segall, R. & Turoff, M.** Published ALN Research Studies (2001), http://www.alnresearch.org/Html/published_aln_research_studies.htm. Accessed 1 Dec. 2001.
2. **Russell, T. L.** The Significant Difference Phenomenon, http://teleeducation.nb.ca/significantdifference/. Accessed 1 Dec. 2001.
3. **Russell, T.L.** The No Significant Difference Phenomenon, http://teleeducation.nb.ca/nosignificantdifference/. Accessed 1 Dec. 2001.
4. **Kulik, J., Kulik, C.** "Computer-Based Instruction: What 200 Evaluations Say," In M. Simonson, S. Zvacek (Eds.), Proceedings of Selected Research Paper Presentations at the 1987 Convention of the Association for Educational Communications and Technology, Ames, IA: Iowa State University, 1987, pp. 18-24.
5. **Fletcher, J. D.** Effectiveness and Cost of Interactive Videodisc Instruction In Defense Training and Education (IDA Paper P-2372), Alexandria, VA: Institute for Defense Analyses, 1990.
6. **Campbell, J. O., Lison, C. A., Borsook, T. K., Hoover, J. A., & Arnold, P.** "Using Computer And Video Technologies To Develop Interpersonal Skills," Computers in Human Behavior, 11, 2, 1995, pp. 223-239.
7. **Campbell, J. O., Bourne, J. R., Mosterman, P. J., & Brodersen, A. J.** The Effectiveness of Learning Simulations for Electronic Laboratories. Journal of Engineering Education Vol. 91, No. 1, January 2002.
8. **Oakley, B.** A Virtual Classroom Approach to Learning Circuit Analysis, IEEE Trans. on Education, 39, 1996, pp. 287-296.
9. **Thaiupathump, C., Bourne, J. R., & Campbell, J. O.** Intelligent Agents for Online Learning. Journal of Asynchronous Learning Networks, Vol. 3, No. 2, November, 1999.
10. **Campbell, J. O.** Automated Lesson Generation for High Volume Computer-Based Instruction. Instructional Design Idea Book 1993, Society for Applied Learning Technology (SALT). Available from the author, olin_campbell@byu.edu, 1993.
11. **Kirkpatrick, D. L.** Evaluating Training Programs: The Four Levels. San Francisco: Berrett-Koehler, 1994.
12. **Phillips, J. J.** Return on Investment in Training and Performance Improvement Programs: A Step-by-Step Manual for Calculating the Financial Return. Woburn, MA: Butterworth-Heinemann, 1997.

VII. ACKNOWLEDGEMENTS

The author thanks Noel Reynolds, Stephen Jones, Scott Howell, Dwight Laws, Steve Brimley, Brian Evans, and Susan Clark for their comments and reviews of this paper.

VIII. ABOUT THE AUTHOR

J. Olin Campbell is Associate Professor in the Department of Instructional Psychology and Technology at Brigham Young University. His work emphasizes cost-effective strategies for individual performance assessment and learning, and design and evaluation of computer-aided learning systems. As Director of Training Operations at WICAT Systems, his teams developed computer-based training for clients including Boeing, ALCOA, AT&T, and the Army Research Institute. The work he directed to develop a highly efficient authoring system saved 17 person years of labor on a large instructional development project. His work includes simulations for technical and interpersonal skills. Dr. Campbell holds a Ph.D. from Stanford, an M.Div. from Union Theological Seminary (NY), and a B.A. from Yale.

Contact: J. Olin Campbell, Brigham Young University, 150-K McKay Building, P.O. Box 25089, Provo, UT 84602-5089; Phone: 801- 378-1171; Fax: 801-378-8672; Email: olin_campbell@byu.edu; Web Page: http://www.byu.edu/ipt/faculty/campbell.htm.

Rethinking Cost-Benefit Models of Distance Learning

Leigh S. Estabrook
University of Illinois
Graduate School of Library and Information Science

- Models for evaluating the benefits of distance education miss several factors, including increased income potential, opportunities for job fulfillment for students who are agile users of distance technologies, and the benefits of training faculty to use new technologies to improve quality of on-campus instruction.

- In University of Illinois Graduate School of Library and Information Science (GSLIS), online courses are a scheduling option, not a separate program. GSLIS is fully integrated into school in costs, fee structure, faculty, students and support staff.

- From its start, GSLIS has had the interest and full involvement of the school, enabling the program to assert LIS leadership, overcome regulatory obstacles, integrate technology, align with field and trends, and take entrepreneurial risks.

- While fee structure is identical to other scheduling options, cost effectiveness requires that a percentage of students are out-of-state.

- Benefits to the school include enhanced faculty proficiency, course offerings in new areas, optimization of instruction, enhanced on-campus technologies, student retention, valuable publicity, and budget increases to variety of areas.

I. INTRODUCTION

LEEP [1] is the nickname given to the Internet-based Master of Science program offered by the University of Illinois Graduate School of Library and Information Science (GSLIS). Students begin the course of study with a required on-campus session during which they are taught one course ("Libraries, Information and Society") and given the technological background necessary to work effectively once they leave Champaign-Urbana. Internet-based classes include both synchronous sessions and asynchronous communication; each faculty member determines how these modes are used. All students are required to come to Champaign-Urbana for a long weekend once a semester. This face-to-face session provides opportunities to use materials that may otherwise be unavailable, to do presentations, to interact with guest speakers, and to continue to build a sense of community.

The courses emphasize group work and projects for which it is important that these students build relationships that enable them to work effectively together electronically. During the times they are not on campus, students work together in chat rooms, on Web-based bulletin boards, and even face-to-face when several live near one another in remote regions. In addition to instructor-authored web pages, students make use of textbooks, coursepacks, electronic reserves, and materials available at libraries near their homes or obtained with the assistance of the Academic Outreach Library. To assure quality, faculty receive release time before and during the first time they teach a new LEEP course. The School also invests heavily in its own technology staff, and a faculty member has administrative responsibility for the program.

Unlike many administrators of asynchronous learning programs in the United States, GSLIS does not treat the LEEP option for the Master of Science as a separate profit center. Instead, LEEP is treated as an alternative mode of class instruction. Resources of LEEP are blended with those of the entire school and, as a result, they benefit the entire school. The impetus for this economic model was bound up in the history of the School's relationship with state and professional regulatory bodies. The results have been significant economic benefits to the School far beyond those originally anticipated. The program has also provided equally important benefits to our students who have been able to move from paraprofessional to professional positions, or to newly created jobs using their technical skills. Those benefits are not, however, easily measured in terms of salary improvement as a noticeable group comes from other highly paid professions. This paper thus seeks to broaden the ways administrators can measure costs and benefits of one asynchronous program. It considers that program as part of the larger academic system and the student as part of a larger professional and personal system of relationships.

II. HISTORICAL BACKGROUND

In 1986, Northern Illinois University was in the process of closing its school of library and information science, and the University of Chicago was threatening to do the same. With an eye to establishing a presence in Chicago and, in the process, saving Chicago's Graduate Library School, the University of Illinois offered a merger with Chicago. Discussions between Provosts at each institution did not, however, end in such a merger, and Chicago closed the Graduate Library School. This left only two American Library Association-accredited programs in Illinois, Rosary College (now Dominican University) and the Graduate School of Library and Information Science at the University of Illinois at Urbana-Champaign (hereinafter referred to as GSLIS).

For the next ten years GSLIS activities in distance/extension education were shaped by struggles with the Illinois Board of Higher Education (IBHE), the state body charged with approving the *sites* at which programs are offered. In 1986 and 1987 the University of Illinois received strong pressure from librarians around the state who wanted library and information science education brought to their geographic regions. The IBHE never formally decided *to deny* site approval, but instead refused to act in a highly charged political debate.

When it became clear that GSLIS would not be given authority to begin offering its master's degree in Chicago in the fall of 1988, the School began a "scheduling option" called Fridays-Only. Still in existence, this option schedules courses on the Urbana-Champaign campus such that students can attend on Fridays only and be assured the courses will be offered that will enable them to complete the Master of Science degree.

In the early 1990's the School began to experiment with technology to support teaching at multiple sites. Jana Bradley (at Indiana) and Geoffrey Bowker (at Illinois) taught a course jointly, with students on each campus enrolled and working together on projects. Judith Weedman (Illinois) and Maurita Holland (Michigan) also taught a course jointly using two-way video.

In early 1995, with expected personnel changes in the IBHE, GSLIS once again initiated a proposal to teach its master's degree program in Chicago. In the end, under strong political pressure, the IBHE formally denied approval of GSLIS's proposal.

Within days of this second refusal to grant site approval to teach LIS courses in Chicago, faculty of the Graduate School of Library and Information Science had approved and sent to the Provost a proposal for an "open access" (i.e., site independent) model for delivering the degree using web-based technologies. The model intentionally avoided any areas that would require state regulation or external approvals. The program was the identical in admissions and course requirements to the accredited on-campus Master of Science program and therefore did not need a separate review by the accrediting body. Tuition charges were also the same to avoid the need for University trustee and IBHE approval. Moreover, by treating the asynchronous program as a scheduling option, the School did not have to seek separate accreditation and could include LEEP in the reaccredidation scheduled for Fall, 1997.

By early January 1996, the School had received the strong support of then Provost Larry Faulkner who wrote to University of Illinois Vice-President Sylvia Manning as follows:

> Dean Leigh Estabrook is proposing to adapt the curriculum leading to the Master of Science in Library and Information Science to utilize multiple technologies and delivery formats including the Internet....I strongly support the concept.... In reviewing the IBHE policies for off-campus programs, it appears that *only campus approvals will be necessary* (emphasis added) in order to implement the curriculum.
>
> ...financial elements need appropriate approvals. First, this curriculum is to be largely self-supporting. In this regard, the tuition generated by the enrollments in the curriculum will need to be dedicated to the Graduate School of Library and Information Science. I will be authorizing the addition of up to five faculty positions based on this assumption....
>
> Second, the technology needs are such that a course technology fee is proposed. I request that the addition of such a fee be considered in the development of the FY98 budget next fall. During the pilot year of FY97, the technology expenses will be underwritten with campus funds....
>
> The master's program curriculum adapted to the Internet and combined with on-campus intensive sessions in the summer promises to be an important pioneering step for the University in utilizing our knowledge about networks and the World Wide Web in meeting the educational goals of both the University and of the students we can serve. (Provost Larry Faulkner to Vice President for Academic Affairs Sylvia Manning, 1/9/96)

The LEEP proposal pleased the University on a number of counts. It successfully avoided the control of IBHE. The program promised to use the University's high technology orientation to the benefit of Illinois residents. It provided the opportunity to engage the University fully in Internet-based distance education at a time when the promises of new technology for education were just beginning to be realized. Illinois administrators were pleased at the idea of being early adopters. So, too, were the GSLIS faculty who desired to exert leadership in this area.

By March 1996, GSLIS had received a commitment for $587,000 in start up funds (over 3 years) and it began recruiting a class of 25, 20 of whom would be from in-state, the goal set by the University. In July 1996, the first LEEP class began with a total of 31. In July 2001, the School began its sixth year of LEEP with 165 students enrolled, 35 percent of whom are from Illinois. Current enrollment exceeds the original target of 125 because of high demand from Illinois residents. The financial model requires approximately 105 out of state students. The program has met its goal of being fully self-supporting through tuition income and, in fact, income is allowing the School to expand in several ways (see below).

The 1995 proposal for Using New Information Technologies to Support Delivery of the UIUC Master's Degree in Library and Information Science is essentially the LEEP program as it is offered today. It, like Fridays-Only, was designed (and continues to be treated) as a scheduling option. It is not separate from the face-to-face option, except for delivery mode. Students on campus, in LEEP, and the Fridays-Only option liberally enroll in each other's sections on a space-available basis. Tuition remains the same. The economic model also remains the same.

By spring 2001 the School was offering 15 LEEP courses per semester during the academic year and 5-7 additional courses during summer session. Expanding the concept of extension, adjunct faculty from around the country contribute significant expertise to the program. Several teach on a regular basis. Because the School allows students from different scheduling options to cross-register, these adjuncts have also allowed the School to offer courses to on-campus students for which campus-based instructors were not available. In most courses LEEP and on-campus students are being educated together.

The program has benefited from an extraordinary staff. In 1997, Professor Linda Smith agreed to become Associate Dean with primary responsibility for LEEP. A retention rate of over 95 percent and the reputation for quality of LEEP can be attributed directly to her attention to the students, her commitment to quality and her recognition of the importance of attending to all aspects of technology support and administration. Early in LEEP development, Vince Patone, a former doctoral student with a background in psychology, assumed responsibility for technology. He now heads the Instructional Technology Office supported by Jill Gengler (formerly a LEEP student) and several graduate assistants, for a total of 4FTE staff. The size of the staff is, in part, due to the way LEEP has become integrated into the fabric of the School. In spring 1999, Patone became director of all instructional technology at a time when it was no longer easy to maintain a boundary between LEEP teaching and technology and that of the rest of the School.

III. THE COST MODEL

As noted above, the cost model for LEEP was initially driven by a need to develop a program that did not require outside approval. This meant the following:

- LEEP is treated as a *scheduling option*, not a different program, nor a separate cost center
- The tuition rate for on campus and LEEP students is the same (although LEEP students do not pay on-campus fees, but instead a fee to the Academic Outreach Office).
- Students have the opportunity to take courses across different scheduling options.
- Faculty teach LEEP *on load* and, by agreement when LEEP was designed, all faculty are expected to teach in the distance program on a regular basis. In return, faculty are given summer money or released time from teaching the first time they develop a LEEP course. The first time faculty offer a LEEP course, it is the only course they teach that semester.

The School retains the tuition income—allocated in the same fiscal year as it is paid. The School also has been responsible for all costs after the initial start up. But because LEEP is fully within the School and monies are fungible, the School had flexibility in LEEP's start-up and was able to absorb early deficits. In its maturity, the School has flexibility in using "profits." The School has neither the overhead nor the formal requirement of keeping all revenues directed to the benefit of those who pay the tuition. The following table summarizes the income and costs for LEEP during its first six years. The data are necessarily rounded estimates since the School has not kept precise budget figures for costs assignable to LEEP.

Table 1: LEEP Budget FY96-FY02

LEEP BUDGET--	FY96	FY97	FY98	FY99	FY00	FY01	FY02
	Start-up	Year 1	Year 2	Year 3	Year 4	Year 5	Year 6
Faculty[1]		$100,000	$180,000	$240,000	$300,000	$250000	$250,000
Adjunct faculty			$24,000	$30,000	$90,000	$120,000	$120,000
Faculty "maintenance"		$5,000	$10,000	$15,000	$20,000	$20,000	$25,000
Summer money[2]		$35,000	$35,000	$30,000	$20,000		
Assistant dean	$10,000	$40,000	$41,600	$43,000	$45,000	$47,000	$17,500[3]
Tech support[4]	$22,000	$60,000	$60,000	$80,000	$100,000	$120,000	$130,000
Graduate and teaching assistants		$20,000	$10,000	$15,000	$30,000	$30,000	$35,000
Mentors[5]		$5,000					
Evaluation[6]		$5,000	$5,000				
Equipment/software[7]	$50,000	$30,000	$25,000	$25,000	$40,000	$60,000	$50,000
Telecommunications		$5,000	$5,000	$5,000	$10,000	$10,000	$40,000[8]
Travel		$1,500	$10,000	$10,000	$15,000	$15,000	$20,000
Supplies, mail, office		$5,000	$15,000	$15,000	$20,000	$20,000	$22,000
Clerk-typist II		$12,000	$13,000				
Admissions clerk		$6,200	$13,500	$13,500	$13,500	$14,000	$14,000
Promotion[9]	$5,000	$5,000	$5,000	$5,000	$5,000	$5,000	$5,000
LEEP coordinator						$18,000	$18,000
Special activities		$1,000	$3,000	$5,000	$5,000	$6,000	$6,000
Academic Outreach			$10,000				
Contingency		$10,000	$10,000				
Campus charges for services [10]						$40,000	$45,000
1. TOTAL EXPENSES	$87,000	$345,700	$475,100	$531,500	$688,500	$731,500	$798,500
2. TUITION INCOME		$93,000	$208,000	$483,410	$730,364	$904,068	$1,300,000
3. CAMPUS SUBSIDY	$87,000	$250,000	$250,000				
Surplus/<deficit>	--	$2,700	<$17,100>	<$48,090>	$41,864	$172,568	$502,500

[1.] This amount reflects entire salary of new faculty. As release time for preparation and for LEEP teaching declines, the cost of faculty salaries for LEEP teaching is beginning to decline proportionally. All faculty are involved in teaching, but the numbers reflect only average salaries of new faculty added because of LEEP.

[2.] Rarely needed as start up by FY01.

[3.] Reflects change in personnel, not change in level of effort.

[4.] FY99 to FY01 increase reflects salary equity adjustments, not added or changed personnel.

[5.] Students did not use or value assigned mentors. Program was dropped.

[6.] Cost of external evaluator in first 2 years. Evaluation is ongoing and reflected in administrative costs for program.

[7.] Does not reflect special university allocations from Sloan grant in FY97and FY98 for special equipment.

[8.] We expect the campus to institute a significant new charge for telecommunications in FY02.

[9.] Reflects only small direct mail efforts. Does not include travel to various conferences at which faculty speak—that cost normally covered under other expenses.

[10.] Instituted under new budgeting system.

In its first three years, as Table 1 shows, LEEP tuition did not pay fully its costs. Despite direct mail, advertising through a variety of listservs, and a variety of presentations at professional meetings by GSLIS faculty, admissions fell short by about 15 percent until this past year. Moreover, the number of outstanding applicants from in-state required admitting a higher proportion of in-state students than our economic model had predicted. Our estimates for cost-recovery were based on an 80/20 percent out-of-state/in-state student population. The percent of in-state students has leveled off at about 35 percent and will likely stay at that level given the School's responsibility to serve the state.

LEEP costs are primarily in salaries. A relatively small amount has been needed for hardware and software purchases even though GSLIS maintains its own servers, its own technical staff and has developed its own ALN software.

The greatest cost is for faculty salaries and support. LEEP allowed the School to increase its faculty size by 5. For each of those individuals there is the added "overhead" of office space, computing, and other support services. Approximately 50 percent of the classes are taught by adjunct instructors who are paid a base of $6,000 per course plus transportation and housing during the one on-campus session. Regular teaching faculty receive, in addition to their regular academic salary, either summer money or release time to prepare initially to teach a LEEP course. This added cost of overall instruction was significant at the start of LEEP, but has declined significantly now that almost all faculty have experience in LEEP teaching and fewer LEEP courses are being taught for the first time.

In the past two years, the cost of technology staff increased by 30 percent. This reflects increases in salaries, rather than an increase in staff numbers, as the School has sought to retain invaluable staff and has "regularized" the status of one intern.

The budget also reflects added administrative costs to support LEEP. This includes costs to process increased applications. Last year, the School hired a doctoral student—a graduate of LEEP—to coordinate LEEP activities, to increase visibility of the program and to assume many administrative tasks that Dean Smith developed in the program's infancy. Campus charges for services and for telecommunications in FY01 and 02 reflect increased charge backs from the campus that are directly associated with LEEP.

Promotion costs are relatively low, since we have discovered that the best promotion is coming from our students and graduates and from the papers and presentations of students and faculty.

Among the other miscellaneous costs are travel and special activities. Adjunct faculty are reimbursed for their travel to the semester on-campus weekend. The travel budget also reflects trips by faculty to make presentations about the program. The "special activities" budget is directed toward a special dinner during the on-campus weekend and other community building activities.

LEEP has obviously become profitable at the bottom line. What these figures do not reflect are other things that LEEP has "bought"— its value to its students and graduates, and to the GSLIS faculty and staff as a whole.

IV. BENEFITS TO STUDENTS

For many LEEP students, GSLIS offers one of few opportunities to earn the masters degree in library and information science in a highly ranked LIS program. Many are bound by location of work or home and do not have access to any of the on-campus programs 54 accredited programs in the United States. The University of Illinois program is consistently ranked among the top one or two in the nation. GSLIS also offers large number of courses that prepare graduates for work in libraries or in information work outside libraries.

In the 1998-1999 academic year, Professor Edward Kingsley Mensah, carried out a study for the University's Vice-president of Academic Affairs, the results of which were published in *Valuing The Returns On Investments In University Of Illinois Online Education: A Case Study Of The Library Education Experimental Program (LEEP)* [2]. Mensah's survey of 59 then-current students asked about current and *expected* income one year after graduation.

Table 2: Current and Expected Income by Type of Job

	In-State	Out-of-State	Librarians	Non-librarians	Overall
N	29	28	31	26	59
Current Income	$31,300	$31,800	$26,600	$38,300	$31,567
Expected	$37,500	$34,900	$29,500	$44,600	$35,261
% Increase	19.4%	9.7%	10.9%	16.5%	14.9%

Expected income reflects the students' perceptions of what they should expect to earn one year after graduation. In fact, there is some reason to believe these estimates are conservative. For a number of years, I have conducted workshops on salary negotiation that is available to LEEP students online. Students who negotiate generally improve their starting salary by 5 to 15 percent over what they expected to earn.

Professor Mensah also looked at the return on investment for graduates working in libraries and those choosing to work outside libraries. He concluded:

> …the private return on investment in LEEP education is $15.23 per dollar invested over the remaining life expectancy of the individual (36 years to 74 years) if she/he works as a librarian in the state. However, if she/he works in a non-library occupation, the private return on dollar invested is $29.52. The returns to the state treasure per dollar subsidy provided by the state are: $8.5 per graduate (librarian) and $20.15 (non-librarian). (mimeograph, p 34-35)

Achieving a higher income is not the only motive of a number of our students and for some of them, a career change may involve a recognized decrease in income. Notable among them is the former commodities broker, former engineer and the approximately one dozen former lawyers who are entering this field because of excitement about the work and/or a desire for a different work environment. In these cases, students are making a conscious decision to take up work with an expected decrease in salary.

Dean Smith has categorized the types of job changes our students seek by enrolling in LEEP. The variety demonstrates the difficulty in interpreting Dr. Mensah's aggregate data. Graduates can by typified as follows:

- Stay at home mothers entering the workforce in professional positions (e.g., a number becoming school librarians; one becoming a bank librarian)

- Paraprofessionals advancing within their organization to higher-paid professional positions (we have examples from a community college, public and university library)

- Paraprofessionals moving into professional positions in other organizations, frequently due to tech skills (two graduates from Atlanta provide good examples: one, a paraprofessional at Emory and was hired to develop digital library capabilities for the Institute for Paper Science and Technology; a second was a paraprofessional in a government law library and was hired to work on Coca-Cola's Intranet. Others include a former legal paraprofessional now working at Tunes.com and a former paraprofessional at the University of Kentucky who now holds a professional position at Harvard)

- Professionals moving into a position more fully exploiting their technology skills (for example a woman moving from doing reference in an academic law library to working at Intel)

- Professionals fulfilling their career goals by changing careers (the primary examples are students moving from corporate sector work and former lawyers, many, but not all, of whom seek positions in law libraries).

An economic analysis of the benefits to students and graduates of these changes awaits a larger pool of graduates, but we can identify a number of less easily measured, but significant benefits to all masters' students at GSLIS. First, all those enrolled in LEEP courses rapidly gain skills in using distance technologies both individually and for work in virtual groups. Second, students on and off campus benefit from extracurricular lectures and workshops, many of which are routinely taped and made available over the Internet. Third, asynchronous learning technologies now permeate and enrich GSLIS teaching and learning for all students. Fourth, students have access to a much broader range of courses offered by new faculty hired with new LEEP-generated income and by adjunct faculty from around the country. Fifth, the student-body is more diverse and provides broader international perspectives.

V. BENEFITS TO THE SCHOOL

LEEP has also had a significant benefit to the School as a whole. For example:

- Because all faculty are expected to teach in LEEP, almost all faculty have become proficient in using asynchronous technologies and, in the process, increasingly use these technologies in their on-campus teaching.

- Because we are able to hire instructors who also live at remote distances, the School now offers to on-campus students, via ALN, courses they would not otherwise have available. This fall, courses in medical reference and government documents are offered—courses for which there are no local instructors.

- Because on-campus and Fridays-Only students enroll in LEEP courses, the School saves the cost of offering 3-4 additional sections each semester.

- Computer upgrades to faculty now occur every 2-3 years, supported by the LEEP budget.

- According to a study by one of the LEEP students (LIS390, summer 2001), the quality of the LEEP technology staff can be credited with retention of 3-5 students each year.

The LEEP costs and budget (in which LEEP tuition is allocated) have had a significant difference to the budget and size of the school as a whole (Table 3). The Graduate School of Library and Information Science is a relatively small unit on the campus of the University of Illinois at Urbana-Champaign. In FY96, when LEEP was proposed, the School's state budget was slightly over $1million. In FY02 it is $3.3 million. The growth is directly attributable to LEEP. Tuition income is a portion of that growth, but it also reflects increased faculty size and a concomitant increased activity in grant-funded research. We also find a dramatic increase in enrollment yield for on-campus students (actually above the desired level), in part generated by the visibility of the School. Perhaps most notable is the fact that the School's percent of the campus academic budget has doubled from .4 to .8 percent, an increase representing more than LEEP tuition and reflecting the increased centrality of the School's role.

Table 3: GSLIS Budget Information FY96 to FY02

ITEM NAME	FY02 est.	FY01	FY00	FY99	FY98	FY97	FY96
Original State Budget (000)	3300	2627	1964	1712	1303	1221	1172
% Group State Budget		0.8	0.6	0.5	0.4	0.4	0.4
Expenditures (000) [1]		.	5279	5128	5074	3751	3776
Deflated state budget/IU paid [2]		.	126	133	126	109	132
On-campus grad students	320	290	256	243	237	240	237
Extramural students	165	129	115	90	53	32	8
Master Degrees conferred		c. 180	150	137	133	114	133
Total Instructional Units		.	9207	7880	6899	7084	6269

[1.]   Includes grants, contracts, gifts and other funds beyond state budget.

[2.]   Deflated state budget/IU paid State budget divided by the Consumer Price Index divided by the Total IUs. The resulting figure is in constant 1982-84 dollars per IU. The CPI used is the monthly, all items, urban consumers CPI based on 1982-84 prices, averaged for the months July-June of each fiscal year. CPI for current year is estimated.

Of particular note is that the increased state budget weighted against the amount of instruction provided by the School has remained relatively constant. This is reflected in the "deflated state budget" (row 4), an important campus measure of the cost of instruction for various programs. The experience of faculty and staff since beginning LEEP is that the School's technological and teaching environment is much richer (Smith, 2001), yet the cost of instruction has not increased.

The economic model for LEEP has focused on improving the school as a whole with the use of LEEP resources, rather than on saving money. We have been able to hire new faculty with expertise in emerging areas; we have increased the range of course offerings. We have been able to optimize enrollment in sections. And this year, the School has taken on a mortgage for an addition to the School's building that doubles its space. None of these would have been possible without LEEP income. Obviously, since the "deflated state budget" has stayed constant while undertaking new initiatives, the direct costs for instruction have declined.

VI. WHAT IF LEEP WERE A SEPARATE COST-CENTER?

We have examined the financial impact of having LEEP as a scheduling option, rather than as a separate cost-center. Were LEEP a cost-center, the School would need to offer at least 4 additional course sections for on-campus students ($45,000); and hire a budget officer to handle LEEP accounts ($35,500). The School would have an additional administrative burden because monies from LEEP tuition would have to be allocated back to LEEP activities, according to the rules of the state. Moreover, it would experience a concomitant loss of benefits to the on-campus and Fridays-Only students. Over time, I expect there will be savings in capital needs for on-campus students. For example, in an on-campus course I will teach this spring, I am considering "virtual" rather than face-to-face sections. The result is a saving of 5 to 7 classroom hours per week. Were the University to adopt such sectioning for even a small number of its regular large-enrollment on-campus courses, the savings would be dramatic.

There are obvious arguments in favor of looking at LEEP as a cost-center, most notably the ability to charge in-state students at the out-of-state rate or even to raise tuition charges for out-of-state and in-state students alike. In FY02, were the 57 in-state students paying out of state rates, the School would yield approximately $290,000 in additional tuition. Based on interviews with students then in the program, Mensah found that librarians, non-librarians, in-state and out-of-state students were willing to pay at least 40 percent more in tuition than that charged in FY98, or in this year's plan, $600,000.

Despite the potential added income, the School has been reluctant to attempt to change its economic model. One reason is that these estimates appear to be high. At the time of Mensah's study LEEP provided a unique opportunity in the country. That is no longer true. Moreover, unlike students in business schools, most of our students pay or borrow for their own tuition. Given increased competition among asynchronous programs in library and information science, and the political and academic considerations at UIUC noted above, it is unlikely students would pay as much as the 40 percent differential they said they would have 4 years ago. Equally important is the fact that we do not see the possibility of differential charging for in-state students given School's obligations, mentioned above, as part of a state-assisted University. Above all, faculty have been persuaded of the benefits of having LEEP fully integrated into the School.

As the introduction to this case notes, the financial model for LEEP was an historical accident, born of the need to avoid state-level permission for its offering. The unintended consequences suggest to faculty and staff of the School that this "integrated" approach has had much greater positive impact on the School, on student learning and on faculty satisfaction than an isolated program would have had. The cost savings are small but not trivial. By avoiding the need for separate accreditation the School saves not only costly process, but enfolds LEEP into any assessments of the master's program as a whole. The benefits include teaching all students and faculty how to use new technologies, adopting asynchronous learning as an on-campus tool, and providing added income to enhance all aspects of the School (including a newly expanded facility).

Obviously this is a case study, without comparative examples, written from the perspective of the person who initially suggested LEEP. Evident to the faculty and to others in the University outside the School is the extent to which the School has dramatically changed since LEEP began. Equally evident in other departments that have tried unsuccessfully to develop degree programs dependent on asynchronous learning is the important of full acceptance and involvement of departmental faculty. The LEEP program that does not distinguish between the have and have-not faculty or students—one in which all benefit from the "profits"—provides a model that suffers under traditional measures of costs and benefits. When the externalities are included, profits seem great. LEEP has infused the entire teaching enterprise with new ways of thinking about instruction. Our on-campus students have benefited from having colleagues from around the globe and from having the opportunity to learn virtually. Faculty and students are energized by the recognition the program has received both within the university and without. And we have been able to assert leadership in unexpected ways, including having the national accrediting body convinced of the possibility of a "virtual" site visit. Each of these benefits derives from the basic economic model that treats LEEP as a "scheduling option."

VII. REFERENCES

1.   Further information about the LEEP program can be found at http://www.lis.uiuc.edu/gslis/degrees/leep.html. And see: Smith, Linda, Faculty Satisfaction in LEEP: a Web-based Graduate Degree Program in Library and Information Science, in Online Education, Vol 2: Proceedings of the 2000 Summer Workshop on Asynchronous Learning Networks. SCOLE, 2000.
2.   **Mensah, E.K.** Valuing The Returns On Investments In University Of Illinois Online Education: A Case Study Of The Library Education Experimental Program (LEEP). http://www.vpaa.uillinois.edu/reports/mensah/.

VIII. ABOUT THE AUTHOR

Leigh Estabrook is professor of library and information science, professor of sociology and director of the Library Research Center at the University of Illinois at Urbana-Champaign. Her current research interests center on the opportunities missed by non-profit higher education by the models of distance education they have adopted. She is principle investigator for a grant from the National Science Foundation to coordinate digital library projects funded by NSF. Estabrook teaches LIS390 (Libraries, Information and Society) to masters students in both the distance and on-campus programs With the Library Research Center she has been involved in a variety of studies including strategic planning for libraries and market research for library vendors. Dr. Estabrook received her Ph.D. for Boston University in sociology, her M.S. in library science from Simmons College and her A.B. in history from Northwestern University. From 1986-2001, a time of dramatic growth in the field, she was dean of the Graduate School of Library and Information Science at Illinois. During that time the School undertook an award winning distance education form of its masters' program, initiated an undergraduate minor in information technology, acquired the Center for Children's Books from the University of Chicago and opened the Information Systems Research Lab.

Contact: Leigh S. Estabrook, University of Illinois, Graduate School of Library and Information Science, 501 E. Daniel Street, Champaign, Illinois 61820-6211. Telephone: 217-333-4209. Fax: 217-244-3302; Email: leighe@uiuc.edu; URL: http://alexia.lis.uiuc.edu/~leighe/

ACCESS ... A FOCUS ON STUDENT SUPPORT SERVICES

World Campus: Setting Standards in Student Services

Jean McGrath
Heather Kiris Middleton
Tamsin Crissman
World Campus
The Pennsylvania State University

- Effective online programs must "unlearn" traditional ideas of supporting students and, instead, determine which support services to offer distance students based on feedback from the students themselves.

- Student support units must remain adaptable to deal with challenges that include improving course completion and retention rates, offering appropriate services, updating student information systems, training and retaining staff, maintaining quality, and becoming cost effective.

- The principles that define quality support online include integration, access, ease and convenience, timely response, accurate information, staff competence, equitable policies and procedures, and customer care.

- The range of services includes administrative, instructional, advising, counseling, and activities and services that promote a sense of community and strong, ongoing relationships. Penn State's World Campus creates a sense of community and connection to the university through many avenues: audio conferences, discussion groups, bulletin boards, program offices, online chats, Penn State logos, web site links, extra curricular resources, a peer mentor program, and a student advisory board.

- Advisors make ethical decisions to make sure that the World Campus and particular program are right for the student based on the student's background and educational and career goals.

I. INTRODUCTION

A. The Importance of Student Support Services

Students seek online learning experiences for a variety of reasons, including but not limited to career change and/or career advancement, job retraining, continuing professional education, degree completion, and self-improvement. Research and experience show that online students are typically over 24 years old, have family and job responsibilities, and are location bound. These students all have different expectations as they approach their learning experiences. The institution's ability to meet those expectations determines whether those experiences will be good or bad.

Student support is an essential component of online learning and can make the difference between a mediocre learning experience and a truly successful experience. Many institutions have neglected student support and given priority to developing web-based courses and opening them for enrollment. Now student support services are being recognized as key to student satisfaction and matriculation.

Accrediting agencies and others are turning their attention to defining standards for online education, including good practices for supporting students studying at a distance. This paper will report the standards and benchmarks identified by the Institute for Higher Education Policy, the eight regional accrediting commissions, and the Western Cooperative for Educational Telecommunications. The documents published by these organizations will be used as a context for the range of services and strategies that Penn State World Campus has implemented as examples of good practice to meet those standards and benchmarks. Included is the background information, discussion on how and why certain decisions were made, lessons learned, and challenges. This is not a research-based case study, but a descriptive case study listing the services that provide student support beyond instruction. A particular focus will be services provided on the Web to students studying online asynchronously.

B. Review of Published Statements, Guidelines, Benchmarks, and Standards

Each student's support needs are different and each student's desire to utilize particular services will differ. Determining what services to offer can be difficult. The support services currently offered by institutions are based on the services offered on campus, the services already in place to assist students in correspondence study or televised courses, the theories of adult education, and/or research. It's the needs identified by the students themselves, however, on which institutions must focus. By examining the identified needs, institutions can determine the necessary student support services to meet those standards.

The statement and guidelines being developed by the eight regional accrediting commissions devote a component to student support. The following are listed in the draft titled *Statement of the Regional Accrediting Commissions on the Evaluation of Electronically Offered Degree and Certificate Programs and Guidelines for the Evaluation of Electronically Offered Degree and Certificate Programs*, September 2000 under Student Support:

- The institution has a commitment (administrative, financial, and technical) to continuation of the program until all admitted students have completed.
- Prior to admitting students into the institution: ascertain by review that the student is qualified to be admitted to the program; inform the prospective student of required access to technologies, technical competence required, all costs of the program and associated payment and refund policies, curriculum design and course time frames, library services and other learning resources, the array of other support services available, arrangements for interacting with faculty and other students, and the estimated time for program completion; and assist the prospective student in understanding the nature and challenges of learning in a technology-based environment.
- Appropriate services to make available, based on the assumption that these students will not be physically present on campus, may include accurate and timely information; preregistration advising; application for admission; course registration; financial aid; secure payment options; academic advising; student intervention; tutoring; career counseling and placement; academic progress information; library resources; training in the use of library

and research techniques; bookstore services; technical support; referrals for student learning differences; physical challenges; and personal counseling.

- Recognizing the importance of a sense of community to students' success and the benefits of a long-term relationship to both the students' and the institution, design and implement strategies of inclusion such as encouraging study groups, make available institutional publications, student government representation, etc.

Quality on the Line: Benchmarks for Success in Internet-Based Distance Education was prepared by the Institute for Higher Education Policy in a project supported by the National Education Association and Blackboard, Inc. Student support benchmarks include assuring that students receive information germane to their programs, including academic requirements, costs, and services available. Students should be provided with hands-on training to use library resources, ongoing technical support, and the opportunity to interact with student service personnel and a structured system to address student complaints.

In 2000, The Western Cooperative for Educational Telecommunications published *Online Student Services Provision: A Guide to Good Practice*. It is a thorough listing of support services that includes good practice recommendations, features to consider, and examples of Web sites that excel in certain areas. Services seen as important to online learning include information for prospective students, admissions, financial aid, registration, orientation services, academic advising, technical support, career services, library services, services for students with disabilities, personal counseling, instructional support and counseling, bookstore, and services to promote a sense of community.

II. BACKGROUND

A. Creation of the World Campus

In his 1996 State of the University speech, Penn State's President Graham Spanier announced plans to appoint a study team to explore the feasibility of a virtual campus that would match the knowledge and teaching resources of the University with the lifelong learning needs of motivated adults, regardless of time or place. There followed an intensive period of development in which many existing processes and systems were adapted and a number of new processes were created to meet the unique needs of this new learning environment.

Penn State proposed two major goals for its World Campus. First, extending educational programs to a rapidly growing number of learners in their workplaces and homes would provide a new pool of qualified students with access to Penn State. Second, through the appropriate application of a new technology-based learning environment, the World Campus would enhance the quality of the educational experience throughout the University. Over time, a successful World Campus initiative would help Penn State improve the productivity of the teaching-learning process and serve as a model for other universities attempting to more efficiently and effectively address the social and economic forces they face in the communities they serve.

In January 1998, thanks in large part to the support of the Alfred P. Sloan Foundation, Penn State's World Campus offered its first four courses to 41 students. The ALN environment was designed using an appropriate mix of technologies to support learner-instructor, learner-learner, and learner-resource interactions. A full range of learner support services including library access, advising, registration/records management, and more buttressed the teaching-learning environment.

B. Initial Goals

The initial World Campus growth goals of 30 programs, 300 courses, and 10,000 annual enrollments by 2003 seemed modest in relation to the explosive interest in, experimentation with, and development of ALN courses throughout higher education. However, given the overriding goal of full institutionalization of World Campus curricula and faculty within a complex, firmly established, and well-proven institutional structure, these goals presented a considerable challenge.

C. Mission of the World Campus

As the single administrative unit for extending Penn State academic programs to off-campus audiences through technology, the mission of the World Campus is to:

- Increase access to Penn State by otherwise under served students;
- Offer high-quality programs that build on Penn State's unique strengths and avoid unnecessary competition with other institutions;
- Create an appropriately interactive and resource-rich learning community;
- Reflect an approach to higher education that meets real market needs and is at the same time financially self-sustaining through full cost recovery;
- Offer a new source of income for participating academic units. [1]

D. World Campus Student Services

The World Campus unit identified as Student Services provides support to Penn State students studying at a distance using correspondence, interactive video, and online delivery methods. A word about nomenclature: The World Campus is part of a broader unit called the Department of Distance Education. Also included in that unit is the Independent Learning program, which evolved from Penn State's century-old correspondence study program. The Department of Distance Education is under the organization called Outreach and Cooperative Extension. It is difficult to discuss services and processes totally within the context of World Campus, so references will be made throughout to Distance Education, the Independent Learning program, and Outreach.

Student Services comprises 35 full-time staff members who perform the functions of a call center, pre-admissions counseling, advising, registration and record management, and technical support. The senior administrators include a director and an assistant director. Student Services was developed many years ago to support students studying by correspondence methodology. Support services were rendered synchronously by telephone and asynchronously by postal mail. Registrations were accepted over the telephone and by mail. Over the last decade, however, the educational and communication technology revolution has changed the way that we interact with students. In the World Campus, electronic mail and the telephone are the preferred methods of communication, and students can use e-mail and the Web to register for courses and pay tuition and fees. In fiscal year 2000-2001, Student Services provided support to students who registered for more than 5100 courses through the World Campus and 17,000 through the Independent Learning program.

Prior to the launch of the World Campus in 1998, the academic policies and business practices implemented by Student Services had been developed, based on the University practices, for students who were enrolled in continuous enrollment Independent Learning courses. Students worked independently in a prescribed time frame that was longer than the traditional on-campus semester. With the launch of the World Campus, Penn State Distance Education was tasked with integrating standard University academic policies and business practices relating to cohort-based courses delivered within a more traditional semester time frame.

III. OVERARCHING PRINCIPLES AND STANDARDS THAT DEFINE QUALITY IN WORLD CAMPUS STUDENT SUPPORT

A key component of the World Campus mission is the integration of the World Campus into the fabric of the University, including the student support activity. Where possible, academic policies and business practices are identical to their on-campus counterparts. In other cases, slight modifications were made to accommodate students not located on campus who could not conduct their business and library research in person.

---

[1] Sections A, B, and C are taken from Thompson, M., Faculty Satisfaction in Penn State's World Campus. *Online Education Volume 2: Learning Effectiveness, Faculty Satisfaction, and Cost Effectiveness,* Sloan Center for Online Education at Olin and Babson Colleges, pp. 129-144, 2001.

It was also necessary to take into account the unique nature of the adult learner studying at a distance, who is busy with family and job responsibilities. Penn State World Campus has done that by using their established experience supporting students in correspondence study as well as their experience with students' changing behavior with the advent of e-mail and the Web.

Adult students studying at a distance must have easy and multiple means of access to services at their convenience. One of the first World Campus accomplishments was to use technology to enhance access to certain services so that they were available 24 hours a day, seven days a week. Experience also showed that students wanted access to live support, especially during the beginning of their relationship with the World Campus. As a result, in September 1999, live support in the call center and records and registration office was expanded to 8:00 a.m. to 11:30 p.m. eastern standard time (Sunday through Thursday) and 8:00 a.m. to 5:00 p.m. (Friday). A year earlier, Technical Support expanded live hours of support beyond 8:00 a.m.-5:00 p.m. to meet student needs. A toll-free number continues to be available for students to use when contacting us.

Expanding hours was a huge cultural change to Student Services, but was necessary for several reasons. World Campus students are located in different time zones and many have jobs or other circumstances that prevent them from contacting us during "normal" business hours.

During this time it was also necessary to add additional Student Services staff to meet the workload; however, there was not enough office space to accommodate new hires, nor were there funds available to purchase more computer equipment. Hiring an evening shift enabled staff to share desks and equipment, and World Campus was able to meet the goal of expanded hourly coverage in the call center and registration services.

The immediacy of electronic communication raised students' expectations regarding response time to questions, fulfilling requests for information, and performing administrative functions. Setting performance standards for prompt and accurate responses with up-to-date information directly impacts student satisfaction and their perception of the quality of services that they receive. The World Campus standard for response is 24 business hours.

Staff competence is crucial to meeting all performance standards. It is important to train staff to do the job that's expected, to develop easy-to-use procedure manuals, to continually develop staff professionally, and to provide performance feedback on areas where improvement is specifically desired. Another requirement is to give staff access to the technology and information necessary to do their jobs. Each World Campus Student Services staff member is required to demonstrate a commitment to improving customer service each year.

All policies and procedures, both academic and business related, are intended to provide unbiased, fair, and equitable treatment for all students. The World Campus academic policies are the same as those used for on-campus students as set by the Penn State Faculty Senate and the Graduate School. While the World Campus business practices are not completely integrated into the Penn State system, they have been modified to meet the needs of the World Campus while being based on the University's practices for on-campus students.

Students also need a mechanism to challenge what they may perceive as unfair treatment with regard to an academic issue or business practice. World Campus regularly convenes a Student Review Committee to hear petitions from students who feel that they should be granted an exception to University policy. The committee members represent Student Services as well as staff from the World Campus instructional design, academic affairs, and business offices. Students are required to provide detailed, written accounts of their situation and extenuating circumstances and to provide documentation if available.

At the World Campus, students are customers and great attention is paid to customer care. Performance standards are set to give students accurate information and good service in a timely manner. Student Services seeks representatives that have personality traits easily transferable over the telephone or via e-mail, such as friendliness, helpfulness, respect, concern, and caring. Once students are enrolled, the goal is to treat them not only as valued customers, but also as perhaps the best spokespersons World Campus can have on its behalf.

The principles, standards, and services that the World Campus embraces are used to establish and maintain a relationship with the student. If students' experiences meet their expectations, a trusting environment will be created, leading to a long-term relationship with the students, successful completion of their program of study, and recommendation of the World Campus to their friends, family members, and colleagues.

IV. RANGE OF SERVICES THAT CONTRIBUTES TO A "QUALITY" PROGRAM

World Campus has classified the support services and strategies used to exemplify quality student support services into three categories: administrative services, instructional support services, and advising and counseling services and resources.

A. Administrative Services

1. Information to Students

Information about World Campus programs, policies, and procedures must be accessible in a variety of formats (e.g. online, print catalog, student guide) twenty-four hours a day. Contact information and hours of operation must be highly publicized. Students should be notified of all policies and procedures that affect them, multiple times through a variety of formats. It is also extremely important to keep all information up-to-date, accurate, complete, consistent, and clear to ensure that, after admission and registration, there are no surprises for the student.

2. Self-Assessment of Readiness to Participate

In addition to providing prospective students all the programmatic information necessary to make an informed decision about seeking admission to a particular program, students should have access to tools that help them assess their readiness to participate in technology-enhanced education at a distance. To be successful in online learning, a student must have the appropriate technology (i.e., hardware, software, and Internet connection), minimum skills to use that technology, and the personal characteristics that lend themselves to learning at a distance. Early in the development of the World Campus, a senior instructional designer on staff with the World Campus designed and developed an online mini-course, *World Campus 101*, in an effort to give students and prospects an idea of what it would be like to learn online. Technology requirements, technology skill level, using library services, available support services, time commitment, etc., are examples of topics addressed. A century of experience in providing information and support to students studying by correspondence informed World Campus about the types of questions students would have, as well as the types of skills they would need. The course needed to be user-friendly and to be based it in the same environment that students would use to learn in the World Campus. There are additional tools that can be developed to help students make a more direct correlation between their individual skills and traits and the skills and traits that most successful distance learners possess (e.g., self-test questions).

Pre-requisite content knowledge is also key. One method for assisting the student in making the determination that their prior knowledge gives them an adequate base for future learning is to pay due diligence to program admission requirements and the correct assessment that the applicant meets those requirements. Students that are applying to World Campus degree programs are accepted by the University's central admissions area, but certificate students are admitted directly by the World Campus. Penn State has found that admission counselors are very beneficial to students in helping to determine qualifications.

3. Web Site Importance

While the original Penn State World Campus Web site helped to produce significant enrollments after its launch in 1998, by the fall of 1999 the site's mission was in need of retooling. Growing competition in the e-learning marketplace meant a shift from "If we offer it, they will come" to "How are we different from everybody else?" For Penn State, that meant investing time and money into an expansion of its newest campus.

Launched in October 2000, the redesigned World Campus Web site laid the foundation for an online learning community that is service based, user driven and built to accommodate new online student resources as they are developed. The site—more people centered than its text-heavy predecessor—allows users to quickly self-identify the best path on the site for their needs. Included among the objectives for the new site were:

- Drive prospects to application,
- Create sense of Penn State community,
- Foster relationships with corporations/associations,
- Help prospective students understand what to look for in a virtual university.

The *Programs & Courses* section allows prospects and students to get up-to-date information about admissions requirements, course schedules, tuition and fees, equipment requirements, etc. "Hot buttons" to applications and information-request forms are on each page. The *Group Enrollments* section provides similar information to organizations and corporations interested in using the World Campus for their staff's training and development needs. A hot button is provided to a form that is fed directly to the Outreach Client Development staff for follow-up.

The *World Campus Community* pages feature profiles of students, faculty members, and staff members; a Student Commons with links to Penn State information (e.g., student organizations, career-development opportunities); and information about how distance learners can enjoy the benefits of membership in the Penn State Alumni Association. It's a priority for the World Campus to reinforce to its students that they're as much a part of Penn State as on-campus students, and the *Community* pages are one section of the new site dedicated to doing that.

In the *Student Services* section, students will find links to the various support resources available through World Campus, included but not limited to advising, student policies, financial aid, library resources, technical support, and World Campus 101. (Hot buttons to financial aid information are located throughout the site since it's one of the top questions receive from prospects and students.) Information on what to look for in an online university is also included in this section.

For Current Students is a portal through which World Campus students can access their courses. Important information such as server maintenance schedules, Penn State Access Account and course materials updates, and holiday hours are posted here as well as on the home page and in the *Student Services* and *Campus News* sections to ensure students are being provided information that directly affects them.

The final two sections, *About Distance Education* and *Faculty Resources*, are designed for scholars/peer institutions and faculty members, respectively. Even so, students and prospects can access the information in both sections if they wish.

Data shows that 77% of World Campus students applied for enrollment directly from the Web site without contacting Student Services for further information. This shows that the Web site's objective of driving prospects to application is working. The Web site also gives students capability for application and registration functions 24 hour a day, 7 days a week, and assists in reducing "live contacts" for a more manageable workload in Student Services.

Keeping the Web site updated is important. In order to do this, World Campus developed the World Campus Web Site Content Ownership Policy and the World Campus Program Page Creation, Revision, and Proofing Process. The Content Ownership Policy identifies the administrative unit that has the ultimate authority for the specific content, and the Creation, Revision, and Proofing Process outlines the process by which pages are created and updated. A specific schedule has been set up for review of each section of the Web site.

Throughout the next year, online student resources such as a World Campus simulated course demo and Peer Mentor program will be developed and implemented on the site.

4. Call Center

After the Web site, the call center may be the most important way to get information to students and prospects. Over the past decade, the Penn State Distance Education call center evolved from two receptionists to the five current customer service representatives. They receive telephone calls, assist callers with level-one information, and respond and manage one of the two e-mail accounts that are publicized in all forms of promotion. Examples of level-one interactions include requests for programmatic information, questions concerning a particular student's lessons and exams, and basic questions about distance education and Penn State in general.

Initially the call center staff's responsibility was to answer telephone calls live, assess the nature of the callers' needs, and then transfer calls to the most appropriate staff member who could best assist them. In 1999 — when World Campus received over 80,000 telephone calls (160,000 total calls if each call was transferred at least once) — changes had to be made in order to give customers the best service possible and manage the increasing workload.

Considering the volume of telephone calls, Student Services wanted to eliminate as many call transfers as possible. Not only did callers not want to be transferred, but it was also necessary to reduce the interruptions to staff doing other work and to eliminate the problem of finding available staff who weren't already helping other customers. With training, the customer service representatives began answering what were deemed level-one questions at the first point of contact with the caller.

Recently the call center initiated a menu-driven automated greeting for the telephone system. Initial reactions have been mixed from both staff and callers. Most callers were thrilled to be able to speak to a live person as soon as the telephone was answered. It was considered a positive way to establish a first impression. Student Services will continue to monitor feedback to the automated system and to assess whether or not the value (e.g., workload improvement) outweighs the drawbacks.

5. Registration, Collection of Tuition and Fees, Bookstore

Registration, payment of tuition and fees, and receiving course materials are the services most frequently used by students. They expect these services to be easy to use, available at times that are convenient, and accessible by multiple means. World Campus students have the option of registering by postal mail, telephone, fax, e-mail, or on the Web. Payment of fees and tuition can be made by cash, check, or credit card either in person or by other means, including the Web.

Course materials are purchased by the student as a separate process from registration. In 2000, the World Campus outsourced course material fulfillment to MBS Direct, a subsidiary of MBS Textbook Exchange. This gave students multiple options in ordering, paying, and receiving materials, and also provided a mechanism for tracking orders. Students now have a book buy-back option through MBS Direct. Out-sourcing also solved several administrative problems, such as the need to keep large quantities of stock on hand to reduce the number of backorders. Space and capacity was freed up to accomplish other activities more in line with what World Campus recognizes as its core competencies.

World Campus is currently developing new initiatives to further improve the registration systems. During this calendar year a new Web-based student information system will be launched to streamline administrative functions and allow even better customer service through the call center and registration office. In the near future, World Campus hopes to develop an automated pre-registration system and tuition payment plan, thus further integrating the campus into the mainstream of the University.

6. Student Record Management

Record management is the maintenance of student records with respect to admission, registration, lesson and exam recording, grade reporting, and transcripting. It is important to have information systems that assist staff to keep accurate records and to supply students with the most up-to-date information about their educational records.

With the onset of online learning, the role of Student Services has changed in the area of records management. Online learning provides the opportunity for students to send assignments directly to the instructor by e-mail or within the learning management system that "houses" the course. Examinations, especially in upper-division and graduate courses, are being replaced by papers and projects. The amount of time spent managing the lessons and exams during the course is greatly reduced, which allows staff to spend more time interacting with the student from the first inquiry to application, admission, and registration. This is where the need for staff talent is greater.

7. Financial Aid

Many distance education students are not eligible under Title IV, Higher Education Act, for student financial assistance programs. The World Campus keeps students informed of options for alternate sources of funding, such as educational loans through Sallie Mae and state and federal job training monies and grants. For students that do qualify for Title IV funding and for disbursement of aid, students are referred to the University Office of Student Aid.

In the future, World Campus hopes to integrate with the University's system that offers students interactive components to assist them in calculating the cost of attendance, to estimate the amount of aid for which they qualify, and to view their financial records with the University.

B. Instructional Support Services

1. Orientation

Orientation is linked closely to prospective student information. Much of the information used by prospects to decide whether or not to apply to a program is the same information they'll need when they prepare to learn online. In addition to providing information to prospective students, *World Campus 101* is an excellent orientation to online learning. Sample lessons and course syllabi are available online for all World Campus courses.

Once students register for a course, they receive a welcome letter by postal mail and an e-mail providing pertinent course information. One week is built into each course as an "orientation week" in which students can obtain course materials and become accustomed to the technology and learning environment before instruction begins.

Future plans include developing a sample World Campus course, through which students can actually experience what it is like to learn online.

2. Library Services

The World Campus was fortunate that the Penn State University Libraries initiated development of a Web site interface and support services for the World Campus through the Innovations in Distance Education (IDE) Project funded by AT&T. The University Libraries has a significant Web presence, and assumes that the student is near a physical Penn State location. Through the IDE Project, the Libraries culled online resources that a distance learner would use and linked them all from one central World Campus page. Here the online student can learn how to become a registered user of the Libraries, locate databases, borrow materials, and effectively perform search strategies for online research. The Libraries' electronic resources continue to grow as more and more full-text databases are put online, now boasting more than 8,000 electronic journals.

Several Libraries services have been developed specifically for World Campus students. In addition to the students' ability to e-mail subject librarians, a librarian has been specifically designated for the World Campus. Because of the needs of World Campus students, interlibrary loan services have expanded to include the delivery of documents and books to the students' homes or offices. This fall semester several World Campus classes will be part of a pilot program that utilizes chat to support live synchronous interaction with the Libraries reference desk.

3. Services for Students with Disabilities

Under the American Disabilities Act, institutions are required to make reasonable accommodations for students with disabilities to enable them to receive an education. Per Penn State policy, all publications and other media developed by the World Campus alert prospects and students to the availability of alternative media on request and to help with access when needed. World Campus Web pages are tested using Bobby, an online tool used to assess Web sites for accessibility by students using screen readers. This tool showed World Campus that the Web site needs improvement in terms of navigation, and the Webmaster is working on that improvement.

Most students initially identify any needs to faculty, who notify World Campus. Students are then referred to the appropriate on-campus department that collects the students' diagnosis and eligibility documentation and informs Student Services of the necessary accommodation(s). With students taking cohort-based online courses, the timing of students notifying the institution of a disability is becoming more crucial. It is critical to know up-front soon as possible if students require accommodation in order to meet their needs without disrupting or delaying their course work.

Currently the World Campus does not have a set process for identifying and tracking students with disabilities. Ideally students should be asked to identify their needs immediately after acceptance, so that their accommodations can proactively be prepared throughout the entire program.

4. Technical Support

Technical Support is provided to prospective students and current students by the World Campus HelpDesk. Prospective students may visit the tech support Web site, take a virtual tour of available resources, and contact the HelpDesk with any questions about their computer systems or their level of computer skills to enable them to make a more informed decision about beginning online learning.

A more systematic approach to providing support is directed to newly enrolled and continuing students. The HelpDesk was designed based on the philosophy that the use of technology in a distance learning environment should merely be a tool to assure that a student receives an enriched learning experience. Technology should not become a barrier causing anxiety or frustration to students or faculty. To overcome this potential barrier, the World Campus HelpDesk relies on superior customer service from a technical support team. To assist in this effort, an online customer service application has been developed to provide effective customer technical support.

The components of the HelpDesk that are accessible by students include *Course Solutions*, *Web Dictionary*, *Tips and Techniques*, *Downloads*, *Contact Us*, and *Take a Tour*. *Course Solutions* lists answers to common technical problems relative to a specific course, which is searchable by course. The *Web Dictionary* lists technical terms that students will see on the World Campus Web site with definitions written in an easy-to-understand, non-technical manner. *Tips and Techniques* is a resource for FAQs, tips, and basic computer tutorials. *Downloads* is a single site that contains legally downloadable software for PCs and Macs that may assist a student in online education. *Contact Us* leads students to a site where they can access support on a one-to-one basis. For ease of navigation, the student has the ability to contact support via electronic mail from each page.

Beginning with the 2001 fall semester, students will have access to online training in Word, Excel, and Powerpoint. This will complement the free Web-based courses already offered by the University.

Through its Web site, the HelpDesk provides students with self-help support 24 hours a day, seven days a week. Students also have the ability to send an e-mail message or leave a message on voice-mail. Live support hours are Monday through Friday, 8:00 a.m. to midnight. Due to decreased use, weekend hours of 4:00 p.m. to midnight have recently been suspended. Live one-on-one support is available through chat and the toll-free telephone number. The HelpDesk is staffed by five full-time employees plus hourly wage students as needed.

Administrative functionality includes a student-problem tracking system that assists staff in providing better support to students. This system enables the technical support staff to have instant access to information about the student, course of study, and related support issues pertaining to the student's immediate technical problem. With the use of this system, each staff member knows which calls are still not resolved and who is working on them. This tracking system also updates the dynamic statistics page that can be accessed by all staff and faculty in the World Campus. The statistics report the numbers of problem reports, how the problem was reported, when reported, the length of time to resolve, and what types of problems are being reported. This allows support representatives to give students information about problems. Instructors can check to see what kinds of problems students are having with their courses, and instructional design staff can see whether or not students are having difficulty with something that a change in design can correct. The tracking of support incidents provides real-time reports to faculty, administration, and course designers by providing online statistical feedback about course delivery. This system allows World Campus to take a proactive approach to resolving technical and design problems before they affect the entire student population.

By integrating technical support into student services, by faculty development, and by planning the design and development of future course initiatives, a flow of information has been created that is frequently overlooked in developing an organizational plan. The technical support team is consulted and provides advice from course/program inception to ensure the success of supporting the particular design during delivery.

During the early planning of the World Campus, it was anticipated that the University's on-campus technical support unit would also support World Campus students. It quickly became apparent, however, that the on-campus unit was not poised to provide support to the unique needs of an online learner at a distance. It was then that the design and development of the HelpDesk began. World Campus chose to develop the HelpDesk in-house rather than out-sourcing for several reasons: (1) World Campus was providing more services to students for a lower rate than commercial vendors; (2) World Campus had more control over the quality of service extended to students; and (3) World Campus staff were able to multitask, serving as developers, trainers, and technicians. The in-house HelpDesk enabled the World Campus to attract better staff and gave staff greater buy-in to the HelpDesk.

The World Campus HelpDesk has proven to be effective in two areas. Since the system was developed in-house, there is no annual upgrade or licensing costs. The infrastructure of the HelpDesk was designed and developed to be scalable to large numbers of students. The efficiencies created by the HelpDesk enable the level of staffing to remain at a minimum. As more students enter the World Campus, the cost of technical support per student decreases.

Through the efficiency of this system, the HelpDesk has achieved a 97% student satisfaction rate with technical support. Almost 90% of the reported problems are resolved within 15 minutes. Satisfied students also increase faculty satisfaction with the support provided. Organizing the HelpDesk as part of the Student Services unit rather than a technical or design unit has reinforced the concept of customer service in defining the HelpDesk mission and designing and developing its Web site.

5. Activities and Services that Promote a Sense of Community

The World Campus Advisory Board and Penn State World Campus Steering Committee affirmed the need for the World Campus to build strong, ongoing relationships with students in order to differentiate the World Campus from its competitors and to enhance the value proposition of distance education to individual students. The goal is to build loyalty to the World Campus, to develop the highest-possible retention rate among students by providing value-added student services, and to ensure that students return to the World Campus as the first choice in meeting their educational needs.

World Campus determined that online communities should connect at the course, program, and university level. Outside of course interaction that consists of audio conference calls, discussion groups, project teams, and bulletin board conferences, there should be "out-of-class" interaction among students in the same program, interaction between students and faculty outside of the classroom, and students feeling a sense of belonging— a connection— to the university community. It was also decided that relationships should be established with the Alumni Association to bring the value of alumni relations to World Campus students and to better serve all Penn State alumni through the World Campus.

Structures and activities that are currently used by the World Campus to encourage interaction with students in the same program include Web sites, called Program Offices, that are intended to simulate connections that may occur in program offices on campuses. Discussions about issues that cut across courses and other topics of mutual interest support connectedness. Included are bulletin boards for discussions, calendars of events, special announcements, visiting lecturers, learning resources, technology tools, library access, etc. To-date, Program Offices have not been as successful as hoped in fostering student communication across a program. As feedback is gathered from students, World Campus will look at ways to improve these offices, perhaps with assistance from the program faculty and advisors. Spring 2002 will be the first experiment for the World Campus with online chat in a program.

Promoting a feeling of "belonging" to the university community and connecting students to Penn State has been an ongoing effort. All student communications and course materials, both electronic and paper, display Penn State logos and other identifying symbols to establish the students' identity as a "Penn Stater." The *World Campus Community* page of the Web site connects students to Penn State by direct links to a Penn State memorabilia store, news articles about Penn State and online learning of potential interest to World Campus students, the latest Penn State sports information, digital Penn State museum and gallery collections, applicable on-campus resources and student organizations, the Alumni Association, and more. World Campus also fosters connectedness by issuing World Campus students identification cards for use in their local communities and by inviting all students to graduation ceremonies held on campus.

World Campus continues to examine the student services and activities that should be developed to ensure that students have access to appropriate extra curricular resources that will contribute to their success and to their long-term loyalty to the World Campus and Penn State. Plans include a peer mentor program, increased Alumni Association activities (both locally sponsored events worldwide and campus events), a student advisory group, and a student newsletter.

World Campus strongly believes that providing students with services and activities that encourage interaction with other students and faculty, and encourage a sense of "belonging" to Penn State will have a direct impact on increased course completion rates and program retention rates.

C. Advising and Counseling Services and Resources

Research indicates that good advising is essential for student recruitment, satisfaction, and retention. The World Campus has committed considerable resources to provide students with pre-admission counseling and advising. The current advising staff includes five full-time advisors and one staff assistant for support and is supervised by the assistant director of Student Services. This staff supports both World Campus students and students studying in undergraduate programs in through Independent Learning. Graduate students are advised by faculty in the specific program's academic home.

There are multiple means of interacting with advisors: postal mail, e-mail, and toll-free telephone number. Currently, the hours of live advisor support are limited to normal business hours. Student Services continually assesses the need to expand those hours.

1. Pre-Admission Counseling

When a potential student first contacts the World Campus, he/she is usually referred to an admissions counselor or advisor, who helps the prospect to understand the University's academic and administrative processes as well as the nature of distance education programs. An advisor can also help the student understand the relationships between the courses and program requirements (general education, requirements for the major, options, electives, etc.).

Adult students frequently want to know how their prior course work will transfer into a program. An advisor may provide pre-application evaluation of transferable credits. Advisors also help students understand the expected standards of achievement, time commitment, and likelihood of success in certain courses or areas of study. Once the advisor begins to develop rapport with a student, that student is assigned to work with the same advisor throughout his or her educational experience in the World Campus.

2. Application and Admissions

In determining how the World Campus should handle the application and admissions process, Student Services took into consideration the unique nature of the adult online student. It was assumed that students would want the ability to apply online at anytime and to pay online as well as via telephone or postal mail. World Campus also developed applications specific to each program with clear directions for completing the application form. Since each program has its own set of requirements and required information, this makes the process of applying less complicated and confusing. The application Web site should describe the process of application and approval, reply to the student when the completed application is received, and enable students to self-track the progress of approval online.

Adult students may not have the exact course pre-requisites as listed in the Penn State Undergraduate and Graduate Degree Programs Bulletins, but may have acquired the comparable knowledge through life and/or job experience. Certain program requirements and course prerequisites may be waived for experience, but careful evaluation must be done to ensure that the potential student possesses the prerequisite knowledge.

There is also an ethical aspect to consider — the balance between encouraging students to apply in order to meet enrollment goals and making sure that the World Campus and particular program are right for the student based on the student's background and educational and career goals. After talking with the student and assessing his or her needs, it is not uncommon to refer the student to another institution or program that is better suited to that particular student.

3. Advising

The World Campus advising unit was established when correspondence study was the only method of distance education delivery. Penn State recognized the need for correspondence study advisors to have the same credentials, experience, and training as on-campus advisors. A distance education full-time academic advising position was created, and the advising function was mainstreamed to reflect University policy.

The University Policy on Advising states: "The basic tasks of the University's academic advising program are to help advisees identify and achieve their academic goals, to promote intellectual discovery, to encourage students to take advantage of both in- and out-of-class educational opportunities, and to become self-directed learners and decision makers." The University Advising Policy was designed primarily for resident instruction of on-campus students. Distance education advisors embrace this policy to ensure that students at a distance receive the same or higher level of advising as provided to on-campus students.

Advisers and students share responsibility for making the advising relationship succeed. By encouraging their students to become engaged in their education, to meet their educational goals, and to develop the habit of learning, advisers assume a significant educational role.

To meet these responsibilities, Distance Education provides each adult student with a primary academic adviser who:

- Helps the student to select and plan a course of study;
- Makes course recommendations, offers advice about courses (content, instructor, lesson submission rate, exams and more), and informs the student about the prerequisites for subsequent courses in the his or her program;
- Provides the student with degree audits and academic progress reports;
- Provides financial aid information;
- Offers encouragement and assists and refers students who are experiencing difficulties with course content, lesson return, and so on;
- Serves as liaison between the distance learner and other University departments.

Advisors must develop a rapport with their students in order to know the students' academic strengths and interests, and to recommend courses (whenever possible) that students will enjoy and in which they can be successful. Advisors also need to understand the challenges faced by individual students, such as health problems, disabilities, family problems, and job pressures.

Adult learners seeking a degree or certificate may have been out of school for a number of years, and are apprehensive about course work. World Campus advisors are ready to reassure and encourage, going the extra mile to make up for the geographic distance between them and their advisees.

Because Penn State Distance Education students can pursue degree programs from anywhere in the world, advisors must be able to communicate effectively with persons who may not be fluent in the English language.

With the advent of online learning, distance learners can shop around the world for their education and make decisions based on program availability, costs, name recognition, accessibility, etc. A major factor that can sway a prospective student to a particular program or school is response time. Adult students expect/demand quick (same day or next day) replies to their calls and e-mails, and they do not have time to be repeatedly transferred to other departments for answers. World Campus advisors provide an exemplary "one-stop shopping" service, acting as liaisons between the adult student and other individuals and departments to provide resolution of questions and problems.

As the number of World Campus programs continues to grow and policies and procedures change, advisors (and all Student Services staff) are challenged to provide adult students with accurate information. This is complicated by the fact that currently our student, course, and program databases don't 'talk' to each other. World Campus is seeking to upgrade current technology to give real-time information access to advisors and all appropriate staff. This will allow for more efficient and accurate responses to inquiries, timely resolution of problems, consistency of information, and reduction in the amount of paper and filing.

In future development efforts, the World Campus plans to incorporate more self-help tools into the Web site (e.g., course and credit transfer guides and increased program audit capabilities). Students will have access to view their own educational records as appropriate, including their particular financial data, and update certain student information, such as their address.

4. Career Services

Adults often have no clear-cut idea of the kinds of academic credentials they'll need to achieve their tentative career goals. When these adults contact World Campus, our advisors function as career counselors, ascertaining the students' educational background and interests, and informing them about the kinds of certificate and degree programs they can earn at a distance. If there is not a good program match at World Campus, the advisor will suggest other colleges or trade schools.

Students currently access career services by a direct link from the World Campus Web site to the on-campus Career Services office Web site. Services available include:
- Help writing a resume and cover letter;
- Online resources such as job-listing services;
- Tips for succeeding in business today;
- Networking opportunities available through the Penn State Alumni Association.

World Campus anticipates developing its own career services Web site over the next few years. Proposed activities include online career fairs, employment opportunities (job listings), resources for locating internships, job-hunting skills, interviewing skills, networking opportunities, self-help tools, mentoring programs online resume writing, critiquing and posting; and developing career plans. The Assistant Director of Student Services has been tasked with moving the advising function forward, including career services.

5. Personal Counseling

To-date the World Campus has not made plans to enter into personal counseling for distance students. We have been working on the assumption, based on the demographics of online learners, that if personal counseling were needed, it would be accessed through learners' local communities (e.g., work, church, or local agencies).

V. EVALUATION OF SERVICES

Gathering feedback information to determine whether students are being offered the proper services in an accessible and useful manner is crucial. The World Campus organizes evaluation under the direction of the Associate Director of the World Campus. Information is collected from students, faculty, and staff through satisfaction surveys, informal student contact, focus groups, student complaints, and benchmarking.

Once evaluation data are collected, it is imperative to have good information flow back to the area of the World Campus responsible for improvement. Penn State designs, develops, and administers programs through program teams that meet monthly. Each program team includes a program manager, senior faculty coordinator, instructional designer, student services representative, and program marketing associate. Expanded team meetings may also include representation from marketing research, client development, and additional faculty. Any member of the team may raise an issue for improvement based on feedback. It is the responsibility of team members to report back to their respective units discussion items, issues, and problems that need resolution. Student support services are reviewed and upgraded, based on feedback, within the constraints of available resources.

This past year World Campus undertook a benchmarking effort with partner institutions in the Alliance of Four (Penn State, University of California, University of Wisconsin, and University of Washington). Student Services was interested in collecting information on which services the Alliance partners offered, how the services were made available to students, how the services were funded, and what each service cost the institution. Since each institution contacted is organized differently with respect to how services are organized within and between the on-campus and ALN units, there was not a one-to-one correlation between services. Because of the differing organizational structures, costs for each of the services are difficult to compare. World Campus was able to determine that it is offering appropriate and comparable services at a cost that is at least as effective as the other institutions.

VI. CHALLENGES AND RESPONSES IN STUDENT SUPPORT SERVICES

A. Services Targeted To Student Population

Many institutions offer student services based on administrators' perceptions of students needs. In turn these perceptions are based on campus services that evolved around the needs of 18–22-year-olds. The challenge is to "unlearn" traditional ideas about supporting students and begin to develop services that apply specifically to adult distant learners. Distance educators must not assume that adults studying at a distance want, need, and will use the same support services as traditional, on-campus students.

A benchmarking study of institutional Web sites conducted last summer showed that most distance student service Web sites link to the on-campus services without an interface to customize the site to the distant student. It becomes apparent rather quickly that students are no longer on the distance education site, but on a site constructed for on-campus students. This can cause feelings of "not belonging" when the site refers a student to a campus location for services, yet the student is prohibited geographically from being on campus.

Trying to offer a full range of services so that everyone has access to all services can be challenging. The key is to remember that the student population is primarily working adults, juggling education and job and family responsibilities, and that they use services on an as-wanted or as-needed basis— and always at a time convenient to them.

Institutions have been concentrating on getting courses and programs on to the web, but their focus must now turn to developing student support services. Valuing and prioritizing services with relation to cost and available resources can be difficult. It is imperative to base your decisions on what students tell you they want and need. World Campus is relying on feedback from students to determine priorities.

B. Course Completion And Program Retention

Students drop or do not re-enroll in courses for a variety of reasons, including (based on student data) life circumstances; personal and professional transitions; lack of sophistication in use of technology; computer hardware and ISP problems; not being suited to the learning environment (independent nature of work, self-motivation); inexperienced teachers; and faulty design. The most commonly reported reasons are job changes and lack of time. Students are older and their lives more complicated. Educational courses seem the easiest thing to sacrifice when one needs to rethink priorities.

Course completion rates for the World Campus have increased from 85% in spring semester 2000 to 95.6% in spring semester 2001. Several factors may contribute to this rate. The facts that students are primarily highly motivated adults who are taking courses in a program and are not casual course takers lead to a commitment to finish the courses. The promotional materials, Web site, and staff are setting the proper expectations for the necessary commitment and rigor of online learning. The last data available for the Independent Learning program lists the completion rate at 69%. An explanation for higher completion rates for cohort-based online courses may be the immediacy of electronic communication and the learning community that forms between and among students and faculty. Communication and the community serve as motivators to keep students engaged and on track with their course work.

The completion rate is increasing. Possible factors to account for the increase include greater expertise in the design of courses, faculty improvement in teaching online, and students becoming more comfortable with the technology.

As students become more experienced in online learning, completion and retention will continue to improve. The World Campus uses two strategies to encourage completion and retention. First, faculty intervention is heavily relied on within each course to encourage students and monitor progress. Second, Student Services communicates directly with students via e-mail during the last quarter of their course, reminding them to register for the next semester and providing a list of available courses in their program of study.

There is another area in which the World Campus is focusing plans for improvements. In addition to a more structured and (where possible) automated communication process with current students (developed in conjunction with Penn State's

97

Outreach Marketing team), World Campus is in the early stages of designing and developing a peer mentor program. Based on the information they provide on their application form, students will be matched based on their selected criteria. It is anticipated that the majority of interaction between peer mentor and learner will take place over e-mail.

C. Student Information Systems

Institutions with distance education programs, particularly those programs that serve both on-campus resident students and students at a distance, have legacy student information technology systems that separate admissions, registration, and other data for on-campus students and distance students. This is particularly problematic for students who are registered both in on-campus and online courses. It is difficult to provide accurate, timely, and complete information to students concerning their academic record; thus, good student support is not being provided. Penn State has the problem of efficiently tracking student enrollments for financial aid purposes and enrollment verification.

Recognizing this as a crucial issue, Penn State has appointed a committee comprised of members from the central University and Outreach that identified the issues of integrating the two legacy systems, and are beginning the development phase to resolve the student aid problems.

D. Staffing Issues

Training and retaining staff, including the expansion of business hours and recruiting staff for the evening shift, has been a challenge. To work with online students, staff need a different skill set. Online learning has changed the daily pattern of student services work since the "old days" of supporting independent learning courses delivered by correspondence study. More time is spent in the pre-admission and pre-enrollment activities than before. Students are submitting lessons directly to the instructor and exams are being replaced by papers and projects, thereby reducing the amount of time spent processing lessons, verifying proctors, and managing exams. Staff must be more oriented to working with students through the issues of understanding program and course requirements and processes for application and registration. Staff find themselves in much more of a service roll, where good written and oral communication skills are critical. Processing students enrollments and records are not rote processes. Each program is different and each student has a different set of circumstances. Staff must be able to use the technology to effectively interact with students and to locate information.

E. Maintaining Quality While Scaling

As the number of online students, programs, and services increase, it can be difficult to maintain the same standard of excellent service to students. Student Services addresses this issue by ensuring that all staff understand the processes for application, admissions, and registration for each program; by setting standards for process performance; by improving student information systems; and by having flexibility and agility in staffing student support positions. Flexibility includes hiring additional staff as necessary and appropriate based on the number of students and cross training staff to be able to put resources where there is the most need at any given time.

F. Cost Efficiency

Becoming cost efficient is a key to the success of a service unit. World Campus continually looks for ways to become more cost effective. A significant amount of resources is committed to staffing student support services. Staff time tracking allows us to monitor the amount of time spent providing each service to students. From that data, the cost of providing each service is determined. These costs coupled with student feedback enable World Campus to focus on streamlining processes and offering essential services. A strategic focus during the next three years is to improve and develop information systems to allow the World Campus to scale without significantly increasing the number of staff.

VII. CONCLUSION

Student support services are a priority and are being given greater attention by the distance education industry. Quality standards and the range of services that should be available to distance learners are being identified. Based on experience and feedback from students and faculty, determine which services students require and would use. Support services and students' expectations and satisfaction should be continually evaluated, so that services can be expanded and improved depending on available resources.

Student will judge the industry by the standards and benchmarks for quality service selected by the distance education profession. These standards need to be incorporated into strategic plans, prioritized, and integrated into work plans so that the strategies for reaching and maintaining these standards become a focus of our institutions.

VIII. REFERENCES

1. **Murgas, S.** World Campus HelpDesk: NUTN 2001 Distance Education Innovation Award, presentation at 19th Annual National University Telecommunications Network Conference, Denver, 2001.
2. **Pennsylvania State University.** The University Policies on Advising (SENATE POLICY 32-00, 32-10, 32-20, 32-30, 32-40). Available: http://www.psu.edu/oue/aappm/B-1.html.
3. **Thompson, M., McGrath, J.** Using ALNs to Support a Complete Educational Experience, http://www.aln.org/alnweb/journal/Vol3_issue2/Thompson.htm.

IX. ACKNOWLEDGEMENTS

The authors wish to acknowledge Heather Kiris Middleton for editing this paper, Jane Ireland and Melody Thompson for reading a draft of the paper and contributing thoughtful comments, and the staff in World Campus Student Services for their tireless efforts in providing good customer service to students.

X. ABOUT THE AUTHORS

Jean McGrath, M.Ed., is Director of the Student Services at Penn State Distance Education/World Campus. As director, her responsibilities include the call center, pre-admissions counseling, advising, registration and records management, and technical support. Jean also instructs a correspondence-based applied mathematics course in the Independent Learning program. Prior experience in distance education includes program planning and program administration. Jean currently serves on the Advisory Board of the National University Telecommunications Network, serves as co-chair of a Distance Learning Community of Practice committee in the University Continuing Education Association, and is a member of the American Association of Collegiate Independent Study.

Contact: Jean McGrath, Director, Student Services, Penn State Distance Education/World Campus, 207 Mitchell Building, The Pennsylvania State University, University Park, PA 16802; Phone: 814-863-8690; E-mail: jwm9@psu.edu.

Heather Kiris Middleton is Assistant Director for Student Services at Penn State Distance Education/World Campus. In that role, she is responsible for collaborating with other DE/WC units to create online resources for distance students, developing strategies for student retention (including communication systems and student support programs), and leading the academic advising team to meet the varied and sometimes complex needs of adult distance learners. Prior to joining Student Services, Heather was Senior Marketing Associate for DE/WC and developed several nationally recognized recruitment publications for the team, in addition to chairing the work group that launched the new award-winning World Campus Web site in late-2000. She earned her Bachelor's degree from Penn State in Writing for the Arts and is working to complete her Master's degree in Adult Education through the World Campus with a focus on distance education.

Contact: Heather Kiris Middleton, Assistant Director, Student Services, Penn State Distance Education/World Campus, 207 Mitchell Building, University Park, PA 16802; Phone: 814-865-3323; Email: hlc2@outreach.psu.edu.

Tamsin B. Crissman is an Academic Advisor in the Department of Distance Education/The World Campus at Penn State University. In that position, she provides academic advising, educational and career counseling, and professional referral services to World Campus and resident instruction students, both traditional and nontraditional. She also provides programmatic information for Master's, Baccalaureate, and Associate degree programs, and for post-baccalaureate, undergraduate, and certificate programs. Prior to joining the Department of Distance Education, Crissman was a Continuing Education Representative at Penn State, where she developed, coordinated, marketed, and delivered credit and noncredit courses, workshops, seminars and training programs to business and industry. Crissman received her Bachelor's degree in Speech Communication from Penn State University; she is currently pursuing her M.Ed. in Adult Education via Penn State's World Campus.

Contact: Tamsin B. Crissman, Academic Advisor, Penn State Distance Education, 207 Mitchell Building, University Park, PA 16802; Phone: 814-865-5403; E-Mail: txw1@outreach.psu.edu

FACULTY SATISFACTION

Online Teaching as a Catalyst for Classroom-Based Instructional Transformation

Peter J. Shea
William Pelz
Eric E. Fredericksen
Alexandra M. Pickett
State University of New York

- In a survey of 255 faculty in 31 colleges, SUNY SLN looked at the effects of conceptualizing, developing, and teaching a complete online course and found 96% of faculty expressed general satisfaction, 74% believing that learning online is equivalent to or better than in other modes:
  - 89% believe that interaction was equivalent or higher online.
  - 88% believe that interaction among students was equivalent or higher online.
  - 62% believe that they know their students as well or better online.
- Online, "all students must think about what they are contributing instead of being put on the spot and just spewing out something." "The interaction is more considered and thoughtful than spontaneous reactions in the classroom. "There is more writing and research done in the Internet class. These activities replace some of the usual lectures found in the brick & mortar classroom."
- "Media don't matter – good instruction matters…"
- Faculty were nine (9) times as likely to report more systematic design of instruction in their online courses, and 85% believe that developing and teaching online courses improves classroom teaching. 85% of faculty feel teaching online will improve teaching in the classroom.
- Students are almost twice as likely to report higher levels of learning online than in the classroom; 87% found online courses equivalent or harder than classroom courses.

I. INTRODUCTION

How does the experience of teaching an online course impact classroom teaching?

In Part I of this paper we present results from a study in which we heard from 255 online teachers from 31 colleges in the SUNY Learning Network about the effects of conceptualizing, developing, and teaching a complete online course on different aspects of their classroom instruction. Questions focused on instructional design, pedagogical reflection, alternative means of instruction and assessment, and the overall effect of online teaching on classroom teaching. Evidence suggests the experience fosters pedagogical review and instructional transformation. Also, a recent sample of these same online instructors revealed that approximately 95 percent are satisfied with online teaching; would teach another online course, and would recommend online teaching to a colleague. Additionally, during the same period, approximately 90% of students reported high levels of satisfaction and learning in this environment. This level of satisfaction and learning was achieved in a unified system comprised of over 1000 online instructors from fifty-three different colleges offering over 1500 online courses to more than 25,000 enrollees across the State University of New York.

Part II of this paper takes a closer look at student satisfaction at one institution participating in the SUNY Learning Network, Herkimer County Community College (HCCC). Through HCCC's Internet Academy, Herkimer has built a model, "locally-branded," online learning program, building upon and complementing SLN support and services. In this section of the paper we report on a campus-level context of wrap-around support and services and faculty reactions to teaching online courses at HCCC. The success of a consortium of fifty-three colleges, such as SLN, depends on the enthusiasm and ownership of its members; the Herkimer Internet Academy provides an excellent example of these qualities. This section of the paper also looks at the effect of developing and delivering an online course on classroom instructional quality and provides additional evidence of the nascence of transformation.

A. Statement of Problem

This paper addresses the complex issue of transforming higher education from a teacher-centered to more learner-centered model. Clearly this is a process that will only occur in stages. One of the first stages is awareness and reflection. What kinds of experiences allow instructors to examine their pedagogy to begin this process? Can developing and teaching an online course serve as a catalyst for instructional review that leads towards instructional change in the classroom? What evidence exists to support the position that well coordinated programs of academic support and training for online instructors allows for the kind of pedagogical reflection that begins the process of educational transformation?

B. Rationale

The SUNY Learning Network (SLN) is the online instructional program created for the sixty-four colleges and nearly 400,000 students of the State University of New York. The primary goals of the SUNY Learning Network are to bring SUNY's diverse instructional programs within the reach of learners everywhere and to be the best provider of asynchronous instruction for learners in New York State and beyond.

Strategic objectives for this initiative are threefold:
1. To provide increased, flexible access to higher education within and beyond New York State;
2. To provide a mechanism for maintaining consistently, high quality online teaching and learning across the SUNY system; and
3. To leverage the resources of the State University of New York system to contain the costs associated with the development, design, and delivery of online education.

Currently, through SLN, fifty-three colleges within the State University of New York offer more than forty complete certificate and degree programs, from associate level degrees through graduate degrees, completely at a distance.

C. Background Information for the Program

The SUNY Learning Network started as a regional project in the Mid-Hudson Valley involving eight SUNY campuses.

Initially, the development and delivery of asynchronous courses was a new activity for SUNY campuses and faculty. With generous support from the Alfred P. Sloan Foundation combined with enthusiasm and resources from SUNY System Administration and participating campuses, SLN has evolved successfully through three stages: proof of concept, proof of scalability, proof of sustainability.

Successful experiences led to an expanded vision and goals for SLN and the scope and objectives of the project have grown substantially. The annual growth in courses, from eight in 1995-1996 to over 1500 in 2000-2001, and annual growth in enrollment, from 119 in 1995-1996 to more than 25,000 in 2000-2001, with courses offered at all undergraduate and graduate levels from fifty-three of our institutions, illustrates that the project has met and in many ways exceeded original projections.

1. Faculty description

Faculty participating in SLN come from all academic ranks, from adjunct to full professor and all types of institutions ranging from small rural community colleges to large urban university centers. Here are some demographics on respondents to the Fall 2000 SLN survey on faculty satisfaction upon which this paper is based:

Table 1: Institution Type

	Frequency	Percent
University Center	15	5.9
University College	33	12.9
College of Technology	13	5.1
Specialized College	18	7.1
Community College	175	68.6
Other	1	.4
Total	255	100.0

Table 2: Reported Faculty Computer Skills Level Before Teaching Course

	Frequency	Percent	Cumulative Percent
High	160	62.7	62.7
Average	85	33.3	96.1
Low	9	3.5	99.6
Zero	1	.4	100.0
Total	255	100.0	

Table 3: Gender

	Frequency	Percent	Cumulative Percent
Female	131	51.4	51.4
Male	124	48.6	100.0
Total	255	100.0	

Table 4: Content Area

	Frequency	Percent	Cumulative Percent
Math/Science	84	32.9	32.9
Humanities	31	12.2	45.1
Business/Prof. Dev.	50	19.6	64.7
Art	6	2.4	67.1
Social Science	44	17.3	84.3
Other	40	15.7	100.0
Total	255	100.0	

Direct support to faculty comes from a variety of sources. Faculty engage in a four-stage faculty development process and seven-step course-design process before teaching online. This following graphic provides details of this process:

Figure 1: SLN Faculty Development and Course Design Process

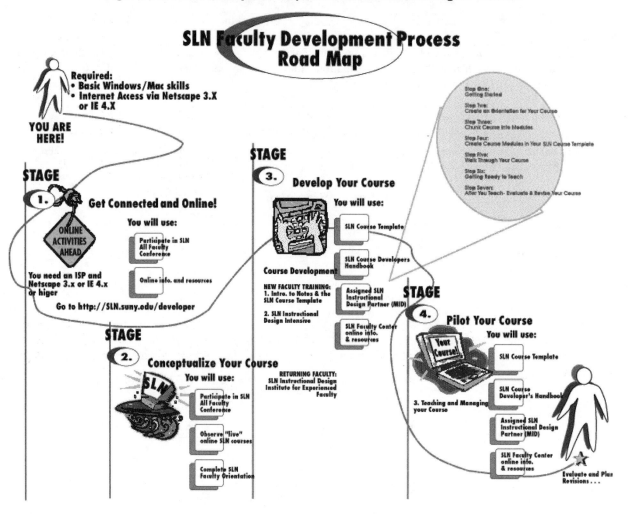

2. Support to Faculty

Support provided to the faculty includes the following:

Table 5: SLN Support: People, Materials, Trainings, and Software

People	Materials	Trainings	Software	Online Resources
SLN Administrative Team	Faculty Developers Handbook and Training Materials 1	Introduction to SLN	Lotus Notes	SLN Website
Instructional Design Partner and Trainers	Training Materials 2	Instructional Design Intensive	SLN Template	SLN Faculty Center
HelpDesk Staff	Training Materials 3	Teaching and Managing Your Online Course	MERLOT Discipline Specific Online Instructional Objects	All Faculty Conference
Experienced Faculty Mentors	Experienced Faculty Training Materials	Experienced Faculty Training	Advanced SLN Media Guide	Live Courses for Observation

In the early years course development was supported centrally, from the Office of the Provost, with both stipends and laptop computers used as incentives to attract faculty course developers. In recent years, these incentives have not been offered centrally and some campuses have begun to provide additional material support. Campuses identify courses and faculty locally, as the do with classroom based offerings. Many campuses have decided to offer complete online degree programs.

II. METHOD

A. Technology and Infrastructure, Hardware and Software:

Technical infrastructure is based on a redundant and highly available, multi-server, multi-location platform. Courses may include text, images, sound and multimedia appropriate to meet course learning objectives. Software, based on a flexible course template was locally developed in the Lotus/Domino Environment.

The following graphic provides additional information:

Figure 2: SLN Infrastructure

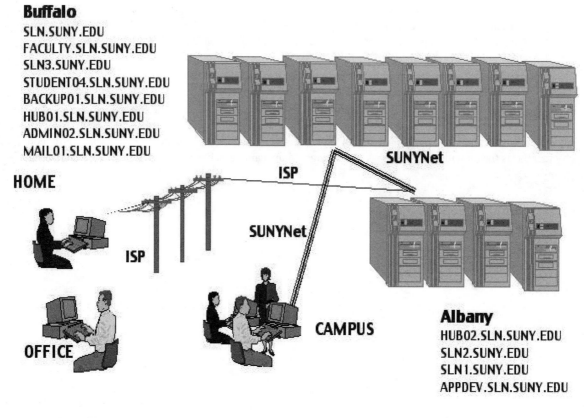

B. Courses

Courses may include text, images, sound and multimedia appropriate to meet course learning objectives. Software, based on a flexible course template was locally developed in the Lotus/Domino. The image below is the new SLN Course Template interface, as seen from a student's perspective on the web:

Figure 3: SLN Course Web Interface

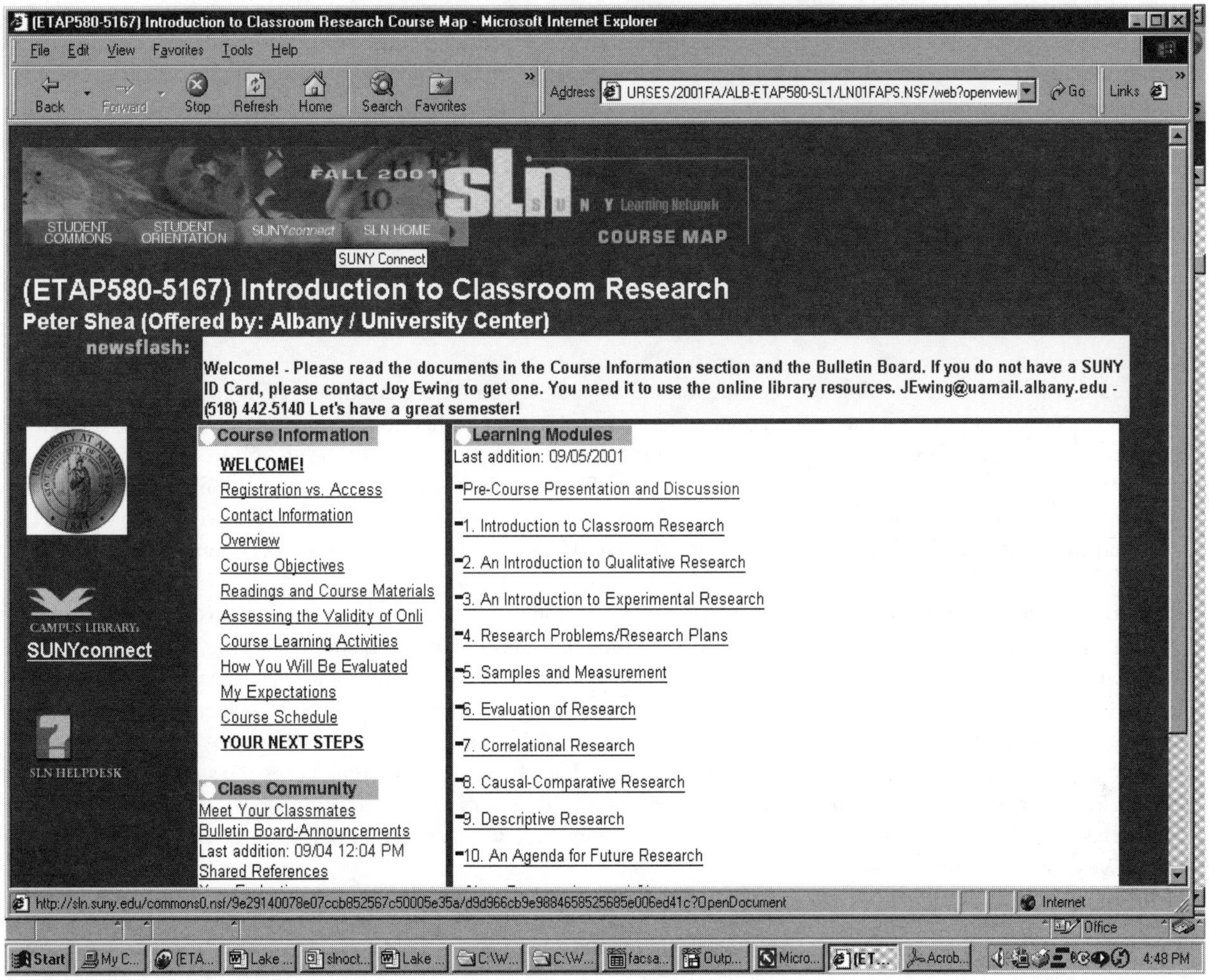

C. Content Delivery

Delivery of courses in SLN is asynchronous and instructor led. Students proceed through the course as a cohort. Faculty course designers participate in ongoing training that highlights the importance of interaction (among other instructional variables). Performance is assessed in many ways (discussion, essays, quizzes, tests, projects, portfolios etc.) and faculty are free to use asynchronous assessment methods that are consistent with their teaching. Occasionally faculty will choose to use proctored examinations (face-to-face meetings) making sure to accommodate students at a distance, by using local proctors.

D. Organization and Evolution

Courses are predominantly faculty developed and taught. A centralized SLN HelpDesk and both centralized and campus-based instructional designers provide technical support. Support is available seven days a week and is widely utilized by both faculty and students.

Again, course development was initially supported centrally with both stipends and laptop computers used as incentives. In recent years, these material incentives have not been offered centrally and some campuses have begun to offer incentives. Courses have been offered a total of fourteen terms through SLN.

III. RESULTS

Ongoing questions about faculty reactions to online education have led us to seek understanding about the effects of online development and teaching on a variety of instructional variables. For example, is the online environment appropriate to a large range of disciplines or do faculty feel that certain subject areas are impossible to implement online? Do faculty who teach online feel isolated from students or that they do not know the students? Do faculty feel that students in the online classroom perform less well than students in the traditional classroom? Do faculty feel that developing and teaching an online course requires more time than traditional courses? Of particular interest— how does the experience of teaching an online course effect classroom teaching?

Through the implementation of a thirty-two question online survey, we heard from 255 online teachers from thirty-one colleges in the SUNY Learning Network. Part of the survey focused on general reactions to online course development and instruction and part focused on the effects of conceptualizing, developing, and teaching a completely online course on different aspects of classroom instruction. These questions investigated online education's impact on systematic design of instruction, pedagogical reflection, and opportunities to consider alternative means of instruction and assessment, and the overall effect on classroom teaching.

Why should we feel that developing and teaching an online course would have an impact on regular class instruction? What evidence exists to suggest a sustained opportunity for pedagogical reflection is allowed through this experience? One piece of evidence - previous surveys indicate that faculty spend a great deal of time and effort on the development and teaching of online courses. In the most recent survey, for example, the most common response to the question - "How much time did you spend developing your online course?" was "More than 120 hours." We suspected that this level of effort might offer opportunities for reflection that would have a positive impact on classroom-based instruction.

It should be pointed out that this development time is not spent alone. All faculty who participate in the SUNY Learning Network agree to participate in rigorous preparatory training, and receive ongoing support during the entire time they teach their courses, both from the trainers, multimedia instructional designers, and a faculty HelpDesk. Training begins with participation in an online all-faculty conference that mirrors the environment in which faculty will eventually instruct. Through participation in this online conference new faculty come together to experience firsthand what they and their students will do in this new learning environment. The all-faculty conference uses the same technology and interface that the new instructors will use, and provides opportunities to discuss a variety of common concerns, observe live courses, and "try out" many of the features and functions they will use in their own online courses, all from the perspective of the student.

Through this experience and through twenty hours of face-to-face training, faculty explore the idea that online instruction does not simply entail mimicking what happens in the classroom, but rather, requires a transformation: a reconceptualization of their course and learning objectives given the options and constraints of the new learning environment. Common issues that arise include how to best create a sense of class community: an environment in which students get to know the instructor, each other, and have ample opportunities for quality interaction and feedback. In order to fully exploit the unique opportunities of online instruction faculty are encouraged to reflect on their instructional goals and then to investigate, with the help on an multimedia instructional designer (MID), how best to translate and achieve those goal online. The faculty HelpDesk provides continuous support to answer technical questions and make the technology as invisible as possible.

Inasmuch as faculty develop and teach their courses with the assistance of face-to-face and online training, with ongoing support of an assigned and dedicated MID and the SLN HelpDesk, we believe there is an opportunity to discover whether the faculty development and course design process, including all the faculty support this process entails, might have an effect on pedagogical reflection and classroom instruction. Results, reported below, are encouraging.

IV. OUTCOMES

"It's very clear to me that the students are the real teachers in online courses– mini lectures; and all the other devices are simply resources that they can call upon. I find it somewhat amusing to read how some entrepreneurs believe that the internet offers them the "advantage" of hiring and using virtuoso teachers. In my opinion these "star" performers are relegated to entertainers on the web. I say again: the real teaching is done through peer discussion with the formal instructor adopting the role of moderator."
Survey Comment from an SLN Instructor

Rather than go into great detail on the more than 8,000 answers we received from the 255 respondents to the thirty-two survey questions, this section will examine the faculty's general reactions to online instruction and greater detail on those responses which provide insight about the effects of the faculty development process, faculty support processes, and online instruction on pedagogical reflection and classroom based teaching. A few comments that were typical of respondents are also included.

A. General Reactions

"Terrific experience! Can't wait to do it again!" Survey Comment from an SLN Instructor

We wanted to get a general understanding of how faulty felt about the entire experience of developing and teaching an online course. The survey asked them to rate their level of satisfaction using a Likert type scale. To the question "How satisfied were you with the experience of developing and teaching an online course?", approximately 96% expressed general satisfaction and approximately 4% expressed general dissatisfaction.

B. Student Performance

"How would you compare your online student's performance to in classroom performance? – online students performed better (they had an incredibly high level of performance that I do not believe I would have had in a classroom environment)." Survey Comment from an SLN Instructor

We also wanted to understand how faculty perceived student performance in online courses as compared to similar classroom courses. To the question, "If you have ever taught this course in the classroom, how would you rate your online students' performance to your classroom students' performance?", respondents were twice as likely to report better performance from their online students then their classroom students. Approximately 33% reported better performance from online students, about 41% reported no difference in performance, and approximately 14% reported better performance from classroom students. The remainder did not teach the course in the classroom.

C. Interaction

"An advantage is the contact with students - they share things I do not believe they would tell me otherwise. The instructor has to be prepared to be available and responsive— I am; and I think as a result the experience is enjoyable for all. Another advantage is the discussion list— timid students are empowered— dominant students are curtailed a bit; and all students must think about what they are contributing instead of being put on the spot and just spewing out something." Survey Comments of an SLN Instructor

"Since I had taught this course a few years in the classroom prior to teaching online I was afraid that it would be difficult to achieve the level of interaction with the students; show as many advertising campaigns; or to be able to interact to any degree with the students. I found that rather inhibit; the online format encouraged personal comments from students; meaningful dialog among students; and excellent student/faculty contact. Through the Bulletin Board; threaded discussions; phone calls ... the student bonded to create a real learning environment." Survey Comments of an SLN Instructor

We feel that importance of interaction in teaching and learning cannot be understated. Through interaction with the instructor, peers, and course content students have the opportunity to negotiate meaning and connect new concepts to previous knowledge. One measure of this important variable is faculty perceptions of interaction. To the item "Compared to classroom based teaching, rate your level of interaction with your online students" online faculty were, again, more than twice as likely to rate their interaction with online students as higher than their classroom students. Approximately 61% felt that their level of interaction with students was higher online than in the classroom, approximately 28% saw no difference, and about 26% thought the level of interaction was lower online than in the classroom. The remainder did not teach the course in the classroom.

We asked a similar question regarding interaction *between* students and found the following results— online faculty were more than twice as likely to rate interaction *between* their online students as higher than their classroom students. About 60% rated interaction between online students higher than their classroom students, about 28% saw no difference and 26% rated interaction between their classroom students as higher than their online students. The remainder did not teach the course in the classroom.

D. Appropriateness of the Online Environment

"In the traditional classroom setting time does not allow for the input and response of each student for every discussion on topics covered. In the online environment each student was required to have input into certain discussions and respond to questions. This allowed me to get to better evaluate the level of the students understanding of concepts and focus on areas that needed clarification." Survey Comments of an SLN Instructor

"I firmly believe that any course can be taught online; (but I also firmly believe that there are some students who should not be involved in online learning)." Survey Comments of an SLN Instructor

We were curious to know whether instructors from different discipline areas had different opinions on the appropriateness of their course content to the online environment. One could hypothesize that certain content areas might not lend themselves to the kind of conversion necessary to success in the online environment. Respondents to the survey taught in the following discipline areas— Math/Science, Humanities, Business/Professional Development, Art, Social Science and others. To the question "Do you think the online environment is appropriate for teaching your course content?" approximately 91% said "yes", about 7% were undecided and about 2% said "no". Of the four respondents who said that the environment was not appropriate, two were professors of Math and Science; one was from Business/Professional Development, and one was from Social Science. Of eighteen who were undecided about the appropriateness of the environment, nine were professors of Math/Science; five were professors of Humanities; three were professors of Business/Professional Development, and one was a professor of Social Science.

E. Knowledge of Students/Isolation

"Getting to know students" is different; interaction is in a different way. Hard to gauge a comparison. In some ways; I thought there was more interaction; but I had a hard time remembering what background went with what student. In the classroom; I had an appearance to attach to the words. Here just a name. I found myself having to keep a "log" on each student to remember simple; notable; important descriptors that would be automatic in the classroom. This made me feel a little more isolated from them; than when I am "in person." Survey Comments of an SLN Instructor

It is natural to be concerned about the effects of teaching online on the degree to which faculty get to know their students and on feelings of isolation. One could certainly hypothesize that the online environment might be cold, sterile, and anonymous. To determine to what extent the faculty became familiar with their students we asked the following question, "Compared to similar courses you have taught in the classroom, how well did you get to know your online students?" Approximately 37% felt they knew their online students better than their classroom students, about 25% felt there was no difference, and 35% felt they did not know them as well. Regarding feelings of isolation we asked the for responses to the following statement, "Developing and teaching this course made me feel isolated from my students." Approximately 73% of respondents expressed disagreement, about 27% expressed agreement.

The majority of the faculty who teach within SLN have never taught an online course before and many report only average computer skills. So we were interested to know about the effect of online course development on faculty understanding of teaching with technology. We asked for reactions to the following statement - "Developing and teaching this online course improved my understanding of teaching with technology." Approximately 97% of respondents agreed, about 3% disagreed.

F. Alternative Means of Instruction, Assessment and Systematic Instructional Design

"I enjoyed this class very much. I was very nervous about this before I started; but the support I received both from my mid and other experienced faculty; and the help desk was very helpful and I am teaching this again. I learned a lot about the type of interactions; and I am making changes in the structure of my course; to hopefully improve it this semester. Like any other course that you teach first time; you need to learn from and make improvements. I am not discouraged at all from the way that things went. I look forward to teaching it again." Survey Comment from an SLN Instructor

"I enjoyed this teaching and learning experience. The students that stayed with the course were very motivated and hard working. I would like to explore new ways and new strategies in teaching using the online format that are not used in the classroom. Perhaps a new pedagogy will be developed so as to not limit ourselves to using the traditional classroom as the benchmark to compare online teaching to. I think we will discover new and more creative ways of facilitating the learning process using this medium. Thank you." Survey Comment from an SLN Instructor

For instruction to become more learner centered, faculty must have an opportunity to consider alternatives to traditional methods and to be able to engage in more systematic design of instruction which incorporates those alternatives. Considering all the time and effort that faculty reported expending, we wondered whether the experience of developing and teaching an online course afforded such opportunities. Apparently it does. Approximately 97% of survey respondents reported that developing and teaching their online course offered them a new opportunity to consider alternative means of instruction, and approximately 93% reported that the experience offered them a new opportunity to consider alternative means of assessment.

Regarding instructional design, we asked the following question, "Think about similar courses you have developed for the classroom— relative to those courses, how likely were you to systematically design instruction before teaching the course?" Respondents were more than nine times as likely to report more systematic design of instruction for their online courses than for their classroom courses. Approximately 58% of respondents reported higher levels of systematic instructional design online, about 37% reported no difference and about 6% reported less systematic design of instruction online.

Although very high percentages of faculty reported that the experience of developing and teaching and online course offered them opportunities to reflect on alternative means of assessment, alternative means of instruction and more systematic instructional design do they transfer that knowledge to the classroom? Since we feel that the process of instructional transformation begins with an opportunity for reflection we asked faculty to respond to this statement, "Developing and teaching this online course provided me with an opportunity to reflect on how I teach in the classroom." Apparently it does. Approximately 94% expressed agreement with this statement. Reflection is, however, necessary but not sufficient. Do faculty feel that this opportunity for reflection will have any impact— will the experience of developing and teaching an online course actually improve the way they teach in the classroom? Results are encouraging— approximately 85% of respondents felt that the online development and teaching experience would improve the way they teach in the classroom.

G. Faculty Support Processes

The following are comments that demonstrate faculty responses to the support processes provided through the SUNY Learning Network:

> *"The greatest single advantage of teaching my courses online has been both the emotional and technical support provided by the SUNY Learning Network staff. Without exception every single person has been professional; helpful; and fully informed on every single aspect of Lotus Notes and Instructional Design. Without the type of support SLN provides it would not be possible to either launch the courses nor to achieve the high quality online courses that I have achieved. The SLN platform provides my Community College the opportunity to advance teaching technologies in a way that would have other wise taken the college years to achieve. BCC faculty and students benefit from the marvelous spirit of cooperation provided by SLN."* Survey Comments of an SLN Instructor

> *"I have found teaching through SLN a great experience. The support and training have been wonderful. Whenever I have encountered a problem; someone has always been there to walk me through to a solution. It has been such a great experience that I am looking forward to teaching in this environment for many years."* Survey Comments of an SLN Instructor

> *I do not know where I would be without Bill Pelz; at H.C.C.C.; and I mean that sincerely. Even though it was a summer course; and he was often out and training; I never felt that I could not access him. He is the best!* Survey Comments of an SLN Instructor

> *"The most positive comments I have are about my MID. He really bailed me out a few times. I really was going to quit; irrespective of the consequences of doing so. He did give me the encouragement and help to continue. He was always responsive; both timely and personally. I always had an answer from him immediately. He did contact me at his own volition to see how I was doing and appreciated the contact. But again; whenever I had problems he was there and I always had the confidence that a solution was an e-mail or phone call away. He is a real treasure for SLN."* Survey Comments of an SLN Instructor

> *I recognize how lucky we are in NYS to have the SLN. I have talked to numerous colleagues across the nation who don't have the support that we do nor a template to use and I know we are truly blessed to have this system. I really would not do it without what SLN provides. It is obvious that your marketing works; most of my students are not local. It is obvious that the template is user friendly for the students since most succeed in using it. It is obvious that you have a lot of technical people who care about the whole systems because generally things work well most of the time. I really do appreciate all that SLN does. I am proud to be part of it and always speak highly of the system. Thanks."* Survey Comments of an SLN Instructor

V. IMPORTANCE OR RELEVANCE TO OTHER INSTITUTIONS

While these results may not be generalizable to all institutions of higher education it is important to note that they were obtained from over 250 online educators from 31 different institutions teaching at the community college, baccalaureate and graduate levels.

Why are these results important? Developing an online learning environment is not a trivial endeavor. A great deal of time, money, and effort must be applied to achieve success. Can online learning be implemented in such a way that both faculty and students report high levels of interaction, satisfaction and learning? From these results (and the results of SLN student surveys) the answer appears to be yes. Can online learning be implemented in such a way that faculty report they have opportunities for reflection on such important pedagogical variables as alternative means of instruction, alternative means of assessment and systematic design of instruction? Again, from these results the answer appears to be yes. Can online learning be implemented in such a way that faculty report that the experience of developing and teaching an online course will allow them to reflect on and improve the way they teach in the classroom. Once again, these results suggest that it can.

Discovering that 91% of 255 online faculty teaching in areas as diverse as Math, Science, Humanities, Business, Professional Development, Art, and Social Science feel that the online environment is appropriate for teaching their course content may be encouraging to institutions just now considering whether and how to implement online education.

For those just getting started who share concerns about the possibility of achieving high levels of interaction online, it may be useful to know that many experienced online instructors feel that they see more interaction both with and between their students than they do in the classroom. For those concerned about the performance of online students it may be encouraging to learn that many experienced online instructors feel that their online student perform as well or better than their classroom students.

For those who are concerned about whether faculty may see professional development benefits from online teaching, it is comforting to know that 97% of our online faculty reported that the experience helped them to better understand teaching with technology. It may also be comforting to read that 85% of faculty reported that the experience will have a positive effect on their classroom instruction.

It is helpful for us to understand that concerns about anonymity and isolation are not unfounded. We have discovered that it may be wise to focus more efforts on finding ways to help faculty to get to know their online students and we will continue to work in this area.

While this information may be useful, it is necessary to admit that much more work remains to be done. Follow-up research with these faculty, in which classroom based instruction is monitored to see if a carry-over effect actually does exist will be necessary. Will faculty actually engage in more systematic design of instruction, and use appropriate alternative means of instruction and assessment in the classroom? This remains to be seen.

It would be foolhardy (and factually inaccurate) to claim that the positive results reported here, were or can be obtained without planning, implementation, evaluation, and revision. But certainly there are lessons that can be learned, and some mistakes that can be avoided, based on the experiences of faculty, academic support staff, and the administration of the SUNY Learning Network.

To achieve these results, in general:

- To assure a consistent interface for student orientation, ease of use, and "ease of support," a flexible, customizable course template is essential.
- Good online instructional practices are independent of software, but not independent of course design.
- In online learning, as in life— just because you can do something doesn't mean you should.
- A well-designed course creatively leverages the options and recognizes the limitations of the online learning environment.
- Just because you are teaching your course online does not mean that all learning activities need to occur online.
- Online learning and/or web enhanced learning does not and should not mean self-paced and "instructor-less."
- When it comes to creating your initial course, first make it "work", then make it "pretty."
- Faculty need to understand the nature of the online environment— this will represent a departure from years of experience and is potentially uncomfortable. Sensitivity to this discomfort is crucial for success.
- Faculty must convert instruction, rather than to try to duplicate the classroom online. Conversion requires "rethinking" how to achieve learning objectives and how to assess online learning within the options and limitations of the new learning environment.
- It is critical to create opportunities for interaction with students and between students.
- It is critical to create and use activities that build a sense of class community.
- Use the structure of the course to convey information about the course, content, tasks, scope and timeframe.
- Provide explicit instructions, cues, and signposts for students.
- Be consistent, redundant, and complete in the structure and creation of your course— complete design and implementation of a course before it is taught allows for greater flexibility while teaching.

- Faculty must create and communicate to the students a reasonable set of expectations for the levels and kinds of interaction, including boundaries required to maintain sanity.

- Keep it simple, computer skill level should not be a barrier to online learning. Consistency of interface allows for diversity of content.

- Successful online teaching and learning is not primarily about technology— it is about people and relationships. Success demands responsive, caring, and understanding, faculty and student support.

- Learner centered online education cannot arise from "trainer-centered faculty training", "HelpDesk-centered faculty support" or "instructional-designer centered instructional design".

VI. FACULTY SATISFACTION AT HERKIMER COUNTY COMMUNITY COLLEGE

Part II of this paper looks at faculty satisfaction information collected through the Internet Academy of one of the intuitions participating in the SUNY learning Network— Herkimer County Community College. This section of the paper provides additional insight into faculty satisfaction and on the impact of online course development and teaching on classroom instructional practices. The success of a consortium of fifty-three colleges, such as SLN, depends on the enthusiasm and ownership of its members— the Herkimer Internet Academy provides an excellent example of these qualities.

The explosive growth of online courses at a rural community college provides an excellent environment to examine some factors which are thought to influence faculty satisfaction with this new higher-education delivery system. Major factors examined include student and professor online interactivity, faculty training and support, and perceived and assessed learning outcomes. The issues of the professor's role in the class and positive transfer of online methodology to the classroom were also investigated. Analysis indicates a high level of faculty satisfaction with online teaching and learning, but also reveals several concerns which merit further study.

Herkimer County Community College (HCCC) is a 2500 student, seventy-five teaching faculty, two-year college located in a rural area of upstate New York. In the spring of 1997 HCCC joined the SUNY Learning Network, an initiative of the State University of New York, with major funding provided by the Alfred P. Sloan Foundation, to assist SUNY colleges and universities to offer asynchronous courses and degree programs. In the fall of 1997 three HCCC faculty members offered asynchronous courses to thirty-six students. The success of those initial asynchronous courses, coupled with the enthusiasm of the faculty members teaching them, got the attention of the college administration, and in the fall of 1999 the college announced the HCCC Internet Academy (IA). The mission of the IA is to offer a variety of degree programs entirely online. Currently HCCC offers thirteen two-year degree programs and two one-year certificate programs online through the SUNY Learning Network. This fall (2001) forty-eight HCCC faculty members will offer eighty-three sections of sixty-seven different courses, with over 1800 student enrollments. Eighty of the eighty-three sections are taught by full time HCCC faculty. It is also important to note that the decision to teach asynchronous courses is voluntary.

Beginning with the fall 1997 term, HCCC faculty teaching asynchronous courses have participated in a "Faculty Satisfaction" survey. It is a web-based survey, the responses are collected anonymously, and the response ratio is between 75% and 90% each term. The results presented below represent aggregate data from the past four years. This paper will focus on three factors thought to influence faculty satisfaction with online teaching and learning: interactivity, training and support, and learning outcomes.

A. Interactivity:

"I've found that there is more student to student interaction (and it's more meaningful) in my Internet courses than in my on-campus courses. I have also found this to be the case with my own student interactions. More interaction with more students."
Annette Yauney – Contemporary Mathematics

116

We frequently hear professors rave about the quality and quantity of student discussions in their online courses. The survey results support this observation.

Q18. How would you characterize the quantity of student-to-student interaction in your online class(es)?

There is more interaction than in the classroom	63%
The amount of interaction is about the same	34%
There is less interaction than in the classroom	3%

"There is significantly more interaction. It is not even close. Students feel much more confident that they will not be negatively sanctioned for expressing their opinions and showing interest in academic matters."
Peter Turner - Macroeconomics

Q19. How would you characterize the quality of student-to-student interaction in your online class(es)?

The quality of interaction is higher than in the classroom	57%
The quality of interaction is about the same	39%
The quality of interaction is lower than in the classroom	4%

Students tend to 'help' each other and make quality comments toward each other. In the classroom, I do not hear these helpful suggestions, but more often I hear negative comments."
Janet Ciccarelli – Business Communications

"The interaction is more considered and thoughtful than spontaneous reactions in the classroom."
Lorraine Martin – English I

Q20. How would you characterize the quantity of student-to-professor interaction in your online class(es)?

There is more interaction than in the classroom	51%
The amount of interaction is about the same	33%
There is less interaction than in the classroom	16%

"I have found that student-student interaction is significantly higher in my online class. Students feel less inhibited to participate in the discussions for a couple of reasons. 1. Nonverbal communication is removed. Students do not see each other and therefore do not become anxious about responding. 2. The student has that all-important 'think time' to develop a response and share it with the rest of the class. Silence is not a problem in the online environment. In the classroom teachers and students can become uncomfortable with silence and therefore try to fill in with incomplete answers."
Peter Fagan – Interviewing Practices and Principles

Q21. How would you characterize the quality of student-to-professor interaction in your online class(es)?

The quality of interaction is higher than in the classroom	49%
The quality of interaction is about the same	42%
The quality of interaction is lower than in the classroom	9%

"The Internet provides for very intense small group discussions which are very different than the traditional classroom. I find the one to one discussion between myself and students to be in-depth, and more complex than in a traditional class. Students who are shy or insecure in a classroom do fine in the virtual group discussion."
Bruce Schwabach – Art Appreciation

B. Training and Support

The SUNY Learning Network provides for thorough faculty training both prior to a professor's first online class (the development cycle) and continually thereafter. Three one-day workshops are required of all new online professors prior to their first online course. During these workshops the trainees learn both the technology and the pedagogy of online teaching and learning. In addition to the workshops, SLN provides a detailed Faculty Developer's Handbook as well as an extensive website loaded with samples, examples, tips and best practices for effective asynchronous teaching and learning. A critical component of the development cycle is the assistance of a Multimedia Instructional Design specialist (MID). The MID works one-on-one with the trainee on course design and assessment issues. There is an SLN HelpDesk which assists faculty and students with technical issues, such as Internet connections and software installation. Finally, many trainees seek the advise and expertise of more experienced colleagues. All SLN courses use a proprietary course management system which was designed specifically for asynchronous higher education by knowledgeable college educators. Much of the training is designed to enable the professors to take full pedagogical advantage of the course management system.

Q10. Which of the following services did you utilize as you developed and taught your first SLN course?

SLN Training Workshops	93%
MID assistance	96%
Developer's Handbook	81%
SLN Help Desk	61%
Experienced SLN Professors	82%

"I could not have done it without the training!"
Janet Evelyn-Dorsey – Introduction to Entrepreneurship

"My course would have been of substantially lower quality without the workshops and MID support."
Timothy McLean – Social Problems

C. Learning Outcomes

It is unlikely that any professor would feel much satisfaction with a methodology which was perceived as inauthentic or ineffective. In addition to the Faculty Satisfaction Survey, HCCC also administers a web-based student survey each term. The results of the student survey are posted to the college Intranet for the faculty to read. The results below are aggregated from the student survey.

Q19. In your opinion, are your Internet-based courses easier or harder than similar classroom-based courses?

Easier	13%
About the same	55%
Harder	32%

Q21. In your opinion, how much are you learning in your internet-based courses?

Less than in the classroom	11%
About the same as in the classroom	57%
More than in the classroom	32%

D. Objective measures of Learning Outcomes

Table 1 shows completion rates of courses taught both in-room and online by the same professor in the 1999-2000 and 2000-2001 academic school years.

Table 1: Course Completion Rates

Term	N	Online	In room	Significance
Fall 1999	13	85.3	91.7	ns
Spring 2000	13	83.2	90.5	ns
Fall 2000	20	91.5	93.1	ns
Spring 2001	19	92.3	94.1	ns

Table 2 shows academic achievement (average GPA) in courses taught both in-room and online by the same professors.

Table 2: Academic Achievement (average GPA)

Term	N	Online	In room	Significance
Fall 1999	13	2.65	2.32	ns
Spring 2000	13	2.68	2.77	ns
Fall 2000	20	2.83	2.57	ns
Spring 2001	19	2.68	2.70	ns

"There is more writing and research done in the Internet class. These activities replace some of the usual lectures found in the brick & mortar classroom."
Bruce Schwabach – Art History

"It's hard to measure. I did give the same competency exam to my in house and online Economics students last year. The online students had a mean score 9 points higher than the in house students."
Peter Turner – Macroeconomics

E. The Professor's Role

Another comment we often hear is that the professor's role online differs in essential ways from the role played in the classroom. Here is some anecdotal evidence that this influences satisfaction.

"Online classes really help the students learn how to learn and become a lifelong learner— more so than the in-class experience can. Therefore the role of the instructor becomes facilitator of the learning process. Some faculty take offense to the title of 'facilitator' but personally like this term. As I learn more about online education I am reminded of an educational practice developed by Maria Montessori. She advocated helping students learn by developing meaningful activities. The student learns by mastery of these activities. A theory developed a century ago is perfect for online education!"
Peter Fagan – Interviewing Practices and Principles

"More time is spent on teaching and guiding learning, very little on discipline (waking students up, admonishing inappropriate behavior, lateness, etc.)"
Janet Ciccarelli – Financial Mathematics

F. Faculty Satisfaction

HCCC professors who are teaching online courses were asked this question: *What is the most satisfying thing about online teaching?* Here is a selection of the responses.

" Not having to physically rush into a room, hope I remembered everything, etc. It is a much more relaxed atmosphere, therefore, my entire focus is on each student. I feel that I give more in my online classes, as I can type faster than I can talk! (Bathroom and snack breaks help also!) Structure sometimes impedes great minds!" Cynthia Gabriel – Modern American Novel

"Participating in a dialogue with a student that continues over several days and in which the student and I both seem to be learning from each other."
Timothy McLean – Social Problems

"There is a certain closeness which develops in the Internet environment. It's sort of like the days of Ham Radio. Someone from far away that you have never seen becomes a comrade."
Bruce Schwabach – Art History

"Unquestionably the enhanced opportunities for student input. While this is typified by the discussions, it also includes things such as relevant websites that students post and submission of their own discussion questions. Students who choose to take full advantage of these opportunities derive a benefit that just can't always be provided in a classroom setting."
Kalman Socolof – Survey of American Television

"I am re-invigorated, less tired, and less burned out. Just ask my family."
Peter Turner – (several online courses)

G. Concerns

Current faculty, were also asked: *What are your concerns about online teaching?* Some of the comments received point to legitimate issues which need to be addressed in order to maximize faculty satisfaction.

"The technology available on the student end. There are some things I would love to try, but they might not be effective for students using slow modems to access my course."
Peter Fagan – Interviewing Practices and Principles

"The authenticity of the work being submitted. After all, how do I truly know that the work is from that particular student?"
Cynthia Gabriel – Modern American Novel

"How will courses be monitored to assure quality?
Mary Green – Anatomy and Physiology

"More screening may be necessary to discourage poorly motivated students who are prone to procrastination from enrollingin online courses. These students would be at risk in any type of educational setting but they are especially likely to fall behind and drop out of an online course."
Timothy McLean – Social Problems

VII. CONCLUSION

As mentioned previously, at HCCC asynchronous teaching on the Internet is a voluntary activity. Accordingly, one indication of faculty satisfaction is the proportion of professors who try it and choose to continue. Of the 49 current HCCC faculty who have volunteered to teach SLN courses, 48 are still teaching them. Two questions on the Faculty Satisfaction survey addressed this issue.

Q24. Overall, how satisfying has your online teaching experience been?

Very satisfying	74%
Somewhat satisfying	26%
Not at all satisfying	0%

Q25. How would you characterize your wishes for future online teaching?

I plan to continue teaching online courses	100%
I plan to stop teaching online courses	0%

Impact on Classroom-Based Instruction

The faculty who go through training and teach online courses learn and implement pedagogical techniques different from those employed in the classroom. When these techniques are subsequently implemented successfully in the classroom, positive transfer has occurred. This could reasonably be a contributing factor to increased faculty satisfaction. From the faculty satisfaction surveys:

Q16. Has developing an online course had any positive impact on your classroom teaching?

A very positive impact	50%
A somewhat positive impact	32%
No positive impact	8%
Does not apply	10%

"I've become much more aware of the importance of relating subject matter to 'real-life' experiences. I'm convinced this is the best way students really learn— or really care— about course content. So, in my class plan, I now have built in questions for each reading whereby students must relate the literature to something from their own lives, from history, tv, movies, song, etc."
Faye Eichholzer– Women in Literature

"The way it has most contributed to the classroom is in the text that I have developed. It has opened up my classroom course to new and different ideas and information which I probably would not have researched if it were not for the Internet course."
Paul Wehrum – Wellness

"Whenever my virtual students start a discussion about a topic that is really interesting, I will take the information from the Internet course and use it as discussion topics in the classroom. I am generating more interesting discussions in the classroom."
Lynton Clark – Introduction to Law Enforcement

"I now include more interactive learning activities, which I think makes my classroom teaching more effective."
Mary Greene– Anatomy and Physiology

At HCCC, everyone currently teaching asynchronous courses has indicated that they plan to continue. In addition, there are potential online professors 'waiting in the wings' for their turns to develop and offer courses online. The HCCC Internet Academy has been a tremendous success, thanks to many contributing factors. As this paper tries to convey, the high level of satisfaction with online teaching and learning on the part of the participating professors is one of these factors. As the comments above attest, we also feel that the experience of developing and delivering online courses through SUNY Learning Network and the Internet Academy has had a positive effect on classroom-based instructional practices and constitute evidence of the seeds of transformation.

VIII. REFERENCES

1. **Swan, K., Shea, P., Fredericksen, E., Pickett, A., Pelz, W., Maher, G.**, Building Knowledge Building Communities: Consistency, Contact and Communication in the Virtual Classroom, Journal of Educational Computing Research, Vol. 23(4), 359-383, 2000.
2. **Shea, P., Fredericksen, E., Pickett, A., Pelz, W., Swan, K.**, Measures of Learning Effectiveness in the SUNY Learning Network, Online Education, Vol. 2, Sloan Center for Online Education, 31-54, 2001.

3. **Fredericksen, E., Pickett, A., Pelz, W., Swan, K., Shea P.**, Student Satisfaction and Perceived Learning with Online Courses: Principles and Examples from the SUNY Learning Network, Online Education, Vol 1, 7-37, 2000.

4. **Fredericksen, E., Pickett, A., Pelz, W., Swan, K., Shea P.**, Factors Influencing Faculty Satisfaction with Asynchronous Teaching and Learning in the SUNY Learning Network, Online Education, Vol 1, 239-270, 2000.

IX. ABOUT THE AUTHORS

Peter Shea is the manager of the TLT @ SUNY Project (Teaching Learning and Technology at SUNY). In this position he is responsible for assisting campuses within SUNY to help faculty use technology in instruction both efficiently and effectively. Currently, he is also director of the MELROT project (Multimedia Educational Resource for Teaching and Online Learning) for SUNY. This project represents a national consortium of 23 higher education systems each contributing to build a database of discipline specific, peer-reviewed, online learning material that can be used by any faculty for free. Before taking over the TLT @ SUNY Project he was the lead multimedia instructional designer for the SUNY Learning Network, where he helped the SLN instructional design team and faculty from 47 SUNY institutions to build well designed online courses. Peter received his doctorate in Curriculum and Instruction from the State University of New York and is also a visiting Associate Professor at the University at Albany, teaching graduate courses in educational research.

Contact: Peter Shea, Director - The Teaching, Learning, and Technology Project, Advanced Learning and Information Services, State University of New York, SUNY Plaza, N303, Albany, NY 12246; Phone: 518-443-5640; Peter_Shea@SLN.suny.edu

William E. Pelz is Professor of Psychology at Herkimer County Community College. Professor Pelz joined the faculty of HCCC in August of 1968, the second year the college was in operation. During his 33 year tenure at HCCC he has served as Chair of the Humanities and Social Science Division and Director of Distance Learning, but has always returned to his first love, teaching. In 1994 he was presented with the SUNY Chancellor's Award for Excellence in Teaching, his most cherished prize. Bill has published an eclectic assortment of scholarly and academic articles, most recently focused on the area of asynchronous teaching and learning. He is currently serving as the Coordinator of the HCCC Internet Academy, and represents The State University of New York in the discipline of Psychology on the national Merlot Project, which is assembling a collection of high quality web content for use in online higher education. He is a vocal advocate for ALNs, and provides training for faculty throughout New York State for the SUNY Learning Network. He is married to Patricia Bielejec Pelz, and has a 21-year-old daughter Leah and a 19-year-old son Matt. You are invited to learn more about Bill, his family and interests, by browsing his website at www.billpelz.com.

Contact: William Pelz, Herkimer County Community College, 110 Reservoir Road, Herkimer, New York 13350; Phone: 315.866.0300 x211; e-mail: pelzwe@hccc.suny.edu.

Eric E. Fredericksen is the Assistant Provost for Advanced Learning Technology in Advanced Learning & Information Services, part of the Office of the Provost in the State University of New York System Administration. He provides leadership and direction for all of SUNY's system-wide programs focused on the innovative use of technology to support the teaching and learning environment. This includes the SUNY Learning Network, the SUNY System's premiere asynchronous learning program and the TLT, Teaching, Learning & Technology program. Eric is also the Co-Principal Investigator and Administrative Officer for a multi-year, multi-million dollar grant on Asynchronous Learning Networks from the Alfred P. Sloan Foundation. He is responsible for the fiscal management, strategic planning, policy development, faculty development, marketing & promotion, student support center, and technical infrastructure. Under Eric's leadership the program has grown from 2 campuses offering 8 courses to 119 enrollments to 47 campuses offering 1500 courses to more than 20,000 enrollments in just five years. Eric received his Bachelors degree in Mathematics from Hobart College, his MBA from the William Simon Graduate School of Business at the University of Rochester and his Master of Science in Education in Curriculum Development & Instructional Technology at the Graduate School of Education at the University at Albany.

Contact: Eric Fredericksen, Assistant Provost for Advanced Learning Technology, State University of New York, SUNY Plaza, Albany, NY 12246; Eric.Fredericksen@sln.suny.edu

Alexandra M. Pickett is the Assistant Director of the SUNY Learning Network (SLN), the asynchronous learning network for the State University of New York under the offices of the Provost and Advanced Learning and Information Services. A pioneer in instructional design and faculty development for asynchronous web-based teaching and learning environments, Ms. Pickett has since 1994 led the development of the instructional design methods, support services, and resources used by SLN to develop and deliver full web online courses. She has spent the past six years conceptualizing and implementing scaleable, replicable, and sustainable institutionalized faculty development and course design and delivery processes that in the 2000-2001 academic year will result in the delivery of 1,500+ courses with 20,000+ student enrollments. One of the original SLN design team members, she co-designed the course management software and authored the 4-stage faculty development process and 7-step course design process used by the network. Her comprehensive approach includes an online faculty resource and information gateway, an online conference for all faculty with the opportunity to observe a wide variety of online courses, a series of workshops for new faculty, instructional design sessions for returning faculty looking to improve their courses, a developer's handbook, a course template, a faculty Helpdesk, online mechanisms for faculty evaluation of SLN services, and an assigned instructional design partner. Today, working with 47 of the 64 SUNY institutions, she has directly supported or coordinated the development of more than 700 SUNY faculty and their web-delivered courses. Her research interests are in faculty satisfaction and the effective instructional design of online courses, and student satisfaction and perceived learning. She has co-authored a number of studies on these topics and has published and presented the results both nationally and internationally. Visit http://SLN.suny.edu/developer.

Contact: Alexandra Pickett, Assistant Director, SUNY Learning Network, SUNY Plaza, Albany, NY 12246; Phone: 518-443-5622; Alexandra.Pickett@sln.suny.edu

STUDENT SATISFACTION

Pace University's Focus on Student Satisfaction With Student Services in Online Education

Dr. David Sachs
Professor Nancy Hale

- Pace University has greatly enhanced the student services that are provided to online students in online testing, support services, and mentoring.

- Using an external evaluator, the University conducts extensive surveying of students.

- These surveys are all done online, are tabulated instantly, and provide a steady stream of feedback to administrators and faculty who are involved in the program.

- Streamlining the surveying process (not too many surveys, too often) enables new ideas to be developed implemented as quickly as possible.

- The Student Information Center at http://support.csis.pace.edu/nactel/infocenter/index.cfm provides students with resources that are quickly and easily accessible. Students can check on and modify their personal information, their company information, take their Math Assessment exams and see their scores, check on their Prior Learning Records, and check on their course registrations, add or drop a course, and request a course transcript.

I. ENHANCED STUDENT SUPPORT SERVICES OVERVIEW

For students in the NACTEL project, student support services focus on a variety of areas. For the past year, these have included:

A. Surveying Students

- Streamlined the surveying process (not too many surveys, too often)
- Surveys to new applicants
- Surveys to new students
- Surveys to returning students

B. Research

- Continued research of other online learning sites
- Focused on the application process
- Focused on the advisement process
- Focused on the registration process
- Focused on tuition assistance for online students
- Focused on financial aid, and
- General Customer Service or Virtual Service

C. Web Site Redevelopment

- Created a sample course
- Prepared a template for staff and faculty bios
- Redesigned the database for course descriptions
- Developed more attractive formatting of the Web site
- Planned for archiving historical information by semester
- Assisted with the initial development of the Student Information Center
- Beginning to work on online, self-paced Tech Help Tutorials and for online self-paced Study Guides

D. Tuition

- Designed automated response email regarding tuition, fees and how to get contact information for Tuition Assistance from companies
- Kept Tuition Assistance information for students up-to-date

E. Communication

- Streamlined and updated all existing communications, targeting both prospective and current students

F. Process Improvement

- Identified breakdowns, and prepared a Process Improvement Review
- In the process of researching contact management software

G. Online Testing

- Fully implemented the proctoring program throughout NACTEL courses

- Continued revision and development of proctoring requirements, guidelines and documents

- More proactive guidance of students throughout the proctor application process

- Standardized various components of the proctored exams (delivery/return methods, exam deadlines)

- New initiatives to provide students with access to proctored exam information directly within their courses

- Continued evaluation of both students and proctors using improved online survey methodologies (in collaboration with IOTA Solutions)

- Monitoring proctored examination status in all courses

- Ongoing communication with students/proctors by providing them with proctor exam information, dealing with conflicts that arise in terms of scheduling an exam and tracking exam completion

- Assisted students in finding a proctor when necessary

- Launched a new online proctor database and application form

II. NACTEL STUDENT SURVEYS

NACTEL students are surveyed in a number of ways. Within their courses, students are surveyed by Pace University after 5 weeks, after 10 weeks, and then after the conclusion of their courses (15 weeks).

In addition, and most pertinent to this case study, students are surveyed by IOTA Solutions, an external evaluator hired specifically to provide online surveys to students. A wide array of surveys has been administered to students. All exams and results are located at: http://www.iotasolutions.com/pace/ and are tabulated and reported almost instantaneously.

The NACTEL Program Improvement Survey focuses on five major areas:

1. The Web Site
2. The Application Process
3. The Registration Process
4. The Course Experience
5. Overall satisfaction with the program

In addition, a second set of surveys focuses exclusively on the Online Testing part of the program. Students are required to have proctors who must verify that they have taken their examinations under the test-taking procedures that were specified by their instructors. There are specific procedures for doing this, all of which are outlined on the Pace University/NACTEL Web site at: http://support.csis.pace.edu/nactel/gotoclass/proctoring.cfm.

As might be imagined, students have a fair amount of anxiety about the proctoring process, and it is extremely important that it go smoothly and effectively. With that in mind, all students and proctors are surveyed about the process, on a continuous basis. Questions about the online testing process focus on:

- Was the proctored exam information clear and understandable?

- How easy or hard was the scheduling process?

- How difficult or easy was it to access the actual examinations?

- Was it necessary to pay the proctor a fee?

- Did the students or the proctors encounter any problems?

- How did the overall proctored examination process go?

- Are there any suggestions about how to improve the process?

Again, the overall thrust of the surveys (which are sent to both the students and the proctors) is to ensure that the services that are being provided are working well and effectively for all concerned.

III. THE STUDENT INFORMATION CENTER

A new feature this year, that continues to improve the services being provided to students in the program, is the Student Information Center. This center, which is located at: http://support.csis.pace.edu/nactel/infocenter/index.cfm provides students with a wonderful array of resources, quickly and easily. Students can check on (and modify) a wide array of information at this site:

- They can check on all of their personal information.
- They can check on all of their company information.
- They can take their Math Assessment exam, and then see what the score is.
- They can check on their Prior Learning Records.
- They can check on their course registrations.
- And if need be, they can add or drop a course and they can request a course transcript.

Automating access to all of this information has dramatically increased the satisfaction level of students in the program. And, it has also reduced the workload (and the opportunity for error) for NACTEL support staff.

IV. TECHNICAL SUPPORT AND THE ONLINE STUDENT SEMINAR

Students in the NACTEL program are, for the most part, individuals working on their own, at great distances from the Pace University campuses. All involved are concerned that hardware and software issues should not get in the way of the educational process. Towards that end, students are provided with technical support as part of their involvement in the program.

First of all, there has been a focus on providing information and resources to the students in a format that is accessible using a 56K modem, and dial-up connectivity to the Internet, with a reasonably current (version 4) browser. In addition, there has been a strong emphasis on getting the students set up technically, before they are in any of their academic courses. Therefore, all entering students are required to take the Online Student Seminar. This one credit course, which takes approximately two weeks to complete, introduces students to all of the technical requirements that are included in the NACTEL program.

In the Online Student Seminar, students encounter:

- Microsoft Office 2000 (Word, Access, PowerPoint & Excel)
- RealAudio
- HorizonLive
- Adobe Acrobat
- Shockwave
- BlackBoard 5.5 – the course management software being used
- Downloading and installing software

Self-tests for all of these are included in the Online Student Seminar. Students encounter examples of each of the programs, and are given a quiz about the content contained within the examples. In this way, they know, and we know, whether or not they are ready to continue in the program. If students need additional help or assistance, it is provided by their instructor or by one or several of the technical support students who answer the NACTEL technical support phone lines and email.

HorizonLive includes a wonderful set of tests within the software. It provides the students with examples of all that they are likely to encounter, and walks them through the process step-by-step.

Again, the focus of all of this has been on how to provide support services to students who may be encountering technical support issues, on their own, for the first time. The underlying premise is that there must be support for the students. And, it is better to localize the need for this support in one course, early in the program. This has enabled most faculty members (and students) the luxury of not having to deal with such problems. It has also meant that when technical problems are encountered, it is early on in the program, in a course that is pass/fail, so there is little or no additional pressure on the students.

V. TUTORING SERVICES AND SMARTHINKING

Pace University's NACTEL program provides students with the opportunity to obtain an AS in Telecommunications. This particular degree requires students to be competent in fundamental math skills. Consequently, there is a math assessment given to all students prior to their entry into the program. Most students take the two math courses that are offered, before taking any of the electronics and telecommunications courses within the degree.

Some of our students need extra help and support while they are taking their math courses. For some of them, it has been many years since they last took math courses. For others, it is probably fair to say that they were not strong math students earlier on in their academic careers.

The concern was (and is) how to provide these students, who tend to do much of their work during the evening or on weekends, with the math support that they need. Consequently, Smarthinking has been engaged to provide tutoring services to math students. The services are available for free to the students and they are available online into the early morning hours. Students are provided with information that tells them where to find the help, and that gives them the userid and password that they need to enter the Smarthinking Web site.

Not all students need the tutoring services. However, for those who do, this has proven to be an invaluable student support service. Some students have told us in their final course evaluations, that without the Smarthinking tutoring services, they would have been unable to successfully pass the math courses.

VI. RESULTS

The following pages describe results from a survey conducted in September 2001 of students in the NACTEL program. The survey provides a good sample of the kind of information that has been collected throughout the three years that the NACTEL program has been in full-scale operation. The survey focuses on five areas:

- The Registration Process
- Online Education
- Online versus Traditional Education
- The Pace University/NACTEL Program
- Demographic Information

Surveys such as this one, throughout the year, are used for continual improvement of the program. It is pleasing to note that for the most part (98%) students responded that they are either very satisfied or satisfied with the overall program. Obviously, there are specific areas that continue to need attention, but overall it appears that the Pace University/ NACTEL program is doing well.

Student Attitudes Report Summary
(Prepared by IOTA Solutions)

The following report contains data from two surveys: the new student survey and the returning student survey. The surveys explored the same topics, but some items are worded differently based on the students' status (i.e., new student attitude items are in the future tense whereas returning student items are in the present tense). This allows for a comparison of expectations and experiences. The following summary uses these various tenses when referring to particular items.

The survey has 5 parts: (1) registration process, (2) attitudes towards online learning, (3) attitudinal comparison of online learning and traditional (i.e., classroom) learning, (4) overall attitudes towards the NACTEL/Pace program, and (5) demographic information. Only returning students were given part 4. For items that were used on both surveys, results are categorized three ways: (1) new student responses, (2) returning student responses, and (3) combined responses (new and returning).

Two email invitations were sent on August 31ˢᵗ 2001 asking students to complete the surveys (one to new students and one to returning students). A total of 103 students responded (38 new and 65 returning).

1. Registration Process
Overall, student attitudes towards the registration process are positive. For items 1N-9N, between 63% and 92% stated they understood the processes "very well" or "well".

2. Online Education
The expectations (new students) and experiences (returning students) of online learning did not differ on many of the individual items. Additionally, most expectations and experiences are positive: 98% "agree" or "strongly agree" that online learning will help or has helped them to balance the demands of school and other aspects of their lives, 88% will or do feel comfortable expressing their opinions online, and 94% expect or experience adequate instructor support. All other items have predominately positive answers accompanied with a higher proportion of "neither agree nor disagree" responses. Further demonstrating the convenience students are experiencing or expecting to experience, 39% of student comments in the following section (Part III) relate to the convenience of online learning, for example:

> "It is such a great convenience not having to go to a school, lugging around books and trying to find parking. I will really love it when winter hits!"

The only item with a comparatively high proportion of negative responses was item 19N/9R: 20% stated it would or does bother them when or if they do not get to know their fellow online students. Interestingly, 30% of new students responded this way while only 14% of returning students did. This difference between new and returning students is statistically significant and demonstrates that students may be able to adapt to any lack of interaction in an online learning environment. A significant difference was also revealed between new and returning students for item 16N/6R: new students expect more interaction than returning students are experiencing. Together, these findings imply that new students expect more interaction than they will likely experience, but this lack may not affect them due to adaptation (i.e., returning students aren't as affected by any lack). To further explore this finding the new students will be tracked over time to explore any differences between their interaction experiences, reactions, and current expectations. Furthermore, 91% feel comfortable expressing their opinions online so any lack of interaction may be due to a lack of opportunity. These findings reveal the importance of giving students a realistic preview of online learning and providing them opportunities to interact with others. Previews will lead students to rely less on adaptation by giving them an accurate idea of what to expect. Additional opportunities for interaction will alleviate any perceived lack.

3. Online vs. Traditional Education
No significant differences emerged between new and returning student responses on individual items. Students do not perceive traditional education to be superior to online education. Only 9% "agree" with the statement that students will not or cannot learn as much online as they would in a traditional course, while 93% "strongly agree" or "agree" that high quality learning can occur without face-to-face interaction. Of the people who agreed with the statement that students

won't or can't learn as much online, only one provided a comment explaining his or her response. It indicates that this student learns not from the medium being used but from the interaction:

> "Q. #13 asks about learning 'as much'; I (maybe not everyone) get a good bit of information from what others ask. Sometimes it has nothing to do with the course work, I learn from the person asking the question."

The student feels he or she could learn as much online as in a traditional course given the opportunity for interaction and question/response sessions. Interestingly, this student "agreed" with the statement that he or she interacts often with other students, which suggests a lack of student-teacher interaction (e.g., question/response sessions).

Students report that online learning requires more motivation and self-discipline than does traditional learning: 69% state that motivation plays or will play a "much greater" or "greater" role in online learning (1% responded "smaller" role) and 44% stated that they will be or are less likely to procrastinate while learning online opposed to traditional learning (6% responded "more likely" or "much more likely", 50% responded "neither more nor less likely"). Additionally, 39% of student comments in this section related to online learning requiring greater self-discipline and self-reliance, for example:

> "Self-discipline is required to a greater degree in online learning. One must also rely on their own ability and resources to figure out problems both technically and academically. The reason for this is that instant access to an instructor is not available as it is in a traditional classroom setting."

28% stated that the workload in an online course will be or is greater than that of a traditional course (71% responded "the same"). 22% stated it will be or is easier to get to know fellow students in an online course compared to traditional, while 26% feel it will be or is more difficult.

4. The Pace University/NACTEL Program

Returning students responded very positively when asked to rate their overall satisfaction with the program: 98% responded "very satisfied" or "satisfied", while the other 2% responded "neither satisfied nor dissatisfied". Comments can be found throughout this report demonstrating students' satisfaction:

> "Everyone at Pace is always very helpful when there is a problem."

> "I would like to thank everyone involved with the program that has allowed me to pursue this degree, which I otherwise would not have access to. The level of quality of both, the faculty and course materials, are far beyond my expectations. Thank you."

5. Demographic Information

No significant interactions were found between the various demographic factors and student attitudes (i.e., students of different ages or with varying Web experience did not differ on their attitudes).

The average age of returning students was significantly higher than was the age of new students. Tracking this term's new students will answer whether or not this is due to older students being more likely to continue in the program while younger students are more likely to drop out.

83% have 3 or more years experience on the Web (only 6% have less than one year). This is encouraging, as a lack of web-experience will become less of a factor in deterring students from taking online courses. 76% do not have online course experience other than with Pace.

97% are taking courses to receive an A.S. Degree in Telecommunications indicating that students are motivated to achieve as much as possible from the program. Additionally, item 41N/33R shows a large proportion of students taking courses for personal and career growth reasons, while only 9% are doing so because of job requirements. Note: the 9% who stated "requirement of their job" also indicated other internally motivating reasons such as personal growth and/or desire to learn more about the telecom field.

VII. CONCLUSION

Pace University has focused on student satisfaction in the NACTEL program since this program's inception. Students are asked early and often (sometimes too often) about how they are doing in their various courses and with our Web site. Methods have been developed, and continue to be developed, that provide faculty and administrators responsible for

NOTE: Results from both the New Student and Returning Student surveys are presented simultaneously. Therefore, two numbers accompany the shared items that appear on both surveys: an "N" follows all new student survey numbers and an "R" follows all returning student survey numbers.

Table 1: Registration Process

Consider your experiences in registering for courses and rate how well you understood:					
Item	Very Well	Well	Adequately	Poorly	Not Applicable
1N. When to register for classes.	22 58%	11 29%	5 13%	0 0%	0 0%
2N. How to register for classes.	21 55%	12 32%	4 10%	1 3%	0 0%
3N. What classes to register for.	18 47%	13 34%	7 18%	0 0%	0 0%
4N. When to order textbooks.	18 47%	9 24%	8 21%	3 8%	0 0%
5N. How to order textbooks.	21 55%	12 32%	3 8%	2 5%	0 0%
6N. How to handle tuition payment to Pace University.	21 55%	10 26%	3 8%	3 8%	1 3%
7N. How to handle tuition reimbursement from my company.	15 40%	10 26%	11 29%	2 5%	0 0%
8N. How to add/drop a course.	11 29%	16 42%	7 18%	2 5%	2 5%
9N. When courses begin.	24 65%	10 27%	3 8%	0 0%	0 0%

Item	Very Good	Good	Adequate	Needs Improvement	Not Applicable
10N. Please rate the promptness in which your questions regarding the registration process were answered.	16 42%	9 24%	5 13%	1 3%	7 18%
11N. Please rate the quality of the student advisement you received.	30 79%	7 18%	0 0%	1 3%	0 0%

Item	Survey	Mean (1-5)	Very Satisfied (1)	Satisfied (2)	Neither S. nor D. (3)	Dissatisfied (4)	Very Dissatisfied (5)
12N. 1R. Overall, my level of *satisfaction with the Registration process* can best be described as:	New	1.79	18 47%	14 37%	3 8%	2 5%	1 3%
	Return	1.61	33 52%	26 41%	3 5%	1 2%	1 2%
	Total	1.68	51 50%	40 39%	6 6%	3 3%	2 2%

13N.
2R. What would you *change or add* to make the registration process more informative and useful?

New Students
- I believe that the systems in place are very good.
- I would like to see a direct link to my company's reimbursement system so, when you register it brings you
  right to the application.
- We need a confirmation for received tuition vouchers.
- A list of what classes to take throughout the year and when you should register for them.
- You should be able to make changes on the classes you registered for in case you made a mistake (in my case).

Returning Students
- I can't think of anything. It was easier the second semester.
- Nothing. I was late registering but I do want to thank Nancy Uhl very much for her assistance in getting me registered so I wouldn't lose any time.
- More updates about when enrollment opens.
- A few more e-mail reminders as to key dates. Sometimes I'm traveling and I have come close to missing some important information.
- I think it would save a step if, with the notification that registration is coming up, Pace would send you a list of courses that would benefit you.
- Have all information available upon registration.
- A list of classes I have taken with the suggested next class or classes.
- I would like to see more information on when certain classes are offered. Say Telecom III is only being offered in the fall. That way I can plan my classes better.
- Include the prerequisites as a drop down menu.
- Instant updating of student information.
- Make an entry on the home page to direct returning students to the proper area for registering.
- Online forms to complete and e-mail to our companies for quicker and hassle free course acceptance.

3R. Is there anything about the Registration process that is confusing?
Returning Students
- Registration here is easy...my company's tuition reimbursement plan is the more difficult process to get through.
- I felt that the Registration process was easy and self-explanatory. It simply involved clicking on the link and going right to the website. No wasted time looking.
- No, I've been registering in classes for two years and the system has become very easy to use.
- Great support from Nancy Treuer.
- The registration is very easy and simple to use.

Take-Away Points:
- Responses to items 1N-12N indicate the registration process is administered well and most students understand the process. There are some issues that need addressing (see next bullet).
- Upon examination of student comments, some predominate issues arose:
  - Negative comments/suggestions related primarily to tuition/reimbursement difficulties. Many of these are due to the payment processes of the company the student works for and not because of Pace University.
  - 15% of negative comments/suggestions related to course information/prerequisite information.
  - 12% of negative comments/suggestions related to textbook purchasing.
- Although further analysis will be needed to determine if the new Web site is more effective, the following comment provides encouraging signs:
  - "Now with the new Web site it's a lot better."

Table 2: Online Education

The following items assess student attitudes towards online learning.   The wording in brackets [ ] indicates wording used for the new student survey (i.e., the wording for new students is in future tense and the wording for returning students is in present tense). Although the items for both groups are not worded exactly the same, comparisons between the two groups provide a method for comparing expectations and experiences.

Item	Survey	Mean (1-5)	Strongly Agree (1)		Agree (2)		Neither A. nor D. (3)		Disagree (4)		Strongly Disagree (5)	
15N. 5R. Taking an online course it has made it [will make it] easier for me to balance the demands of school and other aspects of my life (e.g., work or family).	New	1.30	26	70%	11	30%	0	0%	0	0%	0	0%
	Return	1.35	44	68%	19	29%	2	3%	0	0%	0	0%
	Total	1.33	70	69%	30	29%	2	2%	0	0%	0	0%
16N. 6R. I [will] interact often with other classmates in an online course.	New	2.08	8	22%	20	54%	7	19%	2	5%	0	0%
	Return	2.52	7	11%	25	38%	25	38%	8	12%	0	0%
	Total	2.36	15	15%	45	44%	32	31%	10	10%	0	0%
17N. 7R. I [will] feel comfortable expressing my opinions online via chat, discussion boards or email.	New	1.78	14	38%	17	46%	6	16%	0	0%	0	0%
	Return	1.83	18	28%	41	63%	5	8%	1	2%	0	0%
	Total	1.81	32	31%	58	57%	11	11%	1	1%	0	0%
18N. 8R. I [will] get adequate support from my online instructor.	New	1.62	16	43%	19	51%	2	5%	0	0%	0	0%
	Return	1.60	30	46%	31	48%	4	6%	0	0%	0	0%
	Total	1.61	46	45%	50	49%	6	6%	0	0%	0	0%
19N. 9R. It bothers [would bother] me if I do [did] not get to know other students in my online courses.	New	3.08	3	8%	8	22%	13	35%	9	24%	4	11%
	Return	3.54	0	0%	9	14%	21	32%	26	40%	9	14%
	Total	3.38	3	3%	17	17%	34	33%	35	34%	13	13%
20N. 10R. Access to library resources is [will be] adequate in an online education program.	New	2.14	8	22%	16	43%	13	35%	0	0%	0	0%
	Return	2.43	7	11%	24	38%	31	48%	2	3%	0	0%
	Total	2.33	15	15%	40	40%	44	44%	2	2%	0	0%
21N. 11R. Access to academic support services (e.g., tuition assistance information, academic advisement, tutoring) is [will be] adequate in an online education program.	New	2.03	9	25%	18	50%	8	22%	1	3%	0	0%
	Return	2.02	18	28%	29	45%	17	26%	1	2%	0	0%
	Total	2.02	27	27%	47	46%	25	25%	2	2%	0	0%

22N. 12R. Please provide any other comments you have regarding your perceptions of online learning that have not been addressed above:

New Students
- I enjoy online classes and have been doing it for a while.
- My instructor is very good at responding to questions and comments.
- Encourage even more interaction between classmates.

Returning Students
- Everyone at Pace is always very helpful when there is a problem.
- Nancy Treuer is the best.
- My advisor, Nancy Uhl is absolutely great! Continues to impress me with her promptness replying to e-mails. And her advice is right on target.
- I would like to thank everyone involved with the program that has allowed me to pursue this degree, which I otherwise would not have access to. The level of quality of both, the faculty and course materials, are far beyond my expectations. Thank you.
- Online learning has been very nice. I have a very hectic travel schedule and it has been nice to be able to work on courses when I'm able to (as long as they are within the scheduled timeframe).
- Might want to have videos to watch of important lectures.
- I just started in the spring of this year, so I don't think I've used all the resources available to me yet.
- I would like to see a list of proctors developed for each region, and made available to the students.

<u>**Take-Away Points:**</u>
- Overall, expectations (new students) and attitudes (returning students) towards online learning are positive and there are no differences between new or returning students on most items (see next bullet).
- A significant difference was revealed between new and returning students for items 16N/6R, 19N/9R, and 20N/10R. Returning students had higher mean scores for all three items (indicating they disagreed more with the statements).
  - o 16N/6R – New students expect more interaction than returning students have experienced.
  - o 19N/9R – New students would feel more bothered if they do not get to know their fellow students than returning students have felt.
    - ▪ Assuming returning students had similar interaction expectations as the new students this term, this finding implies that the returning students have adapted to any lack of interaction that they may have been expecting. Following the experiences of this term's new students will further explain this implication.
- The first 5 returning students' comments indicate very positive attitudes towards the program and online learning.

Table 3: Online vs. Traditional Education

The following items assess student attitudes towards online learning compared to traditional learning (e.g., classroom learning). The wording in brackets [ ] indicates wording used for the new student survey (i.e., the wording for new students is in future tense and the wording for returning students is in present tense). Although the items for both groups are not worded exactly the same, comparisons between the two groups provide a method for comparing expectations and experiences.

Item	Survey	Mean (1-5)	Strongly Agree (1)		Agree (2)		Neutral (3)		Disagree (4)		Strongly Disagree (5)	
23N. 13R. Students are not [will not be] able to learn as much in online courses as they would in a traditional course.	New	4.19	0	0%	4	11%	1	3%	16	43%	16	43%
	Return	3.98	0	0%	5	8%	12	18%	27	42%	21	32%
	Total	4.06	0	0%	9	9%	13	13%	43	42%	37	36%
24N. 14R. High quality learning can take place without having face-to-face interaction.	New	1.47	22	61%	11	31%	3	8%	0	0%	0	0%
	Return	1.68	28	43%	32	49%	3	5%	2	3%	0	0%
	Total	1.60	50	50%	43	43%	6	6%	2	2%	0	0%

Item	Survey	Mean (1-5)	Much Less Than (1)		Less Than (2)		Same As (3)		Greater Than (4)		Much Greater Than (5)	
25N. 15R. The workload in an online course is [will be] _____ the workload in a traditional course.	New	3.40	0	0%	0	0%	23	62%	13	35%	1	3%
	Return	3.21	1	2%	0	0%	49	75%	14	22%	1	2%
	Total	3.28	1	1%	0	0%	72	71%	27	26%	2	2%

Item	Survey	Mean (1-5)	Much Easier (1)		Easier (2)		Neither Easy nor Difficult (3)		More Difficult (4)		Much More Difficult (5)	
26N. 16R. It is [will be] _____ to get to know my classmates in an online course compared to a traditional course.	New	3.00	3	8%	6	16%	18	49%	8	22%	2	5%
	Return	3.05	3	5%	10	15%	35	54%	15	23%	2	3%
	Total	3.03	6	6%	16	16%	53	52%	23	22%	4	4%

Item	Survey	Mean (1-5)	Much Smaller (1)		Smaller (2)		Similar (3)		Greater (4)		Much Greater (5)	
27N. 17R. Motivation plays [will play] a _____ role in my success in an online course compared to a traditional course.	New	4.16	0	0%	0	0%	8	22%	15	40%	14	38%
	Return	3.91	0	0%	1	2%	23	36%	21	33%	19	30%
	Total	4.00	0	0%	1	1%	31	31%	36	36%	33	33%

Item	Survey	Mean (1-5)	Much Less Likely (1)		Less Likely (2)		Neither More nor Less (3)		More Likely (4)		Much More Likely (5)	
28N. 18R. I am [will be] _____ to procrastinate about things in an online course than I would in a traditional course.	New	2.32	8	22%	13	35%	13	35%	2	5%	1	3%
	Return	2.52	10	16%	13	21%	37	59%	3	5%	0	0%
	Total	*2.45*	*18*	*18%*	*26*	*26%*	*50*	*50%*	*5*	*5%*	*1*	*1%*

29N. Please add any other comments you have regarding the differences between online education and traditional
19R. education that have not been addressed above:

New Students
*   It is such a great convenience not having to go to a school, lugging around books and trying to find parking. I will really love it when winter hits!
*   I find that having an attitude of wanting to be 'ahead of the game' is better for me to keep me on schedule.
*   Online classes afford me the chance to take classes. I would otherwise not be able to do attend classes at a facility. At least not at this time in my life.
*   Self-discipline is required to a greater degree in online learning. One must also rely on their own ability and resources to figure out problems both technically and academically. The reason for this is that instant access to an instructor is not available like in a traditional classroom setting.
*   Let's be honest here, more people, like myself learn by looking. Although, I think if the books are good and the person has a want to learn that they will. I am good at MATH so I don't have a problem learning on line-in fact I think I procrastinate less than in a traditional class because I am in control of my learning and my education. My success does not depend on what kind of a day my instructor is having. I depend more on myself and on the materials I receive for class.

Returning Students
*   I am much less likely to procrastinate because I have weekly assignments and discussions in which to participate. Additionally I know I must keep up because the course is self-paced to a large extent. I have no one to "get the notes from" or just let the work pile up from beginning to midterm to final as often happens in traditional settings.
*   I believe that students must motivate themselves, either with traditional or on-line learning. Most of the NACTEL students are adults with families and see the need for additional education. Some of us are in the later working years and desire the training or education to assist in our current jobs or advance into a new section of our field. Learning in this manner is very dependent on the student to solve their own time issues and prepare the lessons, put in the effort required.
*   Online studies require more discipline since the student must often "work out" the concepts for himself rather than having class or face-to-face discussion and it sometime requires a lot of "digging".
*   I decided to take this online course for the education, but also because I did not have the time to go to a classroom and I did not feel the need to meet other students. What time I have spent meeting other students and working with them has been good, but outside of course work, I have other things to do.
*   I like being able to juggle work/life with the variable school time. However, sometimes, one week is not enough.
*   I like the on-line classes because it enables me to juggle my work and home life by letting me access the course at odd hours.
*   I spend more time on online courses than traditional courses I have taken in the past.
*   It's all in what you put into it. It's up to the individual to schedule the time to do the "homework".
*   Just the fact that there is no commuting time wasted is tremendous.
*   Less time wasted getting to the classes on the computer as opposed to driving to a site and walking through a building to the class.
*   Q. #13 asks about learning "as much"; I (maybe not everyone) get a good bit of information from what others ask. Sometimes it has nothing to do with the course work, I learn from the person asking the question. As to workload, I had to (am) learn(ing) how to master new technologies just to get my work into the "classroom". I travel in my work, and I had to learn how to bring my classroom with me, and I bought a laptop so I could keep pace.
*   The concept of e-book course books might have merit, for online education.
*   There have been several classes I have taken at the local campus where I never even spoken to other classmates, the discussion board helps out with any interaction needed between students and teachers, I think it is better, sometimes you don't always speak up when you are in a classroom.

Take-Away Points:
- No significant difference emerged for responses to individual items between new and returning students. Combined scores show encouraging trends and attitudes towards online learning:
  - o 78% agree that one does [can] learn as much online as in a traditional classroom.
  - o 93% agree that high quality learning can take place online.
- Majority of student comments indicate students feel online learning is convenient and that it requires increased self-discipline and independence. Individual item responses showed the same trend:
  - o Only 1% indicate motivation plays [will play] a smaller role in online learning compared to traditional learning.
  - o Only 6% indicate they [would] procrastinate more in online learning compared to traditional learning.
  - o Examination of student comments revealed two predominate themes:
    - ▪ 39% related to online learning requiring self-discipline/self-reliance.
    - ▪ 39% related to the convenience of online learning.
- Students were divided in regards to the ease of getting to know other students in an online course compared to traditional courses.

Table 4: The Pace University/NACTEL Program

Item	Very Satisfied	Satisfied	Neither S. nor D.	Dissatisfied	Very Dissatisfied
20R. Overall, my level of satisfaction with the Pace University/ NACTEL program can best be described as:	32	31	1	0	0
	50%	48%	2%	0%	0%

21R. Please provide any other comments or suggestions you have that would help Pace and NACTEL improve the degree and certificate programs.

Returning Students
- Again - I would like to commend the staff and the instructors. They are what made this course so enjoyable
  and as accessible as a traditional learning experience.
- Keep up the good work.
- The course, teachers and overall quality of the learning experience impress me. I have used much of what was taught in the first two classes. I look forward to obtaining my A.S. Degree.
- I think the course is great the way it is.
- Please offer a bachelor's degree soon.
- The only problem I have had, is any time I want to print out any notes or assignments, I get 4 pages of "frames" before the actual notes are printed. Could a link be added for a print version where the headings and links on the side of the screen are not going to print?
- A way to access the final grades online. Since I need the grades to receive my reimbursement for my books, I would rather not wait several weeks before I am able to send it in.

Take-Away Points:
- Students' satisfaction with the program is high.
- Comments can be found throughout this report demonstrating students' satisfaction:
  - o "Everyone at Pace is always very helpful when there is a problem."
  - o "I would like to thank everyone involved with the program that has allowed me to pursue this degree, which I otherwise would not have access to. The level of quality of both, the faculty and course materials, are far beyond my expectations. Thank you."

Part V-Demographic Information

	Survey	Male	Female
30N. 22R. What is your gender?	New	21 55%	17 45%
	Return	40 62%	25 38%
	Total	*61 59%*	*42 41%*

	Survey	Under 18	18-25	26-35	36-45	46-55	Over 55
31N. 23R. What is your age?	New	0 0%	5 14%	13 35%	13 35%	5 14%	1 3%
	Return	0 0%	4 6%	14 22%	28 43%	19 29%	0 0%
	Total	0 0%	9 9%	27 26%	41 40%	24 24%	1 1%

32N. 24R. What is your current job title?

N- 8 (22%) R- 11 (18%) T- 19 (20%)	Customer Services (w/in Telecom)	N- 0 R- 1 (2%) T- 1 (1%)	Operator Services (w/in Telecom)	N- 2 (6%) R- 1 (2%) T- 3 (3%)	Clerical (w/in Telecom)
N- 20 (56%) R- 30 (50%) T- 50 (52%)	Technician (w/in Telecom)	N- 6 (17%) R- 14 (23%) T- 20 (21%)	Management (w/in Telecom)	N- 0 R- 2 (3%) T- 2 (2%)	Employed Outside of Telecom
N- 0 R- 0 T- 0	Student (High School)	N- 0 R- 1 (2%) T- 1 (1%)	Student (College)	N- 0 R- 0 T- 0	Currently Unemployed

	Survey	Citizens	Qwest	SBC	SBC Wireless	Verizon	Other
33N. 25R. What company do you work for?	New	2 6%	3 16%	3 8%	0 0%	27 71%	0 0%
	Return	1 2%	8 12%	21 33%	0 0%	26 41%	8 12%
	Total	*3 3%*	*14 14%*	*24 24%*	*0 0%*	*53 52%*	*8 8%*

If "Other", please specify:
- Pacific Bell
- Avaya
- Florida Power & Light
- Georgia Power Co.
- IPC Information Systems
- PT-1 Communications
- SNET
- SNET/SBC
- Sprint
- United Services Automobile Association

	Survey	CWA	IBEW	None	Other
34N. 26R. What Union do you belong to?	New	21 55%	8 21%	9 24%	0 0%
	Return	31 48%	14 22%	20 31%	0 0%
	Total	*52 50%*	*22 21%*	*29 28%*	*0 0%*

If "Other", please specify:
No responses provided.

	Survey	Less than 1 Year	1 Year	2 Years	3-5 Years	More than 5 Years
35N. 27R. How many years have you been on the web?	New	3 8%	1 3%	4 10%	14 37%	16 42%
	Return	3 5%	3 5%	3 5%	20 31%	36 55%
	Total	*6 6%*	*4 4%*	*7 7%*	*34 33%*	*52 50%*

	Survey	0	1	2	3	4	5	6 or more
36N. 28R. How many online courses have you taken in the past, not including Pace classes?	New	32 84%	1 3%	1 3%	1 3%	0 0%	0 0%	3 8%
	Return	46 71%	7 11%	1 2%	2 3%	3 5%	0 0%	5 8%
	Total	*78 76%*	*8 8%*	*2 2%*	*3 3%*	*3 3%*	*0 0%*	*8 8%*

		Survey	0		1		2		3		4 or more	
37N. 29R.	How many online courses are you taking with Pace in the upcoming semester?	New	1	3%	16	42%	17	45%	4	10%	0	0%
		Return	1	2%	36	57%	25	40%	0	0%	1	2%
		Total	2	2%	52	52%	42	42%	4	4%	1	1%

38N. 30R. Please specify which courses you have taken in the A.S. Degree Program. Please check all that apply:

N- 7 (18%) R- 18 (30%) T- 25 (24%)	AC/DC Electrical Circuits for Telecom	N- 18 (47%) R- 2 (3%) T- 20 (19%)	Academic Skill Seminar	N- 1 (3%) R- 1 (2%) T- 2 (2%)	American Detective Fiction
N- 0 R- 7 (11%) T- 7 (7%)	Business & Technical Communications	N- 7 (18%) R- 3 (5%) T- 10(10%)	Computer Apps for Telecom-97	N- 14 (37%) R- 2 (3%) T- 16 (16%)	Computer Apps for Telecom-2000
N- 0 R- 8 (12%) T- 8 (8%)	Critical Thinking & Problem Solving	N- 0 R- 1 (2%) T- 1 (1%)	Digital & Microprocessor Fundamentals	N- 1 (3%) R- 7 (11%) T- 8 (8%)	English 101
N- 10 (26%) R- 0 T- 10 (10%)	Online Seminar	N- 0 R- 4 (6%) T- 4 (4%)	Physics for Telecom	N- 0 R- 4 (6%) T- 4 (4%)	Solid States Devices and Circuits
N- 6 (16%) R- 15 (23%) T- 21 (20%)	Technical Math	N- 1 (3%) R- 8 (12%) T- 9 (9%)	Telecom I	N- 0 R- 5 (8%) T- 5 (5%)	Telecom. II
N- 0 R- 5 (8%) T- 5 (5%)	Telecom III	N- 0 R- 0 T- 0	Telecom IV		

		Survey	0		1		2		3		4		5		6 or more	
39N. 31R.	How many online courses are you currently taking other than those you've registered for with Pace?	New	32	84%	1	3%	1	3%	1	3%	0	0%	0	0%	3	8%
		Return	46	72%	7	11%	1	2%	2	3%	3	5%	0	0%	5	8%
		Total	98	95%	8	8%	2	2%	3	3%	3	3%	0	0%	8	8%

40N. 32R. Please indicate if you are concentrating on a degree or certificate program, or if you are simply taking one or two courses via the Pace University/NACTEL program?

N- 36 (95%) R- 63 (98%) T- 99 (97%)	Associate of Science in Applied Information Technology, Telecommunications Degree
N- 1 (3%) R- 0 T- 1 (1%)	Introduction to Telecommunications Certificate
N- 1 (3%) R- 1 (2%) T- 2 (2%)	Telecommunications Essentials Certificate
N- 0 R- 0 T- 0	Taking Individual Courses

41N. Please identify your primary reason(s) for applying to the Pace University/NACTEL program. (Please check all 33R. that apply.)

N- 29 (76%) R- 50 (77%) T- 79 (77%)	Receive an A.S. Degree	N- 6 (16%) R- 6 (9%) T- 12 (12%)	Receive a Certificate	N- 19 (50%) R- 31 (48%) T- 50 (48%)	Learn more about telecom field
N- 5 (13%) R- 9 (14%) T- 14 (14%)	Help me enter telecom field	N- 20 (53%) R- 30 (46%) T- 50 (48%)	Get a better job/promotion	N- 6 (16%) R- 12 (18%) T- 18 (18%)	Change careers
N- 7 (18%) R- 19 (29%) T- 26 (25%)	Pay Raise	N- 3 (8%) R- 6 (9%) T- 9 (9%)	Requirement of job	N- 29 (76%) R- 42 (65%) T- 71 (69%)	Personal growth
N- 0 R- 3 (5%) T- 3 (3%)	Other				

If "Other", please explain:
New Students
- Working toward a master's in IT/Telecom.

Returning Students
- Foundation for further degree education.
- I started at Pace because I had a hard time helping my daughters with their homework. Now I'm trying to finish an A.S. Degree because it also has helped me in my job and the NACTEL experience has been great.
- Learn the technical aspect of telecommunications as opposed to the marketing aspect.
- Prerequisite to Bachelor Degree.
- Want job in hometown, only technical jobs likely to be available there.

Take-Away Points:
- Average age of returning students higher than that of new students. Tracking this term's new students will help determine if this is due to older students being more likely to continue than are younger students.
- 83% have 3 or more years experience on the Web (only 6% have less than one year).
- 76% do not have online course experience other than with Pace.
- 97% are taking courses to receive an A.S. Degree in Telecommunications, indicating that they wish to receive the full benefit of the program.
- A high proportion of students are taking courses for personal and career growth reasons, while only 9% are doing so because of job requirements.
  - According to the previous 2 bullets, motivation is not lacking among students.
  - The 9% who stated "requirement of job" also indicated other internally motivating reasons such as personal growth and/or desire to learn more about the telecom field.

the program with information in a timely and efficient fashion. Whenever possible, timely responses are made to the information that students provide.

There has been a focus on how to continually improve all of the processes that students encounter while studying in the program. In addition, there is a continual flow of information back and forth between the students and the faculty about the courses that are being taught. Within the realm of reason, courses have been modified and (hopefully) improved, in response to student feedback.

The goal has been (and continues to be) to keep the student satisfaction level high within the NACTEL program.

VIII. RECENT SURVEY

The following pages include a recent survey (September 2001) of students in the NACTEL program. The survey provides a good sample of the kind of information that has been collected throughout the three years that the NACTEL program has been in full-scale operation. The survey focuses on five areas:

- The Registration Process
- Online Education
- Online versus Traditional Education
- The Pace University/NACTEL Program
- Demographic Information

Surveys such as this one, throughout the year, are used for continual improvement of the program. It is pleasing to note that for the most part (98%) students responded that they are either very satisfied or satisfied with the overall program. Obviously, there are specific areas that continue to need attention, but overall it appears that the Pace University/NACTEL program is doing well.

IX. ACKNOWLEDGEMENTS

Pace University has been fortunate to receive funding through the FIPSE/LAAP program. Funds received from this program have been used to provide significant enhanced student services as well as external evaluation of the Pace University/NACTEL program. Lorraine Kleinwaks, the FIPSE Program Officer, has provided tremendous support for the past two years.

X. ABOUT THE AUTHORS

David Sachs is Assistant Dean and Professor of Office Information Systems in Pace University's School of Computer Science and Information Systems. As Assistant Dean, he has been actively involved in the development and implementation of computer science and telecommunications courses for the corporate community since 1984. As director of the Pace Computer Learning Center, Dr. Sachs is responsible for the many hundreds of days of personal computer, computer science, and telecommunications education that are provided each year to corporations throughout the United States and around the world such as AT&T, IBM, MCI, PepsiCo, The Reader's Digest, Prodigy and others. Dr. Sachs works closely with teachers, administrators and others to think about the most effective ways to introduce technology into public and private schools. Most recently, he has been actively involved in the development of courses to be taught asynchronously over the Internet and the World Wide Web. Dr. Sachs is co-director of the NACTEL project (see http://csis.pace.edu/nactel).

Contact: Dr. David Sachs, Assistant Dean, Pace University, School of Computer Science & Information Systems, 1 Martine Avenue, White Plains, NY 10606; Phone: (914) 763-8820; Fax:(914) 763-9324; Email: dsachs@pace.edu

Nancy Hale is Chairperson of the Technology Systems Department and has curricula and staffing responsibilities for the department's degrees and certificate programs. She has developed curricula and program designs that support the special needs of the adult learner. Prof. Hale was instrumental in the development of CLOUT, an intensive employment-directed education program established in 1991. Professor Hale is co-director of the NACTEL program. As such, she is responsible for the curriculum development, faculty development, and overall student satisfaction with the program. Prof. Hale has co authored two books in end-user computing and regularly presents at conferences on topics related to end user computing and distance education.

Contact: Professor Nancy Hale, Chairperson, Pace University, School of Computer Science & Information Systems, 1 Martine Avenue, White Plains, NY 10606; Phone: (914) 422-4464; Fax:(914) 989-8640; Email: nhale@pace.edu

Student Satisfaction and Reported Learning in the SUNY Learning Network

Peter Shea
Karen Swan
Eric Fredericksen
Alexandra Pickett
State University of New York

- Decades of research on effective learning are synthesized in Chickering and Gamson's "Principles of Good Practice" (1987). The principles are especially demonstrable in online learning, as a SUNY SLN survey of 935 students shows:

    70% reported very high quality interaction with classmates.

    71% of students reported spending more time studying as a result of the increased access afforded by the online format.

    73% reported high levels of interaction with classmates.

    75% reported high levels of interaction with faculty.

    78% reported very high quality interaction with instructors.

    83% reported that the online format helped them improve their ability to communicate effectively in writing.

    85% reported very prompt feedback.

    87% reported that they had received high quality, constructive feedback.

    87% reported being satisfied or very satisfied with their courses.

    90% report learning a great deal.

    90% reported that the instructor provided clear expectations of how students could succeed in the course.

    93.4% reported active participation in their online class.

    94% reported being satisfied or very satisfied with SLN services.

    97% reported satisfaction with the SLN Helpdesk.

- Students were twice as likely to report active participation in online discussion than in classroom.

- Students were twice as likely to report asking for clarification online than in the classroom.

- The "busiest" students report highest satisfaction with online learning, according to reports from students who learn online because of distance or lack of transportation, because of conflict with personal schedule, because the course is not offered on campus, because of family responsibilities or because of interest in technology and the internet.

I. INTRODUCTION

This paper will provide an update on student satisfaction in the SUNY Learning Network (SLN). We will look at the issue of student satisfaction from a variety of perspectives focusing on both the learning environment of SLN and on specific constructs and variables that may promote high levels of satisfaction. From a system perspective we will review the results of student surveys on a variety of issues impacting satisfaction. We interpret these results in light of the strategic objectives of the program, keeping in mind socio-cognitive views of instruction and well established principles of good practice in higher education. As with previous studies of student satisfaction in SLN, and in alignment with predictions from this theoretical framework, results indicate the importance of teacher-to-student and student-to-student interaction. More specifically, these results indicate the importance of both the quantity and quality of faculty-student interaction, of communicating clear expectations about succeeding in courses, and of providing timely, high quality feedback. These are the instructional variables that correlate most strongly with both satisfaction and learning. We also look at survey results that show correlations between the nature of SLN's asynchronous, text-based online learning environment and student's reported depth of thought in discussions, ability to communicate effectively in writing, feelings of isolation, time on task, wasted time, and reported learning. We find good reason to believe that this environment engenders high levels of interaction, participation, satisfaction and learning.

II. RATIONALE

The SUNY Learning Network (SLN) is the online instructional program created for the sixty-four colleges and nearly 400,000 students of the State University of New York. The primary goals of the SUNY Learning Network are to bring SUNY's diverse, high-quality instructional programs within the reach of learners everywhere and to be the best provider of asynchronous instruction for learners in New York State and beyond.

Strategic objectives for this initiative are threefold:

- To provide increased, flexible access to higher education within and beyond New York State;
- To provide a mechanism for maintaining consistently, high quality online teaching and learning across the SUNY system; and
- To leverage the resources of the State University of New York system to contain the costs associated with the development, design, and delivery of online education.

III. BACKGROUND INFORMATION FOR THE PROGRAM

The SUNY Learning Network started as a regional project in the Mid-Hudson Valley involving eight SUNY campuses. Initially, the development and delivery of asynchronous courses was a new activity for SUNY campuses and faculty. With generous support from the Alfred P. Sloan Foundation combined with enthusiasm and resources from SUNY System Administration and participating campuses, SLN has evolved successfully through three stages: proof of concept, proof of scalability, and proof of sustainability.

Successful experiences led to an expanded vision and goals for SLN, and the scope and objectives of the project have grown substantially. The annual growth in courses, from eight in 1995-1996 to over 1500 in 2000-2001, and annual growth in enrollment, from 119 in 1995-1996 to more than 20,000 in 2000-2001, with courses offered at all undergraduate and graduate levels from fifty-three of our institutions, illustrates that the project has met and in many ways exceeded original projections.

IV. METHOD

A. Technology and Infrastructure, Hardware and Software

Technical infrastructure is based on a redundant and highly available, multi-server, multi-location platform. Courses

146

may include text, images, sound and multimedia appropriate to meet course learning objectives. Software, based on a flexible course template, was locally developed in the Lotus/Domino Environment.

B. Content Delivery

Delivery of courses in SLN is asynchronous and instructor led. Students proceed through the course as a cohort. Faculty course designers participate in ongoing training that highlights the importance of interaction (among other instructional variables). Performance is assessed in many ways (discussion, essays, quizzes, tests, projects, portfolios etc.) and faculty are free to use asynchronous assessment methods that are consistent with their teaching. Occasionally faculty will choose to use proctored examinations (face-to-face meetings) making sure to accommodate students at a distance, by using local proctors.

C. Organization and Evolution

Courses are predominantly faculty developed and taught. Technical support is provided by a centralized SLN Helpdesk, and both centralized and campus-based instructional designers. Support is available seven days a week and is widely utilized by both faculty and students.

Course development was initially supported centrally with both stipends and laptop computers used as incentives. In recent years, these material incentives have not been offered centrally and some campuses have begun to offer incentives. Courses have been offered a total of eighteen terms through SLN.

V. RESULTS

A. What Satisfies Students?

In order to best focus our efforts on maintaining this learning environment we have engaged in systematic efforts to evaluate and analyze our online teaching and learning. As a standard part of our operation, every semester we conduct comprehensive surveys of all participating faculty and students through an integrated, web-based data collection infrastructure. To date we have collected data from more than 8000 student and faculty respondents.

How do students who have taken online courses through SLN feel about the experience? For example- is there sufficient interaction with instructors and students to sustain learning? From the students' perspective, how do some of the more than 1000 faculty participating in SLN rate in critical areas of instruction? Do students feel that there is sufficient interaction with other students, or sufficient assistance from academic support staff to attain their learning goals? Do students feel there are any disadvantages to the online format relative to the classroom? For example, does the online format foster or inhibit thoughtful discussion of course topics and effective written communication; is it likely students will ask for help when they don't understand something? Are there downsides? For example do online students find that they waste time due to the distractions of the Internet and thus spend less time studying? Does the online environment make them feel isolated? Finally, how do students feel the environment compares to the classroom overall?

To assess whether SLN has been successful from a student perspective it is necessary to remind ourselves what our "student" goals were. Some of these are outlined in the strategic objectives:

- To provide increased, flexible access to higher education within and beyond New York State; and
- To provide a mechanism for maintaining consistently high quality online teaching and learning across the SUNY system.

We tried to determine whether and to what extent we were achieving these goals through our online student satisfaction survey, which consisted of thirty-three questions. To define high quality teaching and learning in devising the survey, we used both socio-cognitive learning theory (Vygotsky, 1978; Brown, Collins, & Duguid, 1989; Lave, 1988; Bruner, 1990) and principles of good practices in higher education (Chickering & Gamson, 1987; Chickering & Ehrmann, 1995). Approximately one third of the questions we asked were based on the Current Student Inventory (CSI) developed by the Flashlight Program of the TLT Group. In the most recent survey (Summer 2001) we heard back from 935 students, about 26% of student enrollments for that period. We feel the results of the student satisfaction surveys provide some indicators of whether SLN is providing increased flexible access and whether it provides high quality, online teaching and learning, and that these indicators will prove useful to others working on systemic online learning initiatives.

Presented here are some typical comments from the most recent survey of students in SLN that bear on the strategic goal of increased, flexible access and indicate students' levels of satisfaction:

> *"Online courses have literally changed my life. Working fulltime I was unable to continue my college education due to schedule conflicts until the SUNY Learning Network. SLN has made it possible for me to realize a dream by finishing my college education!!!"*

> *"This was my first online course; therefore it was a little awkward at first. My job responsibilities this semester required more travel than normal; taking this class online was a blessing. I worked from Florida and Texas while attending training for work."*

> *"For people who have a less than traditional work schedule; an online course is the way to go. This being my first online course; it was a good experience; worked well into my daily schedule and I believe I learned more than I would have in the classroom setting. Once the stress of a traditional attendance schedule is removed; a much more relaxed atmosphere for learning is created by the ability to sign on and learn during the time frame that fits an individual schedule."*

> *"I love online courses. They have given me the ability to juggle family; career and school. If it weren't for online courses, I would have never gone back to school.... THANK YOU!!! :)"*

Many other comments like these, collected over the past six semesters, testify to some measure of success and student satisfaction in this strategic area.

Another indicator of student satisfaction vis-à-vis increased access can be seen in the differing levels of student satisfaction by distance from their institution. In semester surveys of SLN students in which we ask students about their level of satisfaction with the SLN program we consistently find significantly higher levels of satisfaction from those farthest from campus. It can reasonably be expected that these are the students least likely to have traditional access to the education afforded by SLN. Higher levels of satisfaction are also found among students who report that they are taking courses due to family and personal conflicts which keep them from going to a physical campus, which, again, represent constraints on access. The tables below, based on the most recent sample of 935 SLN students, studying in the Summer of 2001, suggest the importance of increased access on student satisfaction. The scores are based on a Likert-type scale with 1 being highly satisfied and 5 being highly dissatisfied and are in response to the questions "How satisfied are you with the SUNY Learning Network?" and "Why did you decide to take this course online rather than in the classroom?"

Table 1: Satisfaction with the SLN Program by Distance from Campus

DISTANCE	Mean	N	Std. Deviation
On campus	2.09	11	.70
Less than 30 minutes	1.53	389	.66
30 minutes to 1 hour	1.59	214	.68
1 hour - 2 hours	1.57	112	.74
More than 2 hours	1.43	209	.59
Total	1.53	935	.66

Table 2: ANOVA Table

			Sum of Squares	df	Mean Square	F	Sig.
Satisfaction by Distance	Between Groups	(Combined)	6.566	4	1.642	3.796	.005
	Within Groups		402.123	930	.432		
	Total		408.689	934			

Table 4 ANOVA Table

Why Online?	Mean	N	Std. Deviation
Distance or lack of transportation	1.45	128	.59
Conflict with personal schedule	1.50	373	.62
Course not offered on campus	1.74	122	.69
Family responsibilities	1.38	185	.62
Interest in technology/internet	1.78	40	.95
Other	1.71	87	.71
Total	1.53	935	.66

Table 3: Satisfaction with SUNY Learning Network by Distance

			Sum of Squares	df	Mean Square	F	Sig.
Satisfaction with SLN by Reason	Between Groups	(Combined)	15.572	5	3.114	7.360	.000
	Within Groups		393.117	929	.423		
	Total		408.689	934			

These data suggest that students do report higher satisfaction due to increased access. Students who are least able to access the courses due either to distance or to other responsibilities report significantly higher levels of satisfaction with the program.

B. High Quality Online Teaching and Learning

Discussing the other strategic goal for SLN—"to provide a mechanism for maintaining consistently, high quality online teaching and learning across the SUNY system"—requires that we define what we mean by "quality". Again we used socio-cognitive learning theory and principles of good practice in higher education to define and assure quality in the development, implementation and evolution of course design and faculty development in SLN. In brief, for our purposes, socio-cognitive learning theory suggests interaction and active learning are the bases for many of the good practices in instruction at all levels. The principles of good practice are presented below, followed by survey results related to each principle.

1. Good Practice Encourages Contacts Between Students and Faculty

"Being a shy person I am able to think questions and answers through before I respond. In a regular classroom setting I often don't get my question out before we are on to another topic. I really like the online classes. I wish I could complete my degree online..." (survey comment)

It has been suggested that information technologies, "...can increase opportunities for students and faculty to converse" (Chickering & Ehrmann, 1995) and that such conversation is critical to learning and satisfaction. So, we asked students whether they had high levels of interaction with their instructors and other students and about the quality of the interaction. Overall more that 75% of students reported high levels of interaction with their instructors and approximately 73% felt they had high levels of interaction with their online classmates. Additionally, approximately 78% of respondents felt that the quality of the interaction with their instructors was very high and approximately 70% felt the quality of interaction with fellow students was very high. When asked to compare the level of interaction to similar classroom based courses a majority felt there was as much or more interaction with their instructor and fellow students as in similar classroom based courses.

Socio-cognitive principles would predict that the amount and quality of interaction will relate to satisfaction and learning, and our results demonstrate that they do. The tables below show the correlations between students' reports of the quantity and quality of interaction with faculty and with other students and their reports of satisfaction and learning in SLN courses.

Table 5: Correlations between Interaction, Satisfaction, and Learning

		Interaction with Instructor	Quality of Instructor Interaction	Interaction with Fellow Students	Quality of Interaction with Fellow Students
Satisfaction	Pearson Correlation	.631**	.672**	.367**	.401**
	Sig. (2-tailed)	.000	.000	.000	.000
	N	935	935	935	935
Reported Learning	Pearson Correlation	.619**	.631**	.376**	.394**
	Sig. (2-tailed)	.000	.000	.000	.000
	N	935	935	935	935

** Correlation is significant at the 0.01 level (2-tailed).

2. Good Practice Uses Active Learning Techniques

"This was a good experience for me. This course made me do a lot of deep thinking and allowed me to further my education. I cherish the fact that I can learn at this stage of my life. Thanks very much for offering this course." (survey comment)

"I have to tell you that I read the chapters more carefully as it was my responsibility to learn the subject matter. This course has helped me with my concentration skills. I was surprised how much I enjoyed the course. It was a real challenge to me and I love a challenge." (survey comment)

Meaningful learning requires active student engagement. How well do traditional classroom practices do at actively engaging students? Frequently, not very well. Barnes (1980) found that, even among faculty who actively solicited student participation, students only responded 50% of the time when called upon. Karp and Yoels (1988) reported that in classes of fewer than 40, four to five students accounted for 75% of all interactions and that in classes of more than

40, 2-3 students accounted for more than half of all interactions. Stones (1970) in a survey of over 1000 students found that 60% stated that a large number of classmates listening would deter them from asking questions, even when encouraged to do so by the instructor.

In contrast, in the most recent SLN survey, 93.4% of students reported active participation in their online class. To get a sense of how active and in what sense the students engaged in active learning we asked them to compare their levels of participation in online discussions about course material with comparable classroom discussions. We found that students were about *twice* as likely to report active participation in online discussion than in classroom based discussions. Students also reported that they were about *twice* as likely to ask for clarification when they did not understand something online than in the classroom. One side benefit, due to the fact that all of this communication occurred through written means, is that about 83% felt that the online format helped them improve their ability to communicate effectively in writing.

It has been suggested that information technologies allow student and faculty to converse, "…more thoughtfully and safely than when confronting each other in a classroom or faculty office" (Chickering & Ehrmann, 1995) and that this increased comfort and level of thought contributes to learning and satisfaction. We asked students to compare the amount of thought they put into their online discussion comments with those they made in the classroom. We found that about 86% of respondents reported that they put *more* thought into online discussion comments than into comparable classroom discussion, providing support for this hypothesis. As would be predicted, a significant correlation exists between amount of thought invested in discussion responses, and learning and satisfaction.

Table 6: Correlation Between Thought in Discussion Comments, Satisfaction and Learning

		Satisfaction	Reported Learning
Discussion Thought	Pearson Correlation	.262**	.272**
	Sig. (2-tailed)	.000	.000
	N	935	935

** Correlation is significant at the 0.01 level (2-tailed).

To confirm whether online conversations did occur "more safely" i.e. with more opportunity to explore topics that might be difficult to explore face-to-face, we asked students how likely they were to ask an awkward question online as compared to the classroom and whether they were more likely to ask for clarification online than in the classroom. Approximately 69% reported they were more likely to feel comfortable asking an awkward question online. Approximately 40% reported that were more likely to ask for clarification online, which was about twice the rate of those reporting that they were more likely to ask for clarification in the classroom (18%).

Authentic interaction implies that student-participants feel empowered to disagree, not only with each other, but also with the instructor. When asked whether they felt more comfortable disagreeing with the instructor in the online classroom, a large number of students (42%) reported that they did feel more comfortable in this environment.

3. Good Practice Gives Prompt Feedback and Communicates High Expectations

"I absolutely love this class. (The Professor) expects a lot but it's all so clear and interesting that it actually is fun. I've learned so much! I wish more classes were online." (Survey comment)

"I enjoyed this class because the teacher was helpful; she was prompt with answering questions and grading assignments. The teacher was very clear with what she wanted the class to do." (Survey comment)

"What I've appreciated most about this course has been the instant feedback and evaluations; critiques etc. from my professor. It's helped to keep me motivated and striving for better each week of the class. This has been a fantastic experience!" (Survey comment)

"There was very prompt response to discussion threads and test and assignment evaluations. Responses to comments were made within a day in most cases. This encouraged students to discuss with the instructor and other students on a regular basis. It felt like the course was alive; and help was there when you needed it." (Survey comment)

We asked students about the speed and quality of the feedback they received in their online courses. Approximately 85% reported that they received very prompt feedback and about 87% felt that they had received high quality, constructive feedback. Additionally more than 90% reported that the instructor provided clear expectations of how students could succeed in the course. As demonstrated in the table below each of these variables correlates significantly with reports of satisfaction and learning.

Table 7: Correlations Between Satisfaction, Learning, Expectations and Feedback

		Prompt Feedback	Quality Feedback	Clear Expectations
Satisfaction	Pearson Correlation	.592**	.620**	.609**
	Sig. (2-tailed)	.000	.000	.000
	N	935	935	935
Learning	Pearson Correlation	.520**	.569**	.563**
	Sig. (2-tailed)	.000	.000	.000
	N	935	935	935

** Correlation is significant at the 0.01 level (2-tailed).

4. Good Practice Emphasizes Time on Task

"I have learned more from this course than any other graduate course I have taken. There was a lot of work involved; but it only enhanced my understanding of lessons taught and has improved my teaching abilities in the classroom. I have; and will continue to recommend this system to fellow teachers who are trying to obtain a graduate degree. Thank You!!!" (Survey comment)

"I love the learning experiences gained from the online courses. I find that I actually work harder because generally it does take more time and effort to complete the online courses. With this in mind; the time used is very valuable and adds more meaning and depth to the overall learning experience." (Survey comment)

We asked students to think about the format of their courses and the fact that there was "anytime-anywhere" access. Did they feel that this increased level of access resulted in more time studying? Approximately 71% of students reported that they did spend more time studying as a result of the increased access afforded by the online format.

Table 8: Correlation Between Amount of Time Spent Studying, Learning, and Satisfaction

		Satisfaction	Learning
Time	Pearson Correlation	.265**	.294**
	Sig. (2-tailed)	.000	.000
	N	935	935

** Correlation is significant at the 0.01 level (2-tailed).

However, the possibility for wasting time in online courses, due to the distractions of the Internet, is also possible. Approximately 13% of students did report that the online format resulted in more wasted time browsing and about 87% did not.

Wasting time can take other forms. For example, technical difficulties can consume time that would otherwise be devoted to more productive purposes. So we asked students about technical difficulties and their effect on the students' learning and satisfaction. Approximately 88% of students felt that taking a course through SLN was no more technically difficult than taking a classroom based course. We also found that students who were less likely to report technical difficulties were more likely to report higher levels of satisfaction and learning and that students were highly satisfied with the SLN Helpdesk.

VI. RESULTS SUMMARY

Overall approximately 87% of SLN students reported being satisfied or very satisfied with their courses; about 90% report learning a great deal; about 94% reported being satisfied or very satisfied with SLN services; and 97% reported satisfaction with the SLN Helpdesk. When asked whether they would take another SLN course, only 1.7% responded that they would definitely not want to do this. Finally, overall, these 935 students were 1.7 times as likely to report learning more in their online courses (36%) than in comparable classroom-based courses (20.8%), though the majority felt they were equivalent (43.2%).

VII. IMPORTANCE OR RELEVANCE TO OTHER INSTITUTIONS

Are these findings relevant to other institutions? We believe they are useful in a number of ways. Online learning environments are not easy to implement successfully. Effort, coordination, planning and expense are required. If an institution is considering systematic implementation of online education it is useful to know that success, as measured by traditional notions of best practice in higher education, is possible.

In general, although we acknowledge that these results may not be completely generalizable to other systems, to know that nearly 1000 students from 53 institutions from associate level through graduate level programs reported high levels of learning and satisfaction in online courses, offered through a single, unified system, is potentially helpful. We feel the success of SLN demonstrates that it is possible to overcome the complexity and challenges involved in system-wide online learning initiatives, to provide increased flexible access, and to maintain high standards across courses.

For those who are concerned that the online learning is, by its very nature, cold, sterile, and isolating, knowing that the vast majority of these online students reported high levels and high quality interaction with their instructors and other students, and that they were unlikely to report feeling isolated, is potentially helpful. Knowing that the vast majority reported fast and high quality feedback as well as clear expectations for success is also encouraging.

Through Correlational research we have found that a number of variables correlate significantly with high levels of satisfaction and learning. Before embarking on the implementation of new online learning environments it would be wise to consider the following: high levels of interaction with the instructor, and the quality of that interaction, interaction with fellow students and its quality, prompt and high quality feedback on assignments, clear expectations on how to succeed in the course and low levels of technical difficulties are all variables that correlate highly with both satisfaction and learning and, therefore need to be given a high priority in planning and developing an online environment. Perhaps not surprisingly, these are also variables that correlate highly with satisfaction and learning in the classroom.

VIII. IS ALN "AS GOOD AS" THE CLASSROOM?

For those who are concerned about whether the online environment is "as good as" the classroom it is useful to know that it is, at least, possible to attain many measures of equivalence. We see reason for optimism in the knowledge that in the most recent term for which data was collected, nearly 1000 online students from dozens of institutions not only reported high levels of satisfaction and learning, but were also: twice as likely to report active participation in such important activities as discussion of course materials; twice as likely to report asking instructors for clarification; twice as likely to report putting more thought into discussion; twice as likely to report spending more time studying; and nearly twice as likely to report learning more online than in the classroom. We also found that students who had taken four or more classes were no less likely to report high levels of satisfaction and learning in these courses than student who were taking their first course. These results replicate findings from five previous surveys in the period 1998-2001.

IX. REFERENCES

1. **Barnes, M.** (1980). Questioning: The Untapped Resource. Eric Document 1888555. Paper presented at the Annual Meeting of the American Educational Research Association. Boston, MA April 7-11, 1980.
2. **Brown, J. S., Collins, A., & Duguid, S.** (1989). Situated cognition and the culture of learning. Educational Researcher, 18(1), 32-42.
3. **Bruner, J.** (1990). Acts of meaning. Cambridge, MA: Harvard University Press.
4. **Bussmann, H.** (1998) Phatic communion. In Trauth, G., Kazzazi, K. & Kazzazi, K. (Eds.) Routledge Dictionary of Language and Linguistics. London: Routledge.
5. **Chickering, A. W. & Ehrmann, S. C.** (1995). Implementing the seven principles: technology as lever, American Association for Higher Education, retrieved from the American Association for Higher Education web page: http://www.aahe.org/ Bulletin/Implementing%20the%20Seven%20Principles.htm.
6. **Chickering, A. W. & Gamson, A. F.** (1987). Seven principles for good practice in undergraduate education. Racine, WI: The Johnson Foundation, Inc/Wingspread.
7. Flashlight Group Current Student Inventory (1997).
8. **Karp, D. & Yoels, W.** (1987). The College Classroom: Some Observations on the Meanings of Student Participation. Sociology and Social Research, 60, 421-439.
9. **Lave, J.** (1988). Cognition in practice: mind, mathematics, and culture in everyday life. Cambridge, UK: Cambridge University Press.
10. **Stones, E.** (1970) Students' Attitudes to the size of teaching groups. Educational Review, 21 (2), 98-108.
11. **Vygotsky, L. S.** (1978). Mind in society. Cambridge, MA: Harvard University Press.

X. ABOUT THE AUTHORS

Peter Shea is the manager of the TLT @ SUNY Project (Teaching Learning and Technology at SUNY). In this position he is responsible for assisting campuses within SUNY to help faculty use technology in instruction both efficiently and effectively. Currently, he is also director of the MELROT project (Multimedia Educational Resource for Teaching and Online Learning) for SUNY. This project represents a national consortium of 23 higher education systems each contributing to build a database of discipline specific, peer-reviewed, online learning material that can be used by any faculty for free. Before taking over the TLT @ SUNY Project he was the lead multimedia instructional designer for the SUNY Learning Network, where he helped the SLN instructional design team and faculty from 47 SUNY institutions to build well designed online courses. Peter received his doctorate in Curriculum and Instruction from the State University of New York and is also a visiting Associate Professor at the University at Albany, teaching graduate courses in educational research.

Contact: Peter Shea, Director- The Teaching, Learning, and Technology Project, Advanced Learning and Information Services, State University of New York, SUNY Plaza, N303, Albany, NY 12246; Phone: 518-443-5640; Peter_Shea@SLN.suny.edu

Karen Swan (Ed.D. Teachers College, Columbia University) Professor Swan is an associate professor of Instructional Technology at the University at Albany where she also directs the Learning Technologies Laboratory and the Summer Technology Institute. Her research has been focused mainly in the general area of computers and education. She has published and presented both nationally and internationally in the specific areas of programming and problem solving, computer-assisted instruction, hypermedia design, technology and literacy, and asynchronous online learning. Her current research focuses on the latter, on technology integration in English language arts teaching and learning, and on situated professional development for technology integration. Dr. Swan has also written on social learning from broadcast television, about which she co-edited a book, and has authored several hypermedia programs including *Set On Freedom: The American Civil Rights Experience* for Glencoe and *The Multimedia Sampler* for IBM, as well as several online courses which are being offered through the SUNY Learning Network. She is a project director in the Technology Integration Project of the National Research Center on English Learning and Achievement (CELA), and is currently involved with product and usability evaluation for Project VIEW (Virtual Interactive Education Web), research on the CATIE (Capital Area Technology and Inquiry in Education) technology professional development initiative, and design consulting for NYLink online workshops on Information Technology Fluency. Dr. Swan serves on the program committees for several local and international instructional technology conferences, is a member of the ALN Effectiveness Research Advisory Board, and is the Special Issues Editor for the *Journal of Educational Computing Research*.

Contact: Karen Swan, Associate Professor, Educational Theory and Practice, University at Albany, State University of New York, 1400 Washington Ave, Albany, NY 12222; Phone: 518-442-5032; kswan@uamail.albany.edu

Eric E. Fredericksen is the Assistant Provost for Advanced Learning Technology in Advanced Learning & Information Services, part of the Office of the Provost in the State University of New York System Administration. He provides leadership and direction for all of SUNY's system-wide programs focused on the innovative use of technology to support the teaching and learning environment. This includes the SUNY Learning Network- the SUNY System's premiere asynchronous learning program and the TLT- Teaching, Learning & Technology program. Eric is also the Co-Principal Investigator and Administrative Officer for a multi-year, multi-million dollar grant on Asynchronous Learning Networks from the Alfred P. Sloan Foundation. He is responsible for the fiscal management, strategic planning, policy development, faculty development, marketing & promotion, student support center, and technical infrastructure. Under Eric' leadership the program has grown from 2 campuses offering 8 courses to 119 enrollments to 47 campuses offering 1500 courses to more than 20,000 enrollments in just five years. Eric received his Bachelors degree in Mathematics from Hobart College, his MBA from the William Simon Graduate School of Business at the University of Rochester and his Master of Science in Education in Curriculum Development & Instructional Technology at the Graduate School of Education at the University at Albany.

Contact: Eric Fredericksen, Assistant Provost for Advanced Learning Technology, State University of New York, SUNY Plaza, Albany, NY 12246; Eric.Fredericksen@sln.suny.edu

Alexandra M. Pickett is the Assistant Director of the SUNY Learning Network (SLN), the asynchronous learning network for the State University of New York under the offices of the Provost and Advanced Learning and Information Services. A pioneer in instructional design and faculty development for asynchronous web-based teaching and learning environments, Ms. Pickett has since 1994 led the development of the instructional design methods, support services, and resources used by SLN to develop and deliver full web online courses. She has spent the past six years conceptualizing and implementing scaleable, replicable, and sustainable institutionalized faculty development and course design and delivery processes that in the 2000-2001 academic year will result in the delivery of 1,500+ courses with 20,000+ student enrollments. One of the original SLN design team members, she co-designed the course management software and authored the 4-stage faculty development process and 7-step course design process used by the network. Her comprehensive approach includes an online faculty resource and information gateway, an online conference for all faculty with the opportunity to observe a wide variety of online courses, a series of workshops for new faculty, instructional design sessions for returning faculty looking to improve their courses, a developer's handbook, a course template, a faculty Helpdesk, online mechanisms for faculty evaluation of SLN services, and an assigned instructional design partner. Today, working with 47 of the 64 SUNY institutions, she has directly supported or coordinated the development of more than 700 SUNY faculty and their web-delivered courses. Her research interests are in faculty satisfaction and the effective instructional design of online courses, and student satisfaction and perceived learning. She has co-authored a number of studies on these topics and has published and presented the results both nationally and internationally. Visit http://SLN.suny.edu/developer.

Contact: Alexandra Pickett, Assistant Director, SUNY Learning Network, SUNY Plaza, Albany, NY 12246; Phone: 518-443-5622; Alexandra.Pickett@sln.suny.edu

Immediacy, Social Presence, and Asynchronous Discussion

Karen Swan
University at Albany

- Four kinds of interactions support learning—interactions with content, with instructor, with classmates, and with interface.

- Social presence—the ability of learners to project themselves socially and emotionally in a community of inquiry—supports cognition by supporting critical thinking. Social presence makes group interactions appealing, engaging, and thus intrinsically rewarding.

- The equilibrium model of social presence suggests that social presence derives from both the affective communication channels available in a medium and the immediacy behaviors of the participating communicators.

- The affective, interactive, and cohesive immediacy behaviors of students demonstrate the significant correlation of perceived social presence and perceived learning.

- Instructors and designers of asynchronous courses should value course discussions, model and support the development of social presence within courses, and work to build and sustain interactive communities of inquiry in online courses.

I. BACKGROUND

The research reported in this paper grows out of prior research linking student perceptions of satisfaction, learning, and interactions in asynchronous online courses to course design factors, specifically to findings pointing to the importance of active, authentic, and valued online course discussion.

In an empirical study relating course design factors in 73 asynchronous online course to student perceptions of them, Swan, Shea, Fredericksen, Pickett, Pelz & Maher (2000) found that the greater the percentage of course grades that were based on discussion, the more satisfied students were with their courses, the more they thought they learned from them, and the more interaction they thought they had with both their instructors and their classmates. In addition, students' perceptions of interactions with their classmates were related to the average length of discussion responses, and to the required and actual frequency of discussion postings. Other researchers have reported similar findings underscoring the importance of discussion in asynchronous online courses (Hawisher & Pemberton, 1997; Picciano, 1998; Jiang & Ting, 2000).

Indeed, asynchronous discussion seems both a significant factor in the success of online courses and significantly different from face-to-face discussion in traditional classrooms. In online discussion, all students have a voice, and no students can dominate the conversation. The asynchronous nature of the discussion makes it impossible for even an instructor to control. Accordingly, many researchers note that students perceive online discussion as more equitable and more democratic than traditional classroom discussions (Harasim, 1990; Levin, Kim & Riel, 1990). Ruberg, Moore and Taylor (1996), for example, found that computer-mediated communication encouraged experimentation, sharing of ideas, and increased and more distributed participation.

Because it is asynchronous, online discussion also affords participants the opportunity to reflect on their classmates' contributions while creating their own, and to reflect on their own writing before posting it. This creates a certain mindfulness among students and a culture of reflection in an online course (Hiltz, 1994; Poole, 2000). In addition, many researchers familiar with computer-mediated communication have noted what Walther (1994) refers to as the "hyperpersonalness" of the medium. Participants in online discussion seem to project their personalities into it, creating feelings of "immediacy" that build online discourse communities (Gunawardena & Zittle, 1997; Poole, 2000; Rourke, Anderson, Garrison & Archer, 2001).

"Immediacy" refers to perceived "psychological distance between communicators" (Weiner & Mehrabian, 1968). In traditional, face-to-face classrooms, educational researchers found that teachers' immediacy behaviors can lessen the psychological distance between themselves and their students, leading, directly or indirectly depending on the study, to greater learning (Kearney, Plax & Wendt-Wasco, 1985; Richmond, Gorham & McCroskey, 1987, Kelley & Gorham, 1988; Gorham, 1988, Christophel, 1990; Richmond, 1990; Frymeir, 1994, Rodriguez, Plax & Kearney, 1996). They further distinguished between teachers' verbal immediacy behaviors (ie., giving praise, soliciting viewpoints, use of humor, self-disclosure, etc.) and their non-verbal immediacy behaviors (i.e., physical proximity, touch, eye-contact, facial expressions, gestures, etc.).

Indeed, there are several models linking immediacy to increased learning in traditional classrooms (see Figure 1). Learning models suggest a direct relationship between teachers' immediacy behaviors and increased cognitive (Kelley & Gorham, 1988; Gorham, 1988) and affective (Kearney, Plax & Wendt-Wasco, 1985; Richmond, Gorham & McCroskey, 1987, Gorham, 1988) learning. Motivation models posit an intervening variable, state motivation, between immediacy behaviors and learning. That is, these models contend that immediacy behaviors result in students being more motivated to learn the materials being presented, which in turn leads to increased cognitive and affective learning (Christophel, 1990; Richmond, 1990; Frymeir, 1994). The affective learning model of Rodriguez, Plax & Kearney (1996) also posits an intervening variable between immediacy and cognitive learning, but suggests that it is affective learning itself. Regardless of the model posited, however, there is a good deal of research that shows a link between immediacy and learning in face-to-face classrooms.

The immediacy research in traditional classrooms has implications for learning through online communications. Some communication researchers argue that differing media have differing capabilities to transmit the non-verbal and vocal

Figure 1
Models Relating Immediacy to Learning

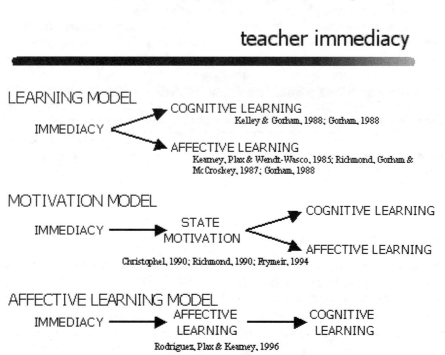

cues that produce feelings of immediacy in face-to-face communication. Short, Williams & Christie (1976) refer to these capabilities as "social presence," or the "quality of a medium to project the salience of others in interpersonal communication." They contend that media with few affective communication channels (such as text-based computer-mediated communication) have less social presence (and by extension promote less learning) than media with a greater number of affective communication channels. Media richness theory (Rice, 1992) reaches a similar conclusion.

Researchers experienced with online teaching and learning, however, contest this view. Participants in computer-media communications, they argue, create social presence by projecting their identities into their communications. What is important, these researchers contend, is not media capabilities, but rather personal perceptions (Walther, 1994, Gunawardena & Zittle, 1997; Poole, 2000; Rourke, Anderson, Garrison & Archer, 2001).

Gunawardena and Zittle (1997), for example, developed a survey to explore student perceptions of social presence in computer-mediated conferences associated with a Global Education course that included participants in both the United States and Mexico. In two separate studies, they found that students rated asynchronous discussion as highly interactive and social. The researchers concluded that course participants created social presence by projecting their identities online and building a discourse community among themselves. What was important, they argued, was student perceptions of the presence of others, not the medium's capacity to capture gestures and intonations.

Richardson & Swan (2001), using a survey adapted from Gunawardena & Zittle (1997), explored perceptions of social presence among students enrolled in Empire State College's online courses in the spring of 2000. They found that students' perceived learning, satisfaction with their instructors, and perceptions of social presence were all highly correlated. Indeed, direct entry regression revealed that students' overall perception of social presence was a predictor of their perceived learning in the courses. In addition, significant correlations were found between perceived social presence and perceived learning for each of the six categories of activities found in Empire State College courses, including activities in which social presence would not seem to be a factor such as lecture, quizzes and tests, and individual papers.

Danchak, Walther, and Swan (2001) developed a model of the development of social presence in mediated educational environments (see Figure 2) which seeks to resolve contradictions between media-centered theories of social presence

(Short, Williams & Christie, 1976; Rice 1992) and perceptual findings (Gunawardena & Zittle, 1997; Richardson & Swan, 2001). They suggest that social presence in mediated environments is a function of both the affective communication channels available and the immediacy behaviors of participants in them. They further argue that participants in environments with less affective communication channels available will evoke more immediacy behaviors to affect a kind of equilibrium of social presence with which they are comfortable.

Figure 2
Equilibrium Model (Danchak, Walther & Swan, 2001)

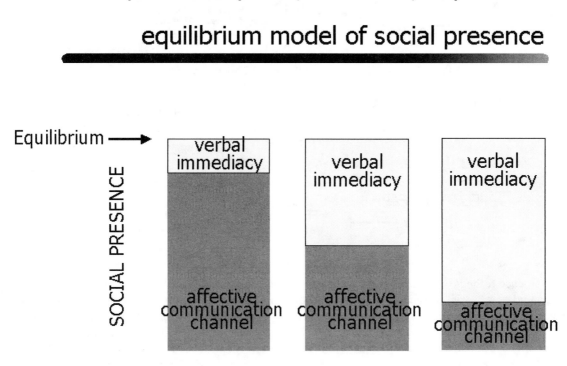

Rourke, Anderson, Garrison & Archer (2001) developed a model of online learning that likewise highlights the importance of the development of social presence in that process (see Figure 3). In this "community of inquiry" model, learning occurs through the interaction of three core components: cognitive presence, teaching presence, and social presence. Cognitive presence is "the extent to which the participants in any particular configuration of a community of inquiry are able to construct meaning through sustained communication." Teaching presence includes subject matter expertise, the design and management of learning, and the facilitation of active learning. Social presence, they contend, supports both cognitive and teaching presence through its ability to instigate, sustain, and support interaction.

Figure 3
Community of Inquiry Model (Rourke, Anderson, Garrison & Archer, 2001)

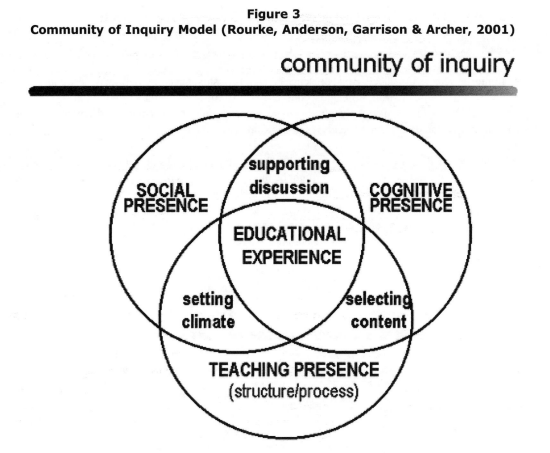

To better explore the importance of the development of social presence in online discussions, Rourke, et al. (2001) developed a template for assessing social presence in computer conferencing. They distinguished among three kinds of social presence responses: affective responses, interactive responses, and cohesive responses. They tested their coding scheme by analyzing sections of discussion in two graduate level courses, and found high interrater reliability for it. They concluded that the template could be useful for the formulation and testing of hypotheses in which social presence is a variable.

The research reported in this paper uses a coding scheme based on the categories developed by Rourke, et al. (2001) to explore the equilibrium model of Danchak, Walther, and Swan (2001).

II. METHODOLOGY

Data was collected from the discussions that took place in a graduate level course in Educational Computing given entirely online in the Spring 2001 semester. The course consisted of four modules that ran sequentially across the semester. In each module, there were three discussions initiated by instructor questions and roughly corresponding to the three weeks students were directed to spend working in each module. Students were required to submit one response to the instructor prompt and two responses to their classmates in each discussion. They could, of course, submit as many responses as they liked, and many participated a good deal more than required.

Data collected consisted of all discussion strands from the first discussion in each module initiated in the first five days each module was open. Two hundred and thirty-five postings in 39 discussion threads, or approximately 10% of all postings in the course discussions, were examined. The average number of words per posting was 82.4 (range = 5 to 562); the average number of responses per thread was 6.05 (range = 0 to 30); and the average interactivity (measured as the depth of responses) was 3.63 (range = 1 to 10).

Students participating in the course ranged in age from 23 to 48 and were about two thirds female. The majority were practicing K-12 teachers, but course participants also included post-secondary educators, librarians, and educational technology specialists.

In order to examine the verbal immediacy/social presence behaviors of students participating in these course discussions, a coding schema was developed (Swan, Polhemus, Shih & Rogers, 2001) based on Rourke, et al.'s (2001) categories and on research on classroom-based immediacy, on social presence in computer-mediated communication, and on indicators emerging from the data. Three categories of indicators were identified.

Affective indicators (Swan, Polhemus, Shih & Rogers, 2001) are personal expressions of emotion, feelings, beliefs, and values (Rourke, et al., 2001). Affective indicators might be thought of as ways of projecting personal immediacy/social presence into online discourse, as ways of making up for the lack of gestures, facial expressions, and/or intonation in face-to-face communication. The affective indicators we coded for included the use of paralanguage, expressions of emotion, statements of values, humor, and self-disclosure. These are listed in Table 1, which gives the code used for the indicator, its definition, examples from the actual discussion, and research sources for its inclusion in the coding scheme.

Table 1
Affective Indicators

affective indicators

paralanguage (PL)	features of text outside formal syntax used to convey emotion (ie. emoticons, punctuation, capitalization)	*Someday . . . . .; How awful for you :-(; Mathcad is definitely NOT stand alone software; Absolutely!!!!!!*	Bussman, 1998; Rourke, et al, 2001; Poole, 2000
emotion (EM)	use of descriptive words that indicate feelings (ie., love, hate, sad, silly)	*When I make a spelling mistake, I look and feel stupid; I get chills when I think of . . .*	Rourke, et al, 2001
value (VL)	expressing personal values beliefs, & attitudes	*I think that commercialization is a necessary evil; I feel our children have the same rights*	emergent
humor (H)	use of humor – teasing, cajoling, understatement, irony, sarcasm	*God forbid leaving your house to go to the library; Now it is like brushing my teeth (which I assure you I do quite well)*	Eggins & Slade, 1997; Rourke, et al, 2001; Poole, 2000
self-disclosure (SD)	sharing personal information, expressing vulnerability	*I sound like an old lady; I am a closet writer; We had a similar problem . . .*	Cutler, 1995; Rourke, et al, 2001; Poole, 2000

Cohesive indicators (Swan, Polhemus, Shih & Rogers, 2001) are verbal immediacy behaviors that build and sustain a sense of group commitment or group presence/immediacy (Rourke, et al., 2001). Cohesive indicators support the development of community. Coded cohesive indicators included greetings and salutations, the use of vocatives, group reference, social sharing, and course reference. They are given in Table 2 which also gives the code assigned to each indicator, its definition, examples from the actual discussion, and research sources for its inclusion in the coding scheme.

Table 2
Cohesive Indicators

cohesive indicators

greetings & salutations (GS)	greetings, closures	*Hi Mary; That's it for now, Tom*	Rourke, et al, 2001; Poole, 2000
vocatives (V)	addressing classmates by name	*You know, Tamara. . . ; I totally agree with you Katherine*	Christenson & Menzel, 1998; Gorham, 1998; Sanders & Wiseman, 1990; Rourke, et al, 2001; Poole, 2000
group reference (GR)	refering to the group as *we, us, our*	*We need to be educated; Our use of the Internet may not be free*	Rourke, et al, 2001
social sharing (SS)	phatics, sharing information unrelated to the course	*Happy Birthday!!to both of you!!!*	Rourke, et al, 2001
course reflection (RF)	reflection on the course itself	*A good example was the CD-ROM we read about*	emergent

Interactive indicators (Swan, Polhemus, Shih & Rogers, 2001) provide evidence that the other is attending (Rourke, et al., 2001), and might be thought of as suggesting interpersonal presence/immediacy. Interactive indicators support interactions among communicators. Indicators we coded for included acknowledgement, agreement, approval, invitation, and personal advice. Table 3 shows the interactive indicators we coded for, together with the code assigned to them, their definitions, examples from the actual discussion, and research sources for their inclusion in the coding scheme.

Table 3
Interactive Indicators

interactive indicators

acknowledgement (AK)	refering directly to the contents of others' messages; quoting from others' messages	*Those old machines sure were something!; I agree that it is the quickest way; I also agree that software can make or break it*	Rourke, et al, 2001
agreement/ disagreement (AG)	expressing agreement or disagreement with others' messages	*I'm with you on that; I agree; I think what you are saying is absolutely right*	Rourke, et al, 2001; Poole, 2000
approval (AP)	expressing approval, offering praise, encouragement	*You make a good point; Good luck as you continue to learn; Right on!*	Rourke, et al, 2001
invitation (I)	asking questions or otherwise inviting response	*Any suggestions?; How old are your students?; Would you describe that for me, I'm unfamiliar with the term*	Rourke, et al, 2001
personal advice (PA)	offering specific advice to classmates	*Also the CEC website might have some references I would be happy to forward*	emergent

Hardcopy transcriptions of online discussions were coded by multiple researchers for each of the fifteen affective, interactive, and cohesive indicators, as well as for the number of words per posting, the number of postings per discussion thread, and the depth of each discussion thread. Participant names were replaced with IDs to preserve subject anonymity, and their genders were noted. Discrepancies between coders were resolved by consensus and reference to the discussion transcripts. Figure 4 shows a section of the coded transcript.

Figure 4
Example of Coded Transcript

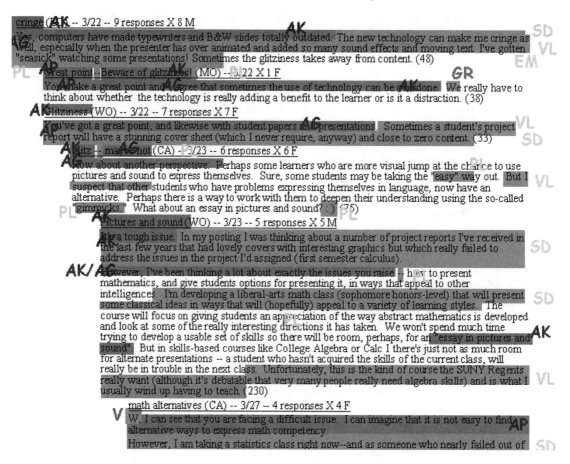

Data analyses consisted of compiling and reviewing raw numbers of indicators across modules and reviewing the findings for patterns of indicator use.

III. RESULTS

We found a great many immediacy/social presence indicators in the online discussions we reviewed, a total of 1,336 (663 affective, 468, interactive, and 235 cohesive) in 235 postings, or an average of almost 6 indicators per posting. Figure 5 shows the raw numbers of responses and indicators across modules. Only one posting had no immediacy indicators in it and that message was not responded to. We believe these findings provide evidence that participants in the online discussions we studied made up for the lack of affective communication channels by employing more immediacy behaviors in those channels that are available to them (Danchak, Walther & Swan, 2001). A closer look at the data supports this notion as well.

Figure 5
Types of Indicators Across Modules

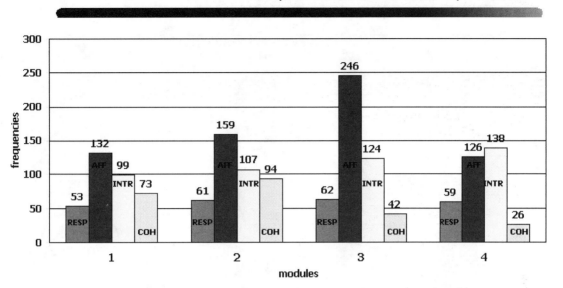

responses & indicators by module

For example, the most frequently used verbal immediacy behavior (254 instances) was the use of paralanguage, the use of text outside formal syntax to convey emotion or emphasis (ie. emoticons, punctuation, capitalization, exaggerated spellings, etc.). It seems reasonable to assume that discussion participants were using paralanguage to take the place of gestures, facial expressions, and aural cues in their conversations. At the other extreme, humor was the least used immediacy behavior. This may be because humor really does necessitate more affective communications channels. It is instructive in this vein to note that no attempts at humor were even made in the discussion we coded from first module.

In the sections that follow, results specific to each category of immediacy indicators are explored.

A. Affective Immediacy Indicators

Affective verbal immediacy behaviors might be thought of as ways of projecting personal presence into online discourse to make up for the lack of gestures, facial expressions, and/or intonation in available in face-to-face communication. Figure 6 shows the raw numbers of affective verbal immediacy indicators found across all the discussion coded. Across all modules, we found an average of 2.8 affective indicators per response. The most frequently used affective indicator was paralanguage with an average of over one indicator per response. As previously noted, the use of paralanguage can be seen as an attempt to reproduce in text some of the affect conveyed in gestures, intonations, and facial expressions.

Figure 6
Affective Indicators Across Modules

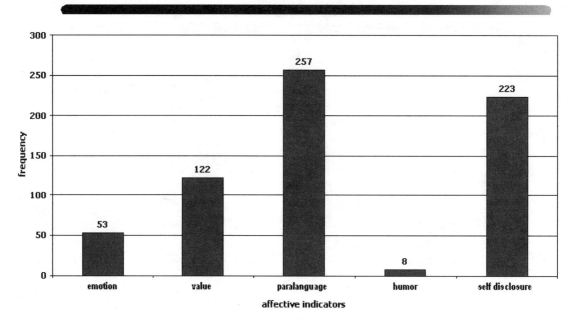

The second most frequently employed affective indicator, with almost one indicator per response, was self-disclosure. Self-disclosure is the sharing of personal information, usually of a vulnerable nature. Self-disclosure is an immediacy behavior frequently noted in the immediacy research as employed by teachers to lesson the gap between themselves and their students (Kearney, Plax & Wendt-Wasco, 1985; Gorham, 1988; Christophel, 1990; Richmond, 1990; Frymeir, 1994; Rodriguez, Plax & Kearney, 1996). It seems to have been employed similarly in the discussion threads we coded. Indeed, self-disclosure seemed to evoke the greatest number and depth of response from other participants. However, humor, another behavior noted in the immediacy research, was very little employed, perhaps because many forms of humor are easily misinterpreted in text-based communication. This finding points to differences between face-to-face and computer-mediated communications.

Figure 7 gives the raw numbers of affective immediacy indicators found in the discussion threads coded in each of the modules of the course. It thus shows the use of these indicators across time. It is interesting to note in this regard the pattern of usage across the modules. It can be seen that the use of affective indicators in general, and paralanguage and self-disclosure in particular, seemed to grow to a peak usage in the third module and to drop precipitously after that. This usage seems to mirror the pattern of discussion in the course in general. Activity in the discussion generally seemed to peak in the third module and decline in the fourth (see Figure 5). The finding suggests that affective immediacy behaviors, at least in this particular course, were an integral part of social interaction, but that in the online environment they took the only available, verbal form. The finding thus supports the equilibrium model of social presence in mediated communication environments.

Figure 7
Affective Indicators for Each Module

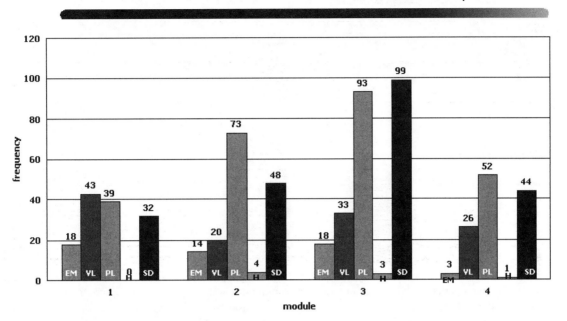

B. Cohesive Immediacy Indicators

Cohesive verbal immediacy behaviors build and sustain a sense of group commitment to support the development of a discourse community. Figure 8 shows the raw numbers of cohesive immediacy indicators found across all the discussion coded. Cohesive indicators were the least used of verbal immediacy behaviors in the discussions we coded. Across all modules, we found an average of 1cohesive indicator per response. The most frequently used cohesive indicator was group reference, the use of words such as "we," "our," or "us" to refer to the class as a group. It is interesting to note in this regard that the use of group reference declined across the modules. It seems possible that the use of such reference became less necessary as a clear classroom community was formed; that is, as participants developed a greater sense of community they felt less need to point to it (Eggins & Slade, 1997).

Figure 8
Cohesive Indicators Across Modules

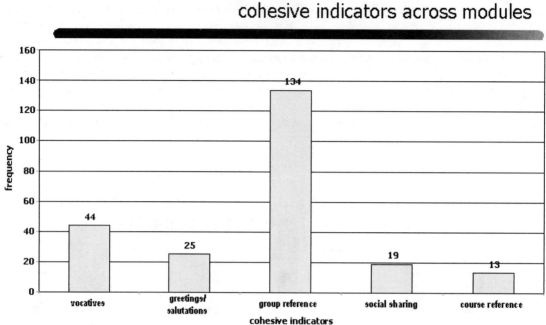

Figure 9 gives the raw numbers of cohesive immediacy indicators found in threads coded in each of the modules of the course. Indeed, it depicts a significant decline in all cohesive indicators by the third and fourth modules, except perhaps in the use of greetings and salutations and vocatives. Greetings and vocatives are immediacy indicators that refer to conversational partners by name. It may be, then, that some of the use of group reference was replaced by personal reference as participants learned and became comfortable using each other's names. This shift in behaviors does not account for the significant decline in most cohesive behaviors across modules, however, or even, for that matter, for all of the decline in the use of group reference. The most plausible explanation remains that discussion participants felt less need to employ cohesive indicators as they felt a greater organic cohesion among themselves.

Figure 9
Cohesive Indicators for Each Module

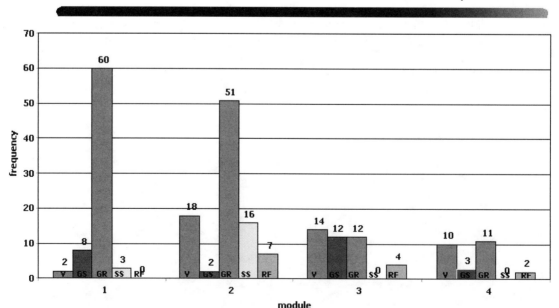

C. Interactive Immediacy Indicators

Interactive verbal immediacy behaviors support interactions among communicators by providing evidence that others are attending to the discourse. Figure 10 shows the raw numbers of interactive verbal immediacy indicators found across all the parts of the modules coded. Across all modules, we found an average of 2 interactive indicators per response. The most frequently used interactive indicator was acknowledgement, which refers to quoting from or referring directly to the contents of others' messages. Discussion participants employed, on average, almost one use of acknowledgement for each response. In addition, agreement/disagreement and approval, taken together, were used almost as frequently. These findings seem to indicate that acknowledgement, agreement, and approval are the glue that holds asynchronous discussion together, an interpretation given further credence by the fact that the use of all interactive indicators continued to increase across modules.

Figure 10
Interactive Indicators Across Modules

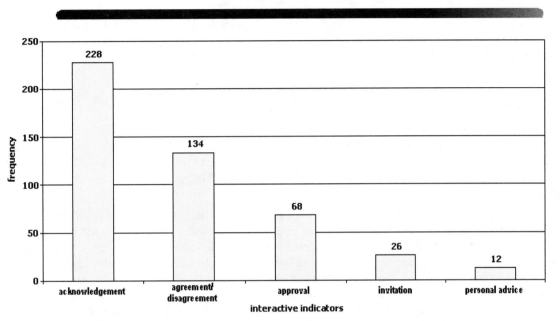

Figure 11 gives the raw numbers of interactive immediacy indicators found in the discussion threads coded in each of the modules of the course. It shows a consistent increase in the use of interactive immediacy behaviors across time. The pattern seems to indicate, at least within the course studied, a growing awareness among course participants of the importance of the use of these indicators. Thus, while cohesive behaviors became less important as the online community came together, the importance of interactive behaviors seemed to grow over time as participants became aware of their usefulness in linking the discussion into a coherent whole.

Figure 11
Interactive Indicators for Each Module

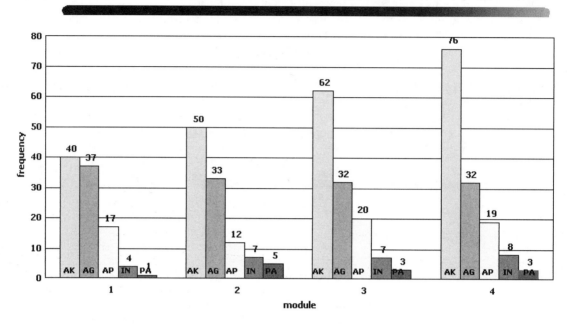

IV. CONCLUSIONS

All these findings lead us to conclude that students participating in the online course discussions we investigated strove to create a community of learning by employing text-based, verbal immediacy behaviors to reduce the psychological distance among themselves. The findings lend support to an equilibrium model of social presence (Danchak, Walther & Swan, 2001) that suggests that social presence derives from both the affective communication channels available in a medium and the immediacy behaviors of the participating communicators. Participants in the course discussions we studied employed more verbal immediacy behaviors then are normally found in traditional, face-to-face classroom discussions. In addition, the equilibrium model makes sense of the patterns of the use of affective, cohesive, and inter-active immediacy indicators that were found in the discussion threads studied. We found that as the course progressed, cohesive indicators declined in importance while the importance of interactive indicators increased. Indeed, taken together, the raw numbers of cohesive and interactive indicators were not significantly different across modules. The use of affective indicators generally mirrored the general flow of the course discussions across time, suggesting that the maintenance of affective presence was integral to the maintenance of community.

The research on teachers' immediacy behaviors in face-to-face classrooms shows links between these behaviors and students' learning. Although some scholars have argued that the lack of affective communication channels in com-puter-mediated communication leads to a loss of immediacy and a corresponding loss in learning, more recent research suggests otherwise. This study supports the latter research but tries to incorporate findings from media theorists by suggesting that participants in online discussions make up for the lack of affective communication channels by engag-ing in a greater number of verbal immediacy behaviors. It posits an equilibrium model of social presence to describe this view.

This model has practical implications for the development and implementation of online courses and for online learning in general, in that it suggests that developers and instructors of online courses should seek designs and strategies that support the development of perceived social presence in these online learning communities. In particular, instructors might use the verbal immediacy behaviors identified to model verbal immediacy behaviors in their interactions with students. Affective and interactive indicators seem most important in this regard.

Of course, this research only looks at a single course; thus it is impossible to generalize from it. While the research supports an equilibrium model, it does not confirm it. Future research should examine discussion in other course contexts to see if the model holds. In particular, it would be interesting to examine courses covering different subject areas and involving differing groups of students. In addition, research exploring the actual, real-time behaviors of students participating in online discussion might reveal more of what is happening in this emergent and fascinating medium.

V. REFERENCES

1. **Bussmann, H.** (1998) Phatic communion. In Trauth, G., Kazzazi, K. & Kazzazi, K. (Eds.) *Routledge Dictionary of Language and Linguistics*. London: Routledge.
2. **Christenson, L. & Menzel, K.** (1998) The linear relationship between student reports of teacher immediacy behaviors and perceptions of state motivation, and of cognitive, affective and behavioral learning. *Communication Education, 47*, (1), 82-90.
3. **Christophel, D.** (1990) The relationship among teacher immediacy behaviors, student motivation, and learning. *Communication Education, 39*, (4), 323-240.
4. **Cutler, R.** (1995) Distributed presence and community in Cyberspace. *Interpersonal Computing and Technology, 3*, (2), 12-32.
5. **Danchak, M. M., Walther, J. B. & Swan, K.** (2001) Presence in mediated instruction: bandwidth, behavior, and expectancy violations. Orlando, FL: Paper presented at the Seventh Annual Sloan-C International Conference on Online Learning.
6. **Eggins, S. & Slade, D.** (1997) *Analyzing Casual Conversation*. Washington, DC: Cassell.
7. **Frymier, A. B.** (1994) A model of immediacy in the classroom. *Communication Quarterly, 42* (2), 133-144.8.
9. Gorham, J. (1988) The relationship between verbal teacher immediacy behaviors and student learning. *Communication Education, 37*, (1), 40-53.
10. **Gunawardena, C. N., Lowe, C. A. & Anderson, T.** (1997) Analysis of a global online debate and the development of an interaction analysis model for examining social construction of knowledge in computer conferencing. *Journal of Educational Computing Research, 17* (4), 397-431.
11. **Harasim, L.** (1990) On-line Education: Perspectives on a New Environment. New York: Praeger.
12. **Hawisher, G. E. & Pemberton, M. A.** (1997) Writing across the curriculum encounters asynchronous learning networks or WAC meets up with ALN. *Jounal of Asynchronous Learning Networks, 1* (1).
13. **Hiltz, S. R.** (1994) The Virtual Classroom: Learning without Limits via Computer Networks. Norwood, NJ: Ablex.
14. **Gunawardena, C. & Zittle, F.** (1997) Social presence as a predictor of satisfaction within a computer mediated conferencing environment. *American Journal of Distance Education, 11*, (3), 8-26.
15. **Jiang, M. & Ting, E.** (2000) A study of factors influencing students' perceived learning in a web-based course environment. International Journal of Educational Telecommunications, 6 (4), 317-338.
16. **Kearney, P., Plax, T. G. & Wendt-Wasco, N. J.** (1985) Teacher immediacy for affective learning in divergent college classes. *Communication Quarterly, 33* (1), 61-74.
17. **Kelley, D. & Gorham, J.** (1988) Effects of immediacy on recall of information. *Communication Education, 37*, (2), 198-207.
18. **Levin, J. A., Kim, H. & Riel, M. M.** (1990) Analyzing instructional interactions on electronic message networks. In L. Harasim (Ed.), *On-line Education: Perspectives on a New Environment* New York: Praeger.
19. **Picciano, A.** (1998) Developing an asynchronous course model at a large, urban university. *Jounal of Asynchronous Learning Networks, 2* (1).
20. **Poole, D. M.** (2000) Student participation in a discussion-oriented online course: a case study. *Journal of Research on Computing in Education, 33*, (2), 162-177.
21. **Rice, R. E.** (1992). Contexts of Research in Organizational Computer-Mediated Communication. In M. Lea. (Ed.), *Contexts of Computer-Mediated Communication*. New York: Harvester Wheatsheaf, 113-144.
22. **Richardson, J. & Swan, K.** (2001) An examination of social presence in online learning: students' perceived learning and satisfaction. Seattle, WA: Paper presented at the Annual Meeting of the American Educational Research Association.
23. **Richmond, V. P.** (1990) Communication in the classroom: power and motivation. *Communication Education, 39* (3), 181-195.
24. **Richmond, V. P., Gorham, J. S. & McCrosky, J.** (1987) The relationship between selected immediacy behaviors and cognitive learning. In M. McLaughlin (Ed.) *Communication Yearbook 10*. Beverly Hills, CA: Sage, 574-590.
25. **Rodriguez, J. L., Plax, T. G. & Kearney, P.** (1996) Clarifying the relationship between teacher nonverbal immediacy and student cognitive learning: affective learning as the central causal mediator. *Communication Education, 45*, 293-305.
26. **Rourke, L., Anderson, T., Garrison, D. R. & Archer, W.** (2001) Assessing social presence in asynchronous text-based computer conferencing. *Journal of Distance Education, 14*, (2).
27. **Ruberg, L. F., Moore, D. M. & Taylor, C. D.** (1996) Student participation, interaction, and regulation in a computer-mediated communication environment: a qualitative study. *Journal of Educational Computing Research, 14* (3), 243-268.
28. **Sanders, J. & Wiseman, R.** (1990) The effects of verbal and nonverbal teacher immediacy on perceived cognitive, affective, and behavioral learning. *Communication Education, 39*, (4), 341-353.
29. **Short, J., Williams, E. & Christie, B.** (1976) T*he Social Psychology of Telecommunications*. Toronto: Wiley.

30. **Swan, K., Shea, P., Fredericksen, E., Pickett, A, Pelz, W. & Maher, G.** (2000) Building knowledge building communities: consistency, contact and communication in the virtual classroom. *Journal of Educational Computing Research, 23* (4), 389-413.
31. **Swan, K., Polhemus, L., Shih, L-F. & Rogers, D.** (2001) Building knowledge building communities through asynchronous online course discussion. Seattle, WA: Paper presented at the Annual Meeting of the American Educational Research Association.
32. **Walther, J.** (1994) Interpersonal effects in computer mediated interaction. *Communication Research, 21,* (4), 460-487.
33. **Weiner, M. & Mehrabian, A.** (1968) *Language Within Language: Immediacy, a Channel in Verbal Communication.* New York: Appleton-Century-Crofts.

VI. ABOUT THE AUTHOR

Karen Swan (Ed.D. Teachers College, Columbia University) is an associate professor of Instructional Technology at the University at Albany where she also directs the Learning Technologies Laboratory and the Summer Technology Institute. Her research has been focused mainly in the general area of computers and education. She has published and presented both nationally and internationally in the specific areas of programming and problem solving, computer-assisted instruction, hypermedia design, technology and literacy, and asynchronous online learning. Her current research focuses on the latter, on technology integration in English language arts teaching and learning, and on situated professional development for technology integration. Dr. Swan has also written on social learning from broadcast television, about which she co-edited a book, and has authored several hypermedia programs including S*et On Freedom: The American Civil Rights Experience* for Glencoe and *The Multimedia Sampler* for IBM, as well as several online courses which are being offered through the SUNY Learning Network. She is a project director in the Technology Integration Project of the National Research Center on English Learning and Achievement (CELA), and is currently involved with product and usability evaluation for Project VIEW (Virtual Interactive Education Web), research on the CATIE (Capital Area Technology and Inquiry in Education) technology professional development initiative, and design consulting for NYLink online workshops on Information Technology Fluency. Dr. Swan serves on the program committees for several local and international instructional technology conferences, is a member of the ALN Effectiveness Research Advisory Board, and is the Special Issues Editor for the *Journal of Educational Computing Research.*

Contact: Karen Swan, Associate Professor, Educational Theory and Practice, University at Albany, State University of New York, 1400 Washington Ave, Albany, NY 12222; Phone: 518.442.5032; kswan@uamail.albany.edu

Student Satisfaction at the University of Phoenix Online Campus

Anthony P. Trippe
University of Phoenix, and
Rochester Institute of Technology

- Everything about the University of Phoenix student experience is oriented toward the adult learner who is seeking life-long learning. Online education encourages learning to be more personal and student centered.

- Students take just one course at a time in a sequenced, intensive (no coasting allowed) 5-6 week term in which they are immersed in a single subject.

- Learning teams play a key role in the academic learning experience of UOP students, providing supplemental learning for content mastery and refining teamwork skills. Learning Teams conduct a team project presented to the class in the form of a written and/or oral report or presentation and cover more material than could be achieved through individual effort.

- Faculty effectiveness is developed by several programs: new faculty selection and basic training; training for the first online course; mentor for the first online course; and workshops on writing, critical thinking across the curriculum, grading, evaluation and feedback, learning teams, copyright infringement, dealing with difficult students, web page development to enhance course presentation, and syllabus preparation.

- When compared to UOP classroom students, the attitudes of UOP online students are much more positive concerning their satisfaction with the course material and with regard to recommending UOP to others.

I. INTRODUCTION

The primary intent of this article is to describe how the University of Phoenix (UOP) Online Campus operates and the relationship between those operations and the success achieved by UOP in leading online learning. Another intent is to examine, through personal experience and research, how policies, procedures and operations at the University of Phoenix Online campus relate to student satisfaction.

A. Introduction to the University of Phoenix

The University of Phoenix is a private, for-profit higher education institution whose mission is to provide high quality education to working adult students. Founded in 1976, University of Phoenix is the largest private institution of higher education in the United States. It offers educational programs and services at 58 campuses and 102 learning centers in 36 states, Puerto Rico, and Vancouver, British Columbia. Combined degree enrollment was 116,800 students as of May 31, 2001.

The University of Phoenix offers associate, bachelor, master, and doctoral level programs as well as professional certificate and customized training programs in a variety of areas. The University offers these programs in the classroom, online, and through distance education including directed study.

The programs are designed to accommodate the adult learner [1], with courses available in the evenings and year round. Small class size, academically qualified practitioner faculty, and outcomes oriented curricula provide students with workplace competence, teamwork practice, and improved communication skills.

At University of Phoenix ground-based campuses, students attend classes at night or on weekends. They are also required to participate in learning teams that meet outside of class at least once a week, and to complete individual homework assignments. At the UOP Online campus, students interact via a computer-based educational delivery system. The Online system has extended the boundaries of the classroom and is an outgrowth of the University's recognition of the technological transformation of the workplace.

Taking just one course at a time, for five or six weeks, students are immersed in a single subject. In this way, the subject matter can be fully explored and more proficiently applied. This course format follows a fast pace, and during these periods of intense study, working adults absorb specific information and relate it to their immediate experiences and background. The course format also integrates collaborative group work in the form of Learning Teams that conduct applied problem-solving tasks. These Learning Teams are a resource from which students obtain and provide support and help among peers. Working adults have no time to waste, and, in comparison to traditional students, they are more systemic thinkers. Thus, the course format assists students to get more done, more efficiently. The courses are taught sequentially, not concurrently, so each course builds upon the previous courses, providing a context for better understanding. The courses also emphasize interactive discussion over lecture because this is the way adult students learn best. In addition, students have access to an online library of research materials and the expertise of their instructor, who is currently working in the field.

Since June of 1990, over 55,000 students have received undergraduate and graduate degrees from University of Phoenix. In 1990, almost 2,500 students received degrees. In 1999, almost 9,000 students received degrees.

The University's educational philosophy and operational structure embody participative, collaborative, and applied problem-solving strategies that are facilitated by a faculty whose advanced academic preparation and professional experience help integrate academic theory with current practical application. The University assesses both the effectiveness of its academic offerings and the academic achievement of its students, and utilizes the results of these assessments to improve academic and institutional quality.

B. Accreditation

The University of Phoenix is accredited by the Commission on Institutions of Higher Education of the North Central Association of Colleges and Schools, 30 N. LaSalle St., Ste. 2400, Chicago, IL 60602-2504; 312-263-0456. [2]

The Bachelor and Master of Science in Nursing programs are accredited by the National League for Nursing Accrediting Commission, NLNAC, 61 Broadway, 33rd Floor, New York, NY 10006; 212-363-5555.

The Master of Counseling program is accredited by the American Counseling Association Council for Accreditation of Counseling and Related Educational Programs. 5999 Stevenson Avenue, Alexandria, VA 22304; 703-823-9800.

C. Additional Academic Program Features

At the University of Phoenix, the opportunity to petition for an Assessment of Prior Learning is one of several degree completion options available to working adult students. The integral place of Prior Learning Assessment within the mission and purpose of the University of Phoenix lies in its compatibility with the needs of the working adult population. The standards and criteria used by the University of Phoenix for assessing prior learning were originally developed in close conformance to the guidelines developed by the American Council on Education (ACE) and the Council for Adult and Experiential Learning (CAEL). The fundamental standards of assessing prior learning have remained unchanged since the establishment of the University's Prior Learning Assessment Center. Through the years, the Prior Learning Assessment Center has achieved a position of distinction in its field and has served as a model for other universities that have chosen to add the assessment of prior learning to their programs.

The University of Phoenix allows each student to take a maximum of 9 credits via the Directed Study format when s/he cannot attend the regularly scheduled classes. When a student works within the Direct Study format, s/he works one-on-one with a faculty member to complete the class. The Directed Study student will do more "individual" work in this setting than the student in the classroom or online setting to compensate for the absence of the Learning Team environment.

D. University Of Phoenix Online Campus

All Online campus interaction is conducted asynchronously so students and faculty participate at their individual convenience. Students complete one five or six-week course at a time, then move on to the next course in the same way as students who meet face-to-face in UOP classrooms. Courses are typically three or four credits each. The courses are organized into five or six learning modules. Each module starts on a Thursday and ends on the following Wednesday. Each module contains reading assignments and problem-solving tasks. Students are required to participate in class discussions by posting substantive messages (at least 350 words on a topic related to the learning module) on at least five of the seven days. A written, weekly summary of individual student learning for that module is required each week.

Students attending the Online campus become active members of a class group of between 8 and 13 working adults. Within most classes, students gather into smaller learning teams for special projects. In addition to participating in the full range of class meeting and learning team activities, students can communicate with instructors, interact with classmates, and conduct research online. Students also access online administrative services including registration, payment of tuition, buying of books, submission of Student End of Course Surveys, printing of grade cards, viewing of the student degree audit summaries and demographic records and even requesting transcripts. A technical support help desk is available 24-hours per day, seven days per week. In addition, an automated attendant technical support line is available to address common issues.

The UOP Online campus enrollment was over 25,000 students in May 2001. This compares to 13,000 students enrolled in May 2000. This increase in student enrollments took place as other distance learning, higher education organizations were closing their doors. Higher enrollments may be attributed to student satisfaction with the policies, procedures and operations of the UOP Online campus. This report will further explore the link between enrollments and levels of student satisfaction.

While convenience and flexibility are key components, the online program does require a high level of discipline and does not allow students to "coast." It challenges their ability to quickly assimilate new ideas, evaluate complex data, think creatively and communicate effectively. It is structured to be a rewarding experience for the adult learner. Everything about the UOP student experience is oriented toward the adult student who is seeking life-long learning.

E. The Online Campus — In the Beginning

In the old days (circa 1990), a new UOP faculty member would watch one class and then be thrown into the fray. There was little mentoring, training, or preparation through formal support systems. Made up of several well regarded leaders, a little band of faculty consultants called the Steering Committee met in San Francisco for about a year. The Committee was instrumental in creating the first training programs. Several members of that crew are still teaching for the UOP Online campus.

The ideas of a Wednesday summary; of substantive participation on five days out of seven, of faculty responding to private student messages within 24 hours, and of the 13 student limit to classes [3] were all hashed out in the Steering Committee [4]. The Committee debated issues like "How do we know students are doing their own work?" and "Really, how many students can be effectively taught in an online section?"

After about the first year of operations, the decision was made for UOP Online to enter the regular UOP governance system and the committee was disbanded.

II. RATIONALE

The following information is presented as part of a case study of the UOP Online campus practices and their relationship to student satisfaction.

A. Online Course Standards and Student Resources

Students have access to a full range of online research libraries and services. During each course, students interact with other students who are often professionals, sharing ideas, debating issues, collaborating and learning from each other's experience. This peer-review process upgrades the quality of student work before it is submitted for review by the instructor. Throughout the class, the faculty facilitator provides guidance and feedback on individual student progress.

Internet access with Microsoft Outlook Express (OE) software allows students to retrieve lectures, questions and assignments from their faculty facilitator and review the information off-line. As an online facilitator, this author uses a combination of MS Word, Excel and PowerPoint files delivered via OE to promote and encourage student learning. This suite of applications is easy to use because the interfaces are familiar to almost anyone who has used a computer and the Internet for other work.

B. Personal Classroom Standards

In all of my courses, students are required to participate in the ongoing classroom discussion. I, like most UOP Online faculty, include participation as one of the components used to arrive at a student's final grade for a course. My normal requirement is that students must contribute a significant input to the class on at least five of the seven days of each week. A significant input is defined as a message of at least 350 words addressing one of the topics covered during that week. Students are encouraged to share their knowledge or experiences or to ask questions that require deeper research into a topic. Not only does this requirement for significant interaction support the principle that students learn from each other, but these regular journals of online discussion assist me to assess student learning. Students earn participation credit for their submissions on a weekly basis. Participation accounts for about 30% of the total course grade. To encourage participation, students receive feedback on their participation style and a grade at the end of each week.

Within the first two weeks of a course, I develop a filter for each student based mainly on individual contributions to the class discussions. The filter is a set of notes in a format which allows for quick retrieval of the information. This filter is another control by which I assess student learning. As we journey through a course, I can easily observe the growth and maturation of each student in learning the specific, required skills. And the filter is useful for detecting plagiarism and cheating. I am often asked how I know that the student on the other end is really who he says he is. I use my filter to examine each participation message and formal written assignment submitted by a student and the moment a marked change in style or knowledge is detected, the filter raises a flag. It is then quick and easy to use a search engine to determine whether the student's material really came from another source. The use of such a filter in the online environment makes it difficult for students to present the work of another while they keep on providing their own inputs. A positive result is that the five out of seven day participation requirement draws the individual student into ownership of the subject material of the course.

III. BACKGROUND INFORMATION

A. Online Student Demographics

The University requires that students be at least 23 years of age to apply and that they have work experience. The average age of entering University of Phoenix students is about 35 years with a household income of $50,000 to $60,000. Almost 60% of entering students have at least 11 years of work experience. An unusually high number—about 60%— of students receive some tuition assistance from their employers.

B. Online Faculty Demographics

University of Phoenix has a dedicated team of over 7400 professional faculty. These faculty hold master or doctoral degrees in the field in which they teach and are employed full-time in their professions outside their University duties. In addition, faculty members:

* average 16 years of business/industry experience
* are approved and certified to teach at the course level
* are evaluated by peers, students, and academic officers
* participate in the curriculum development and revision process
* publish and present papers
* hold office in national professional organizations
* teach because of professional and personal interest

The University of Phoenix Online faculty includes over 1,500 highly qualified instructors from across the country. Because UOP is not limited to those instructors residing in any one geographical area, it can draw from the most qualified in any given field or subject. In addition to impressive academic credentials, UOP faculty also hold high level positions within the fields they teach. This enables them to share valuable, real-world experience which can be immediately applied to student career success. Online faculty teach part-time without interrupting their full-time careers. Courses require about 12 hours of facilitating time per week (3), and are taught asynchronously, so working faculty can teach classes at the times and places that fit their schedules. Courses start every week, and generally run for five or six weeks. A typical class will include eight to thirteen success-driven professionals from various companies and organizations. In addition to facilitating a specific course, by developing course materials, reading various texts, reviewing student research, and participating in class discussions, faculty members expand their own depth of knowledge and sharpen their ability to organize, communicate and lead.

The University of Phoenix encourages and supports its faculty in the pursuit of academic freedom. Faculty members are required to instruct students in the learning outcomes specified by the University's curriculum. However, faculty are encouraged to discuss any additional topics relevant to the course being instructed, regardless of the presence of a topic within the prescribed curriculum.

At UOP, there is, however, a major difference from the traditional University in that shared governance is not present. UOP is organized and run more like a corporation where questions of policy and procedures are discussed in an open forum, but the final decision is made by a manager charged with the relevant responsibility, rather than by consensus opinion.

To ensure that faculty can facilitate a productive and stimulating learning environment, new members must pass extensive testing followed by a training and a mentoring (first course) program. Faculty must meet rigorous standards for both content knowledge and facilitation skills to pass the selection process. After acceptance to the faculty, the training never stops. Additional development courses, continuing education sessions, and ongoing faculty meetings enhance instructional skills and keep faculty up-to-date.

The University of Phoenix views its faculty as facilitators; the instructor and the learner are in a special type of temporary helping relationship. The learner comes to the school because s/he feels the need for increased skills and knowledge to advance professionally. The instructor is there because s/he possesses the subject knowledge and professional expertise necessary to meet the needs of the learner and is a role model as a working professional. Neither party can enact his/her role without the participation of the other. In essence, joint responsibility is placed on both the instructor and the learner in facilitation.

In faculty interviews, it is generally stated that there is also a connection between student satisfaction and student learning. The link appears when the students are challenged by the faculty and interested in the material. UOP stresses to its faculty that students must feel that their instructors know and care about them. In courses where this bridge is built, students become much more motivated to learn.

C. Curriculum

The curriculum is standardized across all of the University's campuses so students who transfer to a classroom campus can make a smooth transition within their chosen programs. Curriculum teams ensure that curriculum is developed and updated using the most current reference materials and textbooks. These teams are composed of representatives from within the University and external partners. The curriculum is embodied in course modules– one for each course. The modules consist of standardized curriculum materials that both students and faculty receive. Course modules set forth the objectives and outcomes of the course, and contain suggested weekly assignments, and supplemental reading materials that relate to the subject being studied. The faculty member's module also contains recommended learning activities and faculty notes.

D. Learning Teams

The University of Phoenix courses are designed to enhance the working adult student's active classroom involvement through a teaching system in which lectures are minimized, and simulations, seminars, group discussions, and student work–related projects constitute the primary methods of learning. Additionally, students group into Learning Teams comprised of three to five students to discuss and prepare solutions for advanced assignments. Learning Team members, by combining their collective resources, talents and experience, and by distributing learning responsibilities, are able to cover more material than could be achieved through individual effort. Learning teams are often responsible for conducting a team project presented to the class in the form of a written and/or oral report or presentation.

Learning teams play a key role in the academic learning experience of students. In addition to providing a supplemental learning environment for mastery of course content, learning teams also provide students with an opportunity to develop and refine teamwork skills needed to succeed in many of today's workplaces.

E. The UOP Library

The University of Phoenix is home to working professionals, and we understand that finding the time to complete research necessary for papers and projects is essential. University of Phoenix students must balance multiple roles in their lives. Flexibility and convenience are requirements and expectations of our students, and the University of Phoenix's library services center around this model of convenience and access.

By using the Online Collection, students, faculty, alumni, and staff have access to millions of full-text articles from thousands of publications right from their desktops— 24 hours a day, 7 days a week.

The University of Phoenix's Library is a gateway to extensive resources that allow users to access, evaluate, and synthesize information. The Online Collection is convenient and easily within reach using the Internet. The University of Phoenix encourages browsing the Digital Library Web site and traveling through its many paths to find information.

Additionally, Library services support the specific learning outcomes of the University's curriculum. The Library accomplishes its mission and supports patrons by providing:
- Research and reference services of the highest quality and integrity.
- Access to services 24 hours a day, 7 days a week.

- Superior customer service that is cost effective, time efficient, and convenient.
- Library holdings and database collections of the finest academic quality that cross all disciplines, degree programs, and educational offerings.

The Library continuously responds to the changing needs of its unique student population and is committed to making available new resources and services. Customer service is provided by a staff of Online Services Specialists and Professional Librarians who offer telephone support 65 hours per week and respond to inquiries submitted via email seven days a week.

F. The Virtual Writing Laboratory

The Virtual Writing Lab is another valuable resource available to students (and faculty). The "lab" is a site where students can send their written materials (papers, projects, and more) to be reviewed by qualified University of Phoenix faculty members and receive feedback. Students simply go to their student web page, click on Services and upload the document to be reviewed in a word (.doc) attachment format.

The lab is not an editing service. Papers are not revised for students. Rather, the work is reviewed and the student receives detailed feedback on how the specific paper can be improved, and how to improve the writing style in general. Feedback is focused on format, grammar, organization, punctuation, and usage, but not course content. Content feedback is the responsibility of the individual course instructor.

The lab is open to all University of Phoenix students in any program, although it was created primarily for those students who require additional writing assistance. A student becomes a candidate for the lab if comments from faculty were received, if the student is unsure of proper language usage, or if the student desires to improve writing skills in general. The lab serves students by providing feedback on all structural aspects of any written assignment. It is *not* intended to serve as a formal tutorial; instead, it provides continuing support to University of Phoenix students as they develop their writing abilities by providing specific feedback on specific work.

G. Training for UOP Facilitators

The University of Phoenix realizes that course rigor is not necessarily defined by the modality as much as it is defined by the faculty member. Therefore, there are several programs at the University of Phoenix to develop, enhance, and ensure faculty effectiveness.

1. New Faculty Selection and Training

Prospective faculty are assessed for their teaching skills, experience, and subject knowledge. Each applicant's academic and professional credentials are first evaluated to determine whether they meet the minimum requirements for faculty appointment. Resumes and other supporting materials including transcripts are reviewed to assure that the candidate possesses the qualifications to be approved to teach at least 1-2 courses. New faculty attend an orientation to familiarize themselves with the University's academic policies, procedures, and philosophy. Additionally, the online campus faculty candidates must pass a four-week training period that introduces them to the University of Phoenix teaching/ learning model. During this time, faculty candidates have an opportunity to present an online lecture, create a syllabus, participate in group exercises, provide feedback on sample student assignments, and observe an online class in action.

2. Training for the First Online Course

For a newly trained faculty member, the first online course can be a tremendous challenge. Therefore, the University of Phoenix Mentor/Internship Program is designed to complement other faculty training programs as an integral component of faculty development. The new faculty member is shadowed in his Internship Course by a mentor who is responsible for assisting with technology (hardware and software) challenges as well as for providing course content support and assistance. The online mentors are assigned to a new candidate faculty member starting two weeks prior to the first class start date. The mentor observes the mentee in class and assists and guides the mentee as appropriate throughout the entire duration of the course. The mentor is also responsible for assisting the mentee with the submission of the final grades.

3. Continuous Online Training

Another of the policies upon which UOP Online is built is the continued training of faculty after the initial training and the mentorship first course. Based on this author's personal experience, the continuous, follow-on training assists a faculty member to grow and become a more confident online facilitator by introducing new techniques and approaches to enhance student learning. Examples of some of the training courses are:

a. The Faculty Writing Workshop

The writing workshop is designed to provide UOP faculty members in all disciplines with the ideas and tools necessary to develop clear writing assignments, to assess student papers effectively, and to help students improve their writing skills. The workshop provides a review of writing principles and includes materials to assist participants in establishing clear grading criteria for written work and providing effective feedback to students. The workshop also covers current UOP writing standards and style guide requirements along with university policies regarding plagiarism. Major topics are Types of Writing at UOP, Essential Elements of Good Writing, Communication of Faculty Writing Expectations, Grading Criteria and Elements, Structuring Written Work, University Policies on Plagiarism and MLA/APA Citation Formats. The workshop includes handout materials that faculty can use in their classes to assist students with their writing assignments.

b. Critical Thinking Across the Curriculum

This workshop helps faculty members understand and utilize the power of critical thinking in any educational process dedicated to understanding the world around and within us. The workshop emphasizes the practical application of critical thinking teaching methods to a variety of curricula. The course topics include The Value of Critical Thinking, Critical Thinking: Purpose and Process and Cross-Curricular Application of Critical Thinking

c. Grading, Evaluation and Feedback

This workshop introduces the potential facilitator to the basics of student performance evaluation, grading and feedback. Through a variety of formats, workshop participants will gain a greater insight into the basic principles of grading written and oral assignments. Topics include Basic Principles of Grading, Designing Written Assignments, Assessing Written Assignments, Assessing Oral Assignments, The Syllabus and Administrative Mechanics of Grading. The participant will be able to identify and utilize tools to determine student grades as objectively as possible, understand the mechanics of grading from an administrative standpoint, and demonstrate the ability to provide constructive feedback on both written and oral student work, on an individual or group basis.

d. Learning Teams

The learning team workshop highlights the philosophy and purpose of learning teams through discussion of the nature of the learning team process. Through class activities, the new faculty candidate learns to facilitate the formation of learning teams and address team conflict issues. Understanding these elements facilitates the University of Phoenix Mission of meeting the educational needs of working adult students through collaborative learning. Topics include The Learning Team Defined, How Learning Teams are Formed, Advantages of Learning Teams, Disadvantages of Learning Teams, Collaborative Learning and Learning Teams, Establishing Guidelines for Team Problem Resolution and The Facilitator's Role in the Learning Team Process.

e. Other Continuous Training Courses

Other faculty training courses address topics such as copyright infringement, strategies for dealing with difficult students, web page development to enhance course presentation materials and a refresher course that reviews the basic principles of the Online Learning Model.

It is the author's opinion, based upon his experiences, that the University of Phoenix's rigorous training of faculty is an important element in student satisfaction and in the success of the University. When a UOP facilitator enters a ground classroom or an online virtual classroom, his or her experience and knowledge of the course content can be communicated because s/he is comfortable in the use of the technology and aware of the presentation techniques which enhance student learning. The virtual classroom environment at the University of Phoenix Online campus may be controlled by the activity of the students, but its foundation is established by the faculty member. The presence of knowledgeable, experienced, personable, confident and most importantly well-trained faculty creates a classroom environment which produces student interaction and ultimately leads to a high level of student satisfaction with the entire learning experience.

H. Faculty Peer Reviews

The University's ongoing system of faculty evaluation provides opportunities for faculty members to request and receive peer feedback. Experienced faculty members perform in-class observations and hold feedback sessions to assist their faculty peers in further developing and enhancing their teaching skills. The Peer Feedback Program provides feedback and sharing among faculty; and the Administrative Review process, along with student feedback, pinpoints the strengths and weaknesses of each faculty member.

I. Student End of Course Survey (SEOCS)

The Student End of Course Survey (SEOCS) provides an ongoing evaluation of the processes managed by the faculty and by the campus administration. Students evaluate the University's support services, facilities, the curriculum, overall educational effectiveness, and learning team activities. They also complete a comprehensive faculty evaluation including handwritten comments regarding the faculty member. Results of student end of course surveys are shared with the faculty member at the end of each course to assist instructors in becoming more effective.

J. Give the Students What They Want – FlexNet and rEsource

The University of Phoenix is going through a review process to revise its Statement of Mission and Purpose in order to emphasize the student-centered focus throughout the entire organization. The proposed language is:

> University of Phoenix serves the educational needs of working adult students and their employers by providing rigorous, relevant academic programs in a variety of professional disciplines. The University is a private, for-profit institution of higher learning dedicated to delivering measurable outcomes to the communities we serve.

When asked about contributions to student satisfaction, the Director of Operations for UOP Online said the most important factors are "...offering quality curriculum, specialized student service teams, end of course surveys (to express their concerns or positive feedback), convenience, quality faculty, flexibility and accessibility as well as interacting with other working professionals together with real world application."

Much of the University of Phoenix success can be attributed to a student-centered philosophy of giving the students what they want. Adult students want a quality education provided at their convenience and with little interference with their job responsibilities and family duties. Several of the ways in which UOP meets these student wants have been discussed above (one-course at a time, evening classes, learning delivered via the Internet, and conveniently located learning centers). However, in an environment of continuous improvement, UOP tests and introduces new learning protocols on a regular basis to further increase student satisfaction.

1. FlexNet

The latest class attendance format that UOP offers students is called FlexNet. FlexNet conducts the first and last workshop meetings for a course in the classroom, and the middle ones are conducted online using the Online software system. FlexNet retains the best of both delivery methods. The FlexNet method was first developed at the Tucson Campus. Several groups have already graduated from programs using the FlexNet feature. The first students were from Mexico in 1998 as the delivery method was not yet approved for financial aid.

Currently UOP is running quite a few FlexNet programs...in Tucson, in Nogales, and in Yuma Arizona. Students and faculty get face time in the first workshop, and meet again for the last session to do oral presentations and wrap up of the course. In Tucson, the classroom workshops are held on a Saturday. The last workshop of a group's current course is conducted in the morning, and the first workshop of the group's next course takes place in the afternoon. This arrangement requires students to be on-campus only once every six weeks. So far, FlexNet has been popular and very successful...students love the mixture of classroom and online delivery. FlexNet is being rolled out corporate-wide. FlexNet is a nice choice for students who are close enough to a campus to attend every six weeks, but far enough away to not want to come every week.

2. rEsource

In recognition of the fact that all students have unique learning styles, the University of Phoenix Online has begun the implementation of rEsource, an exciting new product and the new standard for delivery of student and faculty materials[7]. Implementation across all degree programs will continue through 2002. The rEsource product is a set of learning tools that are designed and presented in a variety of modalities in order to meet the needs of all learners. These materials will be delivered via the Student and Faculty Web on a course-by-course basis. To facilitate this strategic initiative, UOP is partnering with a variety of publishers to provide content and other ancillary services. UOP currently has partnership arrangements with Thomson Learning, Pearson Publishing, McGraw Hill, Course Technology, and John Wiley.

Included in the learning tools is the e-text, a selected "textbook" for each course. In some cases, this material is simply an electronic copy of an existing textbook; in other cases, the e-text is a compilation of material from multiple sources, including chapters from several textbooks, associated selected readings and other printed materials. Students view this material using Microsoft® Reader or by printing all or part of the text from their personal computers.

The rEsource site for a course is not only an "e-Book" – it is a collection of electronically delivered learning resources (one element of which is an "e-text"), which are closely aligned to the course objectives. These collections can be differentiated as visual databases, multimedia libraries and more. For example, instead of a textbook with perhaps 20 chapters from which reading assignments would be chosen for assigned reading, the instructor can assign the specific portions of the e-text to correspond with the number of class meetings or workshops so that the material relates specifically to the learning objectives. PowerPoint presentations that correspond to the course objectives, as well as self-assessments, multimedia activities and current articles from the digital library are available. This allows each faculty member to maintain more distinct focus on course or workshop objectives. Additionally, students have access to an entire reference library of university materials from their desktops or laptops and are able to access their library (with automatic updates) as alumni.

The creation of the electronic rEsource page is intended to foster a dynamic learning climate. It ensures that students will have access to diverse and a larger number of information resources. In addition, online instructors can insure that students have access to the same materials that are tailored to specific course objectives and it allows facilitators to use their subject knowledge to creatively add materials such as PowerPoint presentations or video streams. Material provided via the resource model has real potential to individualize online instruction and promote rich educational experiences that are relevant for today's students.

IV. RESULTS OF RESEARCH

A. Student Satisfaction Factors

As a general measure of student satisfaction based upon student responses, the following information was gathered. This data is not presented as the result of rigorous research on the topic but simply as a list of student-satisfaction elements. To obtain student responses, a request for opinions was posted in the UOP Online Student Lounge. Student response was completely voluntary. The question asked was "What do Online students like about UOP?" Twenty eight responses (written narrative) were received from UOP students. The order (from top to bottom) of the features in the table represents those aspects most liked by students.

Table 1: Student Preferences

UOP Features Liked by Students	Remarks
The convenience of attending class anytime	Almost every student listed this factor
Friendly instructor who gets personal	Lots of interaction with students
Real world related classroom discussions	Other students contribute valuable inputs
Relevance of course material to their jobs	Immediate results from their efforts
Weekly feedback concerning performance	Includes their weekly learning summary
Ease of scheduling classes	No waiting in line or closed courses
Emphasis on learning	No fraternities or sororities, no parties, etc.
The convenience of not going to a classroom	Eliminates traffic, parking and babysitters
Accreditation by recognized organizations	
Availability of financial aid	
One class at a time format	
All assignment and learning information is available at start of a course	
Ordering books and course materials is easy	

The table shows that UOP Online students generally like the same aspects of asynchronous learning as students from almost any other online learning organization.

B. Comparison of UOP Classroom and Online Grades

Specifically for this report, two questions related to UOP Online student *grades* were researched.

Table 2: Grade-Related Question Number One:
Are online student's grade scores equivalent to grades earned by classroom students?

Measurement Factor	Ground Campus	Online Campus
Course No./Level/Credits	POS-568/Masters/3	POS-568/Masters/3
Course Name	Operating Systems	Operating Systems
Total Students in Study	386	423
'A' Grades - % - cum%	270 – 70.0 – 70.0	290 – 68.6 – 68.6
Number of 'A-' Grades	49 – 12.7 – 82.7	77 – 18.2 – 86.8
Number of 'B+' Grades	19 – 4.9 – 87.6	22 – 5.2 – 92.0
Number of 'B' Grades	14 – 3.6 – 91.2	8 – 1.9 – 93.9
Number of 'B-' Grades	5 - 1.3 – 92.5	2 – 0.5 – 94.4
Number of 'C+' Grades	1 – 0.3 – 92.8	2 – 0.5 - 94.9
Number of 'C' Grades	3 – 0.8 – 93.6	3 – 0.7 – 95.6
Number of 'C-' Grades	3 – 0.8 – 94.4	0 - 0 – 95.6
Number of 'D+' Grades	1 - 0.3 – 94.7	0 - 0 – 95.6
Number of 'D-' Grades	2 - 0.5 – 95.2	0 - 0 – 95.6
Number of 'F' Grades	1 – 0.3 – 95.5	2 – 0.5 – 96.1
Number of 'W' Grades	18 – 4.7 – 100.2	17 – 4.0 – 100.1

To answer this question, the grades of two groups of UOP students are compared in the above table. The first group consists of online campus students and the second group is made up of UOP students learning in a traditional classroom.

Comparison of classroom grades and online grades shows little or no substantial differences. The raw data is provided so the reader may use it to make his own evaluation. Even the number of withdraws appears to be equivalent for the two groups. Other research often points to increased 'drop' rates for Online students.

Grade-Related Question Number Two: Do Online students achieve the same 'academic success' as equivalent classroom students?

To answer this question the Grade Point Averages achieved by recent graduates of the online campus were compared to the Grade Point Averages achieved by those recent graduates from the more traditional UOP classroom campuses. The results are:

Traditional classroom campus graduates (total 13,069) since 6/1/00 had an average GPA of 3.68.

Graduates of the Online campus (total 2,072) since 6/1/00 had an average GPA of 3.72.

A Z-statistic is used for testing whether the difference between the two means is significant.

$$Z = \frac{X_1 - X_2}{\sqrt{\dfrac{s_1^2}{n_1} + \dfrac{s_2^2}{n_2}}} = 1.90$$

At the 0.01 confidence level, the difference between the two means is attributed to chance. There is no statistically significant difference between the two means.

C. Comparison of UOP Classroom and Online Attitudes

A great deal of the success experienced by the UOP Online campus is thought to be attributable to how well the policies, procedures and operations meet the needs of the students. This section contains selected results of UOP sponsored student survey research. The data demonstrate the importance of various aspects of the UOP learning experience. Student attitude differences between classroom and online students can be seen in several aspects.

The answers to the following questions were taken from a UOP study [5] that, in part, examines survey responses of students who learn in the on-ground environment as opposed to students who learn in the Online campus environment. The data were compiled from survey responses by 21,500 on-ground and 4,500 online learners. Both groups consist of adult learners. Detailed demographic information on the two groups was not gathered.

The survey instruments for both groups were identical except that the online campus version replaced a classroom rating question with a question about learning in an online environment and added a question about the student's method for internet connection.

Overall Satisfaction Attitude Question: How satisfied are Online students with their UOP learning experience compared to equivalent ground-based campus class students?

These data were reported in terms of the odds of a student answering a question generally in the positive or in the negative. The odds of a student responding with a "yes" or a rating of 4 or 5 (strongly agree) were compared to a "no' answer or a rating of 3, 2, and 1 (strongly disagree). For example, if the odds of a student responding 4 or 5 (strongly agree) to a statement were 5.25 to one — that means that 525 students responded 4 or 5 (strongly agree) to this statement for every 100 who responded with a 3, 2, or 1 (strongly disagree).

The survey instruments grouped questions to measure attitudes toward several areas of satisfaction.

Area I. Overall Satisfaction

Three strategic questions are used by UOP to measure overall student satisfaction.

1. Based on this course, would you recommend the University of Phoenix to other working adults?
>   Classroom response – odds of a "yes" answer are 8.44 to 1
>   Online response — odds of a "yes" answer are 14.34 to 1

2. Would you recommend this instructor to other students?
>   Classroom response odds of a "yes" answer are 7.97 to 1
>   Online response odds of a "yes" answer are 7.91 to 1

3. Did this course meet your expectations?
>   Classroom response odds of a "yes" answer are 5.29 to 1
>   Online response odds of a "yes" answer are 9.43 to 1

The attitudes of online students are much more positive concerning their satisfaction with the course material and with regard to recommending UOP to others [6]. Student attitudes about specific faculty members are nearly identical for classroom and online groups. This aspect of the UOP learning experience is explored further in the next area.

Area II. Faculty

1. The instructor demonstrated expertise and professional experience in the subject.
>   Classroom response odds of a 4 or 5 (strongly agree) answer are 3.69 to 1
>   Online response odds of a 4 of 5 (strongly agree) answer are 5.30 to 1

2. The instructor's presentation of the course material contributed to the course objectives.
>   Classroom response odds of a 4 or 5 (strongly agree) answer are 2.88 to 1
>   Online response odds of a 4 of 5 (strongly agree) answer are 3.35 to 1

3. The instructor organized and managed this course effectively.
>   Classroom response odds of a 4 or 5 (strongly agree) answer are 2.62 to 1
>   Online response odds of a 4 of 5 (strongly agree) answer are 2.70 to 1

Again, as in the Area I responses, it is difficult to see any real difference in student satisfaction with respect to faculty activities. Perhaps, Online faculty members are perceived by their students as having better expertise and experience than their classroom counterparts. These data may also point to the need for further research into the differences in *actual* levels of experience and expertise possessed by classroom and online facilitators.

Area III. Curriculum

1. Sufficient time was allocated to learn the course content.
>   Classroom response odds of a 4 or 5 (strongly agree) answer are 1.87 to 1
>   Online response odds of a 4 of 5 (strongly agree) answer are 2.08 to 1

2. Individual assignments were appropriate for the course.
>   Classroom response odds of a 4 or 5 (strongly agree) answer are 2.37 to 1
>   Online response odds of a 4 of 5 (strongly agree) answer are 3.06 to 1

3. The requirements for this course were generally more difficult than other UOP courses.
>   Classroom response odds of a 4 or 5 (strongly agree) answer are 0.78 to 1
>   Online response odds of a 4 of 5 (strongly agree) answer are 2.44 to 1

Student attitudes toward course timing and assignments showed little difference between those in the classroom and those online. Remember, a large part of the UOP course content, schedule and learning measurements are provided to faculty in the UOP-written course modules. However, an overwhelming difference in student attitudes toward a course's degree-of-difficulty exists between classroom and online students. This author believes much of the difference arises from a general belief, by inexperienced online students, concerning the nature of distance learning. In general, before students actually take courses online, they expect to encounter an easy, lightweight learning experience. When they realize the rigor and workloads are the same as classroom courses, they respond by indicating the difficulty level exceeded their expectations.

Area IV. Educational Effectiveness

1. The course contributed practical knowledge I can use in my current job.
> Classroom response odds of a 4 or 5 (strongly agree) answer are 1.76 to 1
> Online response odds of a 4 of 5 (strongly agree) answer are 0.56 to 1

2. The course strengthened my problem-solving skills.
> Classroom response odds of a 4 or 5 (strongly agree) answer are 1.57 to 1
> Online response odds of a 4 of 5 (strongly agree) answer are 3.43 to 1

3. My learning team was a valuable part of this course.
> Classroom response odds of a 4 or 5 (strongly agree) answer are 2.74 to 1
> Online response odds of a 4 of 5 (strongly agree) answer are 1.35 to 1

By more than three to one, classroom students feel that their new knowledge can be immediately applied to their current job. But by two to one, online students think the new knowledge improved their ability to solve problems. And, classroom students respond twice as often that the learning teams activities contribute to their new learned knowledge. These large differences in student attitudes, observed between the two groups, may point the way to improved, more effective techniques for managing learning in the online environment. For instance, the learning team technique may be a better learning tool when it takes place face-to-face. Team projects and cooperative activities may not work as well at a distance.

Area V. University Services

1. During this course, administration and staff at my campus were helpful.
> Classroom response odds of a 4 or 5 (strongly agree) answer are 0.77 to 1
> Online response odds of a 4 of 5 (strongly agree) answer are 2.47 to 1

2. I received my textbook(s) in a timely manner.
> Classroom response odds of a 4 or 5 (strongly agree) answer are 1.58 to 1
> Online response odds of a 4 of 5 (strongly agree) answer are 2.82 to 1

3. During this course I received accurate and appropriate information from my Academic Counselor/Advisor.
> Classroom response odds of a 4 or 5 (strongly agree) answer are 0.49 to 1
> Online response odds of a 4 of 5 (strongly agree) answer are 0.88 to 1

4. During this course, I received accurate and appropriate information from my Financial Advisor.
> Classroom response odds of a 4 or 5 (strongly agree) answer are 0.35 to 1
> Online response odds of a 4 of 5 (strongly agree) answer are 3.40 to 1

Note that the online student responses to these four questions were much more positive than those of classroom students. The responses point to another basic difference between the two groups of learners. Both groups are adult learners with common needs, but the perception of how UOP meets those needs is markedly different. The survey responses point to basic attitude differences between classroom and online students and indicate what satisfies their needs. In the asynchronous environment of the online student, a response within 24-hours is probably much more satisfying than the same 24-hour response to a classroom student. Programs such as the FlexNet class attendance format assist in closing the gap in student perceptions of how well University services meet their needs.

V. CONCLUSIONS

Several areas in which students are impacted by University policy, procedures and operations are included as part of this research. The research examines student satisfaction with respect to faculty, curriculum, educational effectiveness, University services and the overall UOP experience. The results indicate that a great deal of the success experienced by the UOP Online campus can be attributed to how well the policies, procedures and operations meet the needs of the students. The data presented also demonstrate the existence of differences in the levels of student attitudes among students in a traditional classroom setting and students in the virtual Internet environment. These differences can be used to define policy, develop procedures and implement operations tailored to the specific learning environment of the student.

VI. REFERENCES

1. **Gross, Ronald** (1991), Peak Learning, ISBN: 0-87477-610-4, published by G. F. Putnam's Sons, New York.
2. **University of Phoenix** (2000), University of Phoenix http://www.phoenix.edu/catalog/
3. **Biner, P.M., Welsh, K.D., Barone, N.M., Summers, M. and Dean, R.S.** (1997), The Impact of Remote-Site Group Size on Student Satisfaction and Relative Performance in Interactive Telecourses, American Journal of Distance Education, vol.11, no.1, 1997, pp.23-33.
4. **White, Ken W. and Weight, Bob W.** (2000), The Online Teaching Guide, ISBN 0-205-29531-2, Published by Allyn and Bacon, Needham Heights, MA.
5. **University of Phoenix** (2001), Student End-of-Course Survey Report December 1, 2000 – February 28, 2001, Internal Report released August 2001.
6. **Thomerson, J.D. and Smith, C.L.** (1996), Student perceptions of the affective experiences encountered in distance learning courses, American Journal of Distance Education, vol.10, no.3, 1996, pp.37-48.
7. **Muirhead, Brent, McAuliffe, Jane and LaRue Marla** (2001), Online Resource Page: Using Technology to Enhance the Teaching and Learning Process, UOP Internal Discussion Paper.

VII. AUTHOR INFORMATION

Anthony Trippe is an adjunct faculty member at the University of Phoenix and has been facilitating courses for almost four years. He was trained as a classroom facilitator by the San Diego Campus of UOP and approved for about ten graduate and undergraduate courses including Project Management, Operating Systems, Computer Architecture, Statistics, Strategic Planning and Computer Programming. He has facilitated approximately a dozen classroom courses at four of the learning centers of the San Diego Campus. Subsequently, he trained to facilitate courses for the Online Campus, and in 1998, he facilitated courses for both the San Diego campus and the Online Campus. After moving to Rochester, New York to be close to his grandchildren, he continues to facilitate courses for the Online Campus since there is no UOP classroom campus near to Rochester. In his "day" job, he is a faculty member at the Rochester Institute of Technology where he teaches in the Electrical, Computer and Telecommunications Engineering Technology Department. To date, he has taught two distance courses for RIT and approximately forty courses for the UOP Online Campus. Much of the information presented in this paper is derived from his personal experience as a teacher and facilitator in both the classroom and on the Internet.

Contact: Anthony P. Trippe, Rochester Institute of Technology, Computer Engineering Technology, 78 Lomb Memorial Drive, Rochester, New York 14623; E-Mail: a_trippe@cast-fc.rit.edu; Phone: (716) 475-6537; URL: www.rit.edu/~aptiee